EDWARD WILSON
OF THE ANTARCTIC

EDWARD WILSON.
From the picture by Hugh G. Riviere.

EDWARD WILSON
OF THE ANTARCTIC

NATURALIST AND FRIEND

BY

GEORGE SEAVER

WITH AN INTRODUCTION BY

APSLEY CHERRY-GARRARD

LONDON
JOHN MURRAY, ALBEMARLE STREET, W.

First Edition . . . October, *1933*

Reprinted . . . . October, *1933*

Reprinted . . . . November, *1933*

To
O. F. W.

Contents

vii

Contents

Illustrations and Maps

Note

With the exception of the frontispiece and the final portrait,
all the illustrations are from Dr. Wilson's own sketches.

Maps

Introduction

By APSLEY CHERRY-GARRARD

Thy friends are exultations, agonies,
And love, and man's unconquerable mind.
WORDSWORTH.

IF this book succeeds in showing what kind of man Bill was, it will give you courage ; and this is what the world has wanted since he died, and never perhaps so much as now. When things for which men have worked for centuries are being destroyed ; when those who have done most for the longest time are being sacrificed ; when no one who has any intelligence and does not live in a monastery can but be deeply stirred by the chaos which threatens, you will read here the story of a man who, however appalling the conditions, and whatever the dangers, in the face of starvation and more than once of inevitable death, just went on doing his job.

I have two nightmares which still come to me on windy nights. The first originates one night on the *Terra Nova* when Bill and I were sleeping on top of the ice-house. I dream that I am navigating a ship out of Havana Harbour and have gone to sleep without laying a course. I wake (apparently) to find the ship just running on to a great headland, and I wake (actually, or so it seems in my dream) shaking Bill to ask him what I am to do.

xi

We had a habit of doing that.   In the second nightmare I am asleep in my bunk at Cape Evans ; the
hut door opens, letting in its mist of cold air, and
the Polar Party walks in, shaking the snow from
their clothes and the ice from their faces.   Scott
is there, and Bill with his usual cheery grin, and
Birdie Bowers, just utterly done.   Titus Oates and
Taff Evans are not there.   The disappointment of
finding that it is only a dream will last for days.
There is another of us survivors who has much the
same dream, I find.

On the evening of Thursday, July 26, 1910, a
group of probable young men were gathered at
the bottom of the cliffs of uninhabited South
Trinidad Island with a very big sea dividing them
from their ship.   They were immensely keen, eager
to prove themselves in the first nasty fix we had
got into, and fussily active when there was not
much to be done until a life-line could be floated
in from a boat.   One man alone was unmoved
and idle, sitting quietly on a rock and eating a
biscuit.   This was Wilson, and he told me afterwards that he had cramp : a bad start for swimming
out into that boiling surf.   Many of that band are
now famous and dead—Pennell, who commanded
the *Terra Nova* so efficiently after the shore parties
were landed, and brought the survivors back a
year after the tragedy and victory of the Pole :
Atkinson, who commanded the Main Party during
that last and most ghastly year, when God alone
knew what was best to be done : Bowers, perhaps the hardest man who ever sledged : Oates,
who walked out to try and save his friends.   As
time went on these men began to stand out and

they with their companions agreed in an affection
and admiration for Wilson which amounted to love.

What they did has become part of the history
of England, perhaps of the human race, as much
as Columbus or the Elizabethans, David, Hector
or Ulysses. They are an epic.

What was it then that gave Bill such a position
among such men? Looking back, I am sure it was
character, combined with an immensely high standard of work, most unselfishly done ; men such as I
have named have an intuitive recognition that there
is something good in a man like Bill. But at the
time I had not the curiosity to inquire. During those
two years, mostly sledging, when Bill and I lived in
daily companionship I feel now that I wasted a lot
of time. I knew him straight away as a famous
explorer, a tried naturalist and artist, and no doubt
a skilled doctor, and accepted him as such. Sledging we discussed the *Discovery* Expedition and
various polar and outside problems for weeks, and
then when we had been out for some time conversation became less and less until we spent as a
party many days with hardly a word beyond the
usual ' Camp,' ' Time to get up,' and so on. We
reached a time when if someone started a new topic
it was a relief to get away from thoughts of food
and crevasses and tracks and distances and depôts
and weather and frost-bites. If I had that time
over again I should want to find out from Bill how
he grew up, why he thought this and that, and I
might have learned something of the great faith
which I now believe was at the foundation of his
greatness and how it came. All this I hope to
learn now from this book.

How far was his courage based upon his faith?
After all, courage alone will not take you far in the
Antarctic as we knew it in its old man-hauling days.
The lady gave the bus-conductor a penny and said
'How far will it take me?' 'To the door of the
Ritz,' was the answer, 'but it will not take you
far inside.' Courage, or ambition, or love of
notoriety, may take you to the Antarctic, or any
other uncomfortable place in the world, but it
won't take you far inside without being found out;
it's courage: and unselfishness: and helping one
another: and sound condition: and willingness
to put in every ounce you have: and clean living:
and good temper: and tact: and good judgment:
and faith. And the greatest of these is faith, especially a faith that what you are doing is of use. It's
the idea which carries men on. There, if I am not
mistaken, you have Bill Wilson.

Not that we knew anything of his spiritual life.
The man upon whom we threw our troubles and
our worries, as well as our aches and pains, who
was to us such a happy companion, never revealed
to us the depths of religious feeling which is apparent
in those letters and diaries of his which I have read.
When we were going to die on the slopes of Terror
we sang hymns because they were easier to sing
than *La Bohême* and it was a good thing to sing
something. You must not think of Bill as a
'religious' man. It has come almost as a shock
to some of us to learn now for the first time that he
held a service to himself up in the crow's nest every
week. But after reading some of these letters I begin
to realize why Bill made no comment when, after
years of preparation and months of racking toil, he

reached the Pole only to find that the Norskies had been there first.

It is literal truth that this was a happy expedition. It was happy because the main sledging men—and always it is sledging which counts—either had in themselves, or developed as they went on, a fair share of the qualities I have mentioned. And it is probable that the habit of putting the expedition first and the rest nowhere which lasted some of us through some pretty ghastly days (especially during that last year) was largely imitative. It was imitative of Bill, with Pennell and Bowers a very close second. He told me one day, ' I thought I could work ; but I can't keep up with Pennell,' and in one of his letters he writes of Pennell as ' by far the most capable man on the whole expedition.' That is most interesting, because Pennell is unknown to the general public. Most men's usefulness is in inverse proportion to their notoriety.

Cowardice is catching ; that is why men are down on cowards : they are frightened of them. But courage is catching too. These men handed down their spirit unconsciously and with cheerful generosity. It was easy to be brave when Bill and Birdie were near ; it would have been difficult to run away. This was imitative too. It is curious now to look back upon these letters and diaries and see how much depended upon religion with the man as a go-between.

For this question of the search for knowledge and its relation to religion is the real psychological interest of this book. Man says, ' I trust in God ' and immediately a crevasse opens and swallows him up. Supposing he said, ' God ! If you give me

another night like that I'll go over to the other
camp '? Lawrence did that in Arabia and carried
his Arabs to victory.[1] This want to find out will
take men almost anywhere : it took us to Cape
Crozier, and Wilson to the South Pole and to his
death ; men weave it into their religion, and what
its place there may be has been a subject of war,
persecution, martyrdom, suffering and death
throughout the ages.

After all, these simple old-fashioned days of man-
hauling in Polar regions gave a man very little of
personal gain. As often as not when he got home,
if he did get home, he was told by some arm-chair
critic who becomes an ' authority ' by saying so,
that he ought to have done something quite
different. Once you took it on, sledging with the
same men month after month and year after year,
you're for it : for better, for worse, in sickness and
in health : and in sickness there was suicide—
sometimes ; it was the only way out. There were
no cushy wounds, no cheering crowds, no restaurants nor hospitals, no wireless nor women. There
was something outside a man which forced him to
these things, and this may well be called religion.
The nearest modern approach is the lone sailor who
goes away for years in a little boat, like Slocum, or
Gerbault, or Captain Voss. It is all changed now,
and rightly changed : if men wish to cross the
Antarctic continent they should wait for an aero-
plane to show them the way. But the world is so
much the poorer.

And Wilson was convinced he had more work
to do, although down South we knew little of those

[1] *The Seven Pillars*, pp. 394–5.

deep feelings which are revealed in his letters and diaries and which were the foundations of his character. We saw then his serenity, his courage, and his sympathy. For of course that sympathy, which in a way is love, was at the bottom of the devotion he got from us all. Whatever was the matter you took your trouble to Bill and, immediately, he dropped what he was doing, gave you his complete attention, and all his help. If you were doing your best he would do his best for you : though maybe you could not reach his standard, he was immensely tolerant of your shortcomings : he treated you as an equal even if you were not so. In a way he who lies in the snow of the Barrier was like Mallory who lies on the snow of Mount Everest. But Mallory was burning with a kind of fire, an ardent impatient soul, winding himself up to a passion of effort the higher he got. Bill was not like that : he was calm, unchangeable, serene, plugging along with a certain neat smartness and with a ready smile. Indeed, he was a gallant kind of gentleman upon whom you could lean. And so men did lean upon him, and no doubt he loved them for it, and liked them to come again. It was a proof to himself (could we have doubted) that he was doing some good.

Birdie Bowers was the most indomitable person I have ever met. I have seen him in the most terrible situations ; a few times I have seen him more than anxious, I think I have seen him afraid : there used to be a curious breathless catch in his voice when he was really worried. But I have never, never seen him dismayed. I am sure that when he came to die himself, after watching and helping two of his friends who were dying on the way, he was as resolute, dogged, and helpful as ever. I uncovered his body, and I think he just died in his sleep.

I just can't imagine Birdie leaning on anyone or anything : even upon Wilson. But as far as it was possible for Birdie to carry his troubles to anybody, I am sure he took them to Bill. At a time like the Winter Journey we three were not men of whom there could be any question of consciously shirking anything we could do. It came to a question as to which could help the others most ; with their harness, with the cooker, the matches, the primus, the lashings of the door or the food bags, getting into our sleeping-bags or our harness, with straps in packing or unpacking the sledge. Birdie slept more than Bill or me, and was undoubtedly the strongest. I think he still had the most initiative left when we got in. On the other hand, Birdie and I both slept on the march : and somehow or other Bill on his longer trace ahead kept awake : at any rate he kept the course, so far as it could be kept in the darkness.

I really believe that through all the horrors of the Winter Journey Wilson thought almost nothing of his own sufferings ; the times when the conditions were too much for him stand out as exceptional. One night when a blob of burning blubber shot into his eye and he thought his eye was gone, he was quite unable to stifle his groans : that is the only time I can remember when his feelings of pain became too much for him. And I can remember one thing after another in which he helped me, perhaps night after night. I am sure that he

often and often helped when I did not realize, so
secretly even from himself was it done. When the
tent had gone, and the roof of the tent had just
that second blown away, in the midst of that howling
blizzard and the savage thunder of that great wind,
I tried to help him into his sleeping-bag (being
already half into my own), which was nearly all he
had left, but he would not be helped. ' Get into
your own,' he shouted, and leaned over until his
mouth was against my ear. ' Please, Cherry,' he
said, and his voice was terribly anxious. He was
worrying about us but not a bit about himself.
Long before, he said one night : ' I never meant
to bring you out into this, shall we go back ? '
All he said when I came tumbling down an ice-fall
in the middle of the Cape Crozier pressure was :
' Cherry, you *must* learn to use an ice-axe.' Another
man would have sworn heartily, and later said to
Birdie, ' Really, Cherry is the limit.'

Wilson was almost an invalid when he was chosen
as second doctor of the *Discovery* Expedition. He
must have made a great impression upon Scott, for
he was chosen with Shackleton to be his companion on the Southern Journey. Scott and Wilson
saved Shackleton's life, and got him in alive,
although they themselves had scurvy. This journey
led to an understanding between these two men :
it became a friendship which endured to death.

In a post-war world where ideals have been
smashed by the million and disillusion has won the
temporary day, where men and nations live on
jealousy and fear, it is almost impossible, though
inexpressibly pleasant, to get back into that atmosphere where a number of men (such as those whom

I have named) risked their lives and all that was dear to them for an ideal. 'We are weak, writing is difficult, but for my own sake I do not regret this journey, which has shown that Englishmen can endure hardship, help one another, and meet death with as great a fortitude as ever in the past. We took risks, we knew we took them ; things have come out against us, and therefore we have no cause for complaint. . . .'

When I first knew Wilson it was certain that he and Scott were going South again if possible : they wanted to finish the job. I do not know whether Scott would have gone again without Wilson. Wilson in going again contemplated a visit to Cape Crozier in winter to get the embryo of the Emperor Penguin and possibly made an agreement with Scott that this journey should be attempted. Then came the Last Expedition. By the start of the Depôt Journey Scott wrote that Wilson ' has by sheer force of character achieved a position of authority over the others whilst retaining their warmest affection,' and Wilson wrote of Scott, ' There is nothing I would not do for him. . . .'

During the Depôt Journey Scott had a very bad time. Calamity came upon calamity : the collapse of the ponies ; then the loss of faith in the dog-teams : in the middle of the journey he was chatting with Meares of what they would do on the Plateau, but when we had a team down a crevasse he lost faith in them for the Beardmore and the way they lost condition alarmed him. Then one on top of the other came the breaking up of the sea ice with men and ponies going out to sea, the apparent loss of two men who had been left

at Hut Point, and the news that the *Fram* with
Amundsen (who had left Norway to go to the
North Pole) had been found in the Bay of Whales.
I have never seen Scott so distressed as he was
during this time. I saw also how wise and well
balanced was Bill's influence, though his anxiety
was as great as that of Scott. I remember getting
to the *Discovery* Hut utterly done after the sea ice
business and Bill came out and caught hold of me
—' I don't think I have ever been so pleased by
anything in all my life,' he said, and his voice
showed how moved he was.

Then came the time at Hut Point, leading a kind
of Swiss Family Robinson life, using any scrap we
could find from the *Discovery*, and waiting for the
sea ice to freeze a way to Cape Evans. For us it
was a jolly time, but for Scott, especially when he
discovered that much of Glacier Tongue had disappeared, a period of anxiety as to the safety of
the Hut at Cape Evans and those in it. Scott told
Wilson and myself to prepare for an attempt to
reach Cape Evans by crossing the icefalls on Erebus :
but this was given up after a talk with Bill. Several
times we prepared to cross the newly frozen ice to
Cape Evans, and several times Scott, after a quiet
talk with Bill, gave up the idea as too dangerous.
One evening we even prepared to start the next
morning, but the whole ice moved away to sea on
the tide without any wind during the night. In a
way I was thankful to see it gone.

Walking with me on the slippery ice-slope which
ended in a cliff and open water Wilson asked me
whom I would take for a third on the Winter
Journey. There was never any doubt whom we

both wanted and Bowers was asked that evening.
We had a few weeks of preparation at Cape Evans
during which Wilson painted many of the most
beautiful water-colours he did, most of them sunsets from Hut Point during the period of waiting.
They are perhaps the best water-colours he ever
did, showing the clear colour and clean brushwork
of a man who was quite fresh and to whom it was
a joy to get back to his paint-box. Two pictures
of Erebus hanging side by side in the Polar Research
Institute, Cambridge, one painted on April 28,
1911, after the Depôt Journey, the other on August
12, 1911, after the Winter Journey, will prove this.
The latter is the work of a tired man.

Almost more beautiful are his pencil drawings,
the delicacy of which suited the snow mountains,
drifts, and cornices before him. It is as a specialist
that he shows the strata of the rocks, the weathering
of a berg or glacier, the striations of an ice-wall,
and the details of pack-ice. There is a dramatic
quality in some of these drawings which his water-
colours possess, but in a smaller degree. Many of
these sketches were made in low temperatures and
perhaps in a wind, slipping his hands out of his
mitts for a minute or two at a time. Many were
done at a camp halt, or even at a pause on the
march, sometimes with his eyes in torture from
snow blindness. Most interesting are those made
in the darkness of winter, the pencil biting hard
into the paper to make a mark which could be
seen. How they bring it all back : better than all
the photographs in the world.

I suppose Bill had spent a good deal of thought
upon details before we started on the Winter

Journey. At any rate we changed over, almost in
a night, from sledging as it had been done before,
when we took pride in getting a meal twenty
minutes after dropping our harness, to an absolutely
new routine. Latterly it took us some four hours
to get up in the morning (so called), and sometimes over an hour to get into our bags. This
showed his adaptability, and failure would have
meant serious frost-bite. He never hurried, insisted that if our hands were frost-bitten we must
drop everything to get them back (we could not
do this for our feet) and was quite content to take
such time as was necessary to do each job as it
came along. This man was so highly strung that
it was the greatest trial to him in civilization to
face a crowd or new people or to pay a week-end
visit : here where quick decisions had to be made
at any moment, he appeared quite calm. I saw
him impatient only once, when I tried to pull him
up an ice cliff by the Alpine rope : the rope had
bitten into the snow cornice so that for all my
pulling it was slack below. All through the
journey he was quite self-controlled, and although
the strain upon his nerves must have been great,
he appeared to be unmoved. As we approached
Cape Evans and the hut that last night in pitch
darkness, he and Birdie had quite an angry argument as to where Cape Evans was : that was because the strain was coming off. I remember that,
because it was the only time.

It was Bill who made us stay seven hours in our
bags and at long last told us we might get up. As
a doctor he judged when his feet or mine were
frost-bitten and then we had to camp. But Bowers

had almost as much share in the leadership for the
journey as Wilson. We formed a kind of committee, I being quite prepared to do what they
thought best. How anybody wrote anything I
don't know ; but Wilson wrote quite a diary and
Bowers kept the meteorological log perfectly and
handled all the instruments. I have mentioned
that we discussed going back : the real difficulty
is that once you get started on a thing of this kind
you can't go back. ' I think we're all right as long
as we have our appetites,' said Bill.

The weeks flew after the Winter Journey. I had
a walk with him one day on the sea ice when we
discussed what we were going to do about the third
year. Bill said he was going to stay if Scott stayed ;
he seemed to think it was Scott's job to go home,
but that it was most doubtful whether the Polar
Party could get back before the ship was forced
to leave, which would probably be about the middle
of March. There was a tremendous amount to be
done between the two journeys and I know that
Bill sat up many a night writing till dawn.

There's a nice film taken on the Barrier of the
three of us and our ponies leaving Safety Camp
on the Polar Journey. Nobby and Bill were a good
pair, and Nobby lasted better than any other pony
until he was killed at the horrible camp in the
Gateway ; he was the only survivor of the Depôt
Journey and had therefore adapted himself to a
Barrier life. There was even a question whether
Bill should lead Nobby part of the way up the
Beardmore ; thank goodness he didn't. That last
day of pony flogging to get the depôt in under the
mountains was a necessary nightmare. Wilson and

I did most of Scott's camp work on the Barrier once the tent lining was thrown over the bamboos ; Scott wandered off to inspect the ponies and discuss their chances. I am sure that he was right : he had all the burden and anxiety of leadership. From One Ton Camp we did our fifteen miles a day pretty regularly, marching by night. As often as not Bowers and Oates were called into our tent after hoosh for a conference, about weights and ponies and so forth. Bowers was always for keeping weights and banking upon the ponies lasting ; but Victor his pony, ' as gentle as a dear old sheep,' had to be killed for want of food in 83 South. Owing to Oates' skill and care even the worst crocks among the ponies did better than had been hoped. ' I congratulate you, Titus,' said Bill in the Gateway, ' And *I* thank you, Titus,' said Scott. That was after 428 miles and the end of the Barrier Stage.

After the Winter Journey November weather on the Barrier seemed like heaven ; before we started it was impossible to imagine such pleasant conditions. We saw little of the Gateway and Mount Hope as we came up to the Glacier, owing to thick weather, but I remember one day when it cleared and we saw those great ranges of beautiful mountains, and Wilson said : ' Well ! The man who stood here and saw that for the first time and plugged into it did a pretty fine thing.' He was, of course, referring to Shackleton.

Shackleton entered the Glacier on slippery ice. We went in on the deepest soft snow, into which our heavy sledges sank to the cross-bars, and acted like snow ploughs. This was due to the great blizzard which hit us when a few miles away from the Gateway. We were working against Shackleton's averages and dates ; this blizzard had not only put us behindhand but had made the surfaces upon which we were to make up for lost time appalling. I am sure that tremendous pull to the Cloudmaker took it out of the men frightfully, and much more than was realized at the time. Scott had the strongest team, including Wilson, Oates and Seaman Evans. They took more care with their runners than any other team, often unloading and turning up their sledge in camp to get rid of any ice ; they impressed one to watch them on the march : there was a solidity and rhythm about them and when they faced and man-handled their sledge you felt it just had to come ; but Oates was limping slightly from an old wound in South Africa on the top of the Glacier, and Atkinson, who knew him best, told me he did not want to go on. Sometimes during those Glacier marches we felt when we camped that we could not go on again. It was the lunch mug of tea which did it ; it lasted me just one and a half hours and they were the best part of the day's march. After some days the doctors, Wilson and Atkinson, had a talk with Scott that we must have a more definite routine.

Scott had settled on man-hauling, and we plugged up that Glacier against time, in fine weather and in thick ; no party returned or could return by the same way they had gone up. For instance, we left our Middle Glacier Depôt somewhere under the Cloudmaker without getting proper land bearings for it : we had to, the clouds were down on the mountains. Some day, every mile surveyed, dog-teams will be taken up and down the Glacier with plenty of food, lying up in thick weather and avoiding the ice-falls. But to take dogs through some of the places we all went through on our way down, when we could not see the ice-falls which we skirted on our way up, until we were into them, and then did not know whether we were too far to the right or left, is sheer impossibility. It seems quite an ordinary thing to take it for granted nowadays that Scott should have taken dogs, and that Amundsen was better equipped than Scott. Those who criticize Scott for relying on man-haulage should go down the Beardmore : I notice they never have. It is 120 miles up, and 120 miles down : and sometimes forty miles across to go wrong in. Take some dog-teams down in thick weather and then talk about it, and not before. There are miles and miles in it where you can drop St. Paul's and the *Terra Nova* and never know they had gone down.

Scott took on his own team to the Pole, adding Bowers from the Last Supporting Party at the last moment. But four days before all that party had depôted their ski and Bowers had to pull some 350 miles on foot in the middle of a team on ski. That he did it and still remained one of the strongest members of the team shows his immense strength : he was unconquerable. But fine as that team was— and it was as good as anything which ever got into harness—we hear of trouble immediately the Last Supporting Party left them : heavy surfaces, sandy snow and falling crystals. The party was feeling the cold, but the temperatures were no lower than expected. From this time onwards things went wrong.

As things got worse Bill's work as a doctor became heavier. As temperatures fall work takes longer and longer to do. In such conditions an enormous amount depends upon the care a man takes of himself ; the idea of a team dashing gallantly through every difficulty is absurd. Wilson had to look after himself and at the same time devote time to others. We know he was also their adviser and friend. He would be later in getting into his sleeping-bag after a meal, he was losing heat which would help him through the night, and his bag would be all the more difficult to thaw out. He had additional responsibility.

What was wrong has been discussed fully and with great care in the last chapter of *The Worst Journey in the World*. The fact which has to be faced is that although these men had full rations they starved to death. The ration was the best that any party had eaten to date, and in those days was considered to be generous. It was vitamin free, but nothing was known about vitamins until a few months after we left England. The party did not die of scurvy. Wilson says nothing about scurvy, and he knew the symptoms as well as anybody ; Atkinson, a specialist in scurvy, examined the bodies while I was with him, and he was emphatic that there were no scurvy symptoms. Nor did they die of the low temperatures, except in so far that they would have lived if the temperatures had remained high.

We found these men starved to death. The shock of finding them where they were was so great that the fact that we had never imagined that they could be short of food was clean forgotten at the time. Years after I came to wonder how they could have been short of food when we knew they had so much ; to my great surprise I found that they had eaten their full rations or more than their full rations all the time except for a few days on the Beardmore Glacier. Meanwhile Atkinson had the food values worked out, according to post-war knowledge. The results were staggering, and a summary of them is in the *Worst Journey*.

These men did not make their distances because they became weak. They became weak because, according to post-war standards, the values of their food were insufficient for them to work under the conditions which they actually met until the end of February, without loss of strength. The conditions on the Barrier in March were far worse than they imagined to be possible ; ' the facts above enumerated were as nothing to the surprise which awaited us on the Barrier.'

The conditions on the Barrier in March were ' −30 in the day, −47 at night pretty regularly,' with no wind or northerly winds, that is, in their faces. Since our return Simpson's Meteorological Report has shown that owing to excessive radiation from the snow surface a cold layer of air is formed in calm weather near the ground which may be many degrees colder than the air above it. It becomes as it were colder than it ought to be. This, however, can only happen during an absence of wind ; when a wind blows the cold air is swept away, the air is mixed, and the temperature rises.

It seems to me that the sudden and unexpected cold which proved their undoing on the Barrier came with the dipping of the sun in the south.

The specialists say that the conditions which these men met were exceptional ; nine times out of ten the party would have come through. This will be proved some day and I should like to put it on record that I believe the conditions which obtained would be met in the same region almost every year : for the sastrugi and snow surfaces show that this is probably a comparatively windless area. Shackleton got in just, and only just, in time.

This is one of the great tragedies. When men who are truly great get into these messes they think more and more of others, and less and less of them-selves. One wonders what Napoleon would have done under similar circumstances. What these men did and what they wrote inspired the world. There was no trace of selfishness, no regret for themselves, no blame of others. There was, it shines through all we know and read, all human help for their companions, and thought for those who would be left.

And of the three who died together in that tent Scott and Bill were complementary one of the other, and the chance which brought them together meant more than anyone could have foreseen. Their partnership organized the discovery of the last con-tinent ; for when they came to it men had wintered in the Antarctic, but never travelled beyond its fringe. Truth to tell, they knew little about it and their first sledging was all wrong ; as the Ice-Quartermaster said of another expedition, ' There they goes ; they knows nothing, and fears nothing.' Yet within some fourteen years it was possible to carry out journeys of some two thousand miles, and for this Scott was mainly responsible and Wilson was always at his right hand. I do not think many people know what Scott did (they think of him merely as a hero) and I do not think people will ever know how much Wilson meant to Scott and to the South.

Scott was a very sensitive man. Some of the jobs he undertook, such as the begging of money in civilization or the driving of animals down South, were torture to him. The man with nerves gets things done : but he has a rotten time in doing them. Had he not been so highly strung and had he not had Wilson by his side to soothe him, I wonder whether so much would have been done : certainly it would have been done with much more wear and tear.

It is the great good fortune of England that Scott wrote—could feel so deeply and express his feelings —as he did. Those words which Scott wrote when he was dying, forced out of him by the circumstances and by his sense of duty, are part of England. Of this I am sure ; the unselfishness, the sacrifice, the fight against hopeless odds immortalized by Scott in that last message and in those letters which he wrote as he died, had their effect upon the Great War and will go on having their effect for many years unknown.

They pitched their last camp perfectly (I suppose they knew) and it was upon the line of cairns between depôts. But cairns and marks on the Barrier are drifted up and disappear so quickly that these men must have died without any certain knowledge that what they had done would be known. Scott when he wrote those words could not know that they would ever be read. And as

he wrote his greatest friend lay dying by his side.
'His eyes have a comfortable blue look of hope
and his mind is peaceful with the satisfaction of
his faith in regarding himself as part of the great
scheme of the Almighty. . . .' Those who knew
Bill know that it would be so : and when you
have read this book you will know it too.

APSLEY CHERRY-GARRARD.

LAMER, 1933.

Foreword

THE thanks of the author are due first and last to Mrs. Wilson who has given into his hands letters and journals, besides some copied extracts of personal letters to her, which cover the whole period of her husband's life. Use has also been made of an unpublished Memoir by his father. From the material thus provided a separate volume could be written on Dr. Wilson as a naturalist alone, to say nothing of his activities in other directions ; and to select from it just that amount required for a biography has necessitated the exclusion of much that is of great interest.

Then to Dr. Leonard Huxley, for his judicious and sympathetic help in revising the manuscript. The completion of the book in its much-reduced form is largely due to him. It proved to be one of the last tasks to which he gave the benefit of his long experience and of his keen personal interest.

Also to Mr. Cherry-Garrard, not only for his Introduction, helpful suggestions, and for permission to quote from *The Worst Journey in the World*, but also for the use of a valuable map of his own making.

The illustrations that appear in this book are from sketches which have been selected as far as possible as representative of Dr. Wilson's art at different periods of his life, but they cannot do

even approximate justice to its range and ver-
satility. His finished pictures of Antarctic scenery
and fauna alone number upwards of four hundred :
some of these may be seen at the Scott Polar
Research Institute in Cambridge, and at the Royal
Geographical Society's Institute, South Kensington.

G. S.

CHAPTER I

Early Years and Cheltenham College

Words must always fail me when I talk of Bill Wilson. I believe he really is the finest character I ever met—the closer one gets to him the more there is to admire. Every quality is so solid and dependable ; cannot you imagine how that counts downhere? Whatever the matter one knows that Bill will be sound, shrewdly practical, intensely loyal and quite unselfish. Add to this a wider knowledge of persons and things than is at first guessable, a quiet vein of humour and really consummate tact, and you have some idea of his values. I think he is the most popular member of the party, and that is saying much.

CAPTAIN SCOTT.

TWENTY years ago the name of Dr. Edward A. Wilson was on the lips of thousands of his countrymen who were profoundly moved by the story of the great South Polar tragedy. He was known as the right-hand man of both Captain Scott's expeditions to the Antarctic, and in some indefined way it was guessed that he was also the soul of them, but he has ever since remained a somewhat shadowy figure moving in the background of those large events. But history would remain incomplete unless he took his rightful place in the foreground of that group of pioneers, and it is the purpose of this book to show how wholly he came to deserve the above-written tribute of his comrade and leader.

I

The second son of Dr. Edward Thomas Wilson
and Mary Agnes (*née* Whishaw) his wife, he was
born at Cheltenham on July 23, 1872, where
'Westal,' the home of his upbringing, was to be
his home to the end of his life. On his father's
side he could look back to a long line of Quaker
ancestors, and from them he seems to have inherited their distinguishing characteristics of industry, modesty, fine culture and quiet self-posses-
sion. *Res non verba*, the family motto, appropriate
to the family as a whole, might seem indeed to
have been specially chosen for him.

For those who affirm that 'the boy is father to
the man' it will be of interest to trace in the characteristics of his early years, which his father's
memories and his mother's diary have preserved,
some of the qualities that were conspicuous in his
manhood.

From infancy a cheerful disposition and a sense
of personal independence appear to have developed
side by side with a strongly emotional temperament that was with difficulty got under control.
'He is the brightest and jolliest of all our babies,
but subject to violent outbursts of temper, and
then he will brook no contradiction.' Already at
two years old 'he is his Father's boy, and his love
for him is most beautiful.' His mother pronounces
him 'the pride of the bunch' but notes that 'he
has comic fits of earnestness during which no one
can succeed in making him smile.' At five years
old 'he is fearless, brave and independent' and
though 'tears are always near the surface,' yet
'nothing can interfere with his own happiness or
with his favourite pursuits.'

These traits foreshadow the deliberate discipline
of strong emotions by which in after life he attained
the fullness of his powers : a serenity of temper
and a tenacity of purpose which obstacles served
only to enhance.

At the close of his third year he was noticed
as 'always drawing,' and a little later his mother
began to give him lessons with the pencil, ' and
he is never so happy as when lying full length on
the floor and drawing little figures in every con-
ceivable attitude, which are full of action and all
his own, for he disdains the idea of copying anything.' His earliest scrap-book rather prophetically contains the picture of some explorers in the
Arctic regions, and for the midnight sun a disc
is neatly cut out of the sketch and filled in with
orange-hued transparent paper in order to give
the requisite effect of light, which he evidently
realized his colours could not. At the age of seven
he began the practice, which continued all his life,
of drawing his own Christmas cards for the family ;
and two years later these little pictures display
such facility, decision, animation and originality
as to make it a matter for surprise that so obvious
a talent was not fostered ; but the fact remains
that beyond the ordinary school curriculum Wilson never received any training in pencil or brushwork in his life.

Concurrently with his devotion to art developed
a passion for collecting shells and fossils, butterflies and dried flowers, ' anything he can lay his
hands upon ' ; at the age of nine he informed
his father that he had quite made up his mind to
be a naturalist, and, having invested a sovereign

given to him in skinning- and stuffing-tools, took
his first lessons in taxidermy. He much preferred
a country ramble to school games, and the welfare of the occupants of his cabinet and aquarium
was more absorbing than any lessons. Yet he
appreciated the discipline of his preparatory school
at Clifton where he says that he was ' made to
work and not allowed to look about him.'   So
anxious was he to learn that he chose to sit with
his back to his favourite ' beasties ' which included
not only the usual collection of silkworms, mice,
butterflies, eggs, shells and fossils, but curiosities
of all kinds such as grass-snakes, newts, frogs,
beetles and other insects, with ingenious devices
for housing them. The masters fortunately looked
with lenient eyes on the scientific vagaries of their
boys, with the result that there was a regular
menagerie in the schoolroom.

He took kindly to the sports, however. As he
wrote long afterwards, at the start of the great
Southern Journey in 1902, ' my strength is in my
legs.' A letter home at the end of a term, when
he had won prizes in the high jump and long
jump, is characteristic :

the chap who might have beaten me has measles. I'm
sorry he's got them because he's rather a jolly chap.
. . . Every fellow finds that when he is here he can
think of such a lot to do in the hols, but when they come
he never does anything ; and I feeling the same have
written down a lot of things that I can do very easily
indeed.

Though he was quite definite in the matter of
his special wants, they were even in his boyhood
simple and never extravagant, and he took pleasure

in doing with less pocket-money than his parents allowed him ; and while his letters from school are full of information about his own pursuits, they are also marked by a rare instinct of courtesy and a consideration for the interests of the rest of the family at home. At the same time too he had a sense of good sportsmanship unusual in a boy of thirteen, and could not endure anything destructive or merely predatory in the way of collecting : he would never allow himself or a friend to *rob* a bird's nest, or to take more than one egg out of four. In manhood collections of any sort became abhorrent to him, and he was content to watch the birds, and note the number of eggs in their nests.

On leaving Clifton he was tried unsuccessfully for a scholarship at Charterhouse, but he always remembered his preparatory school with gratitude :

I failed to get a scholarship but learned a first-class morality. From the year 1884 when I went to Wilkinson's school at Clifton I have had an increasing disgust for impure talk, impurity in every shape,—a thing for which I shall always be grateful to that wonderfully high-toned school. I never heard a dirty word or a doubtful tale or jest there, and when I came into the thick of it afterwards I never had any share in it.

In later life when his lot was sometimes thrown in an environment where refinement was lacking and vulgarity confused with wit, the level look in Wilson's eyes and the for once unsmiling face proved more disconcerting than any words ; and the would-be humorist was abashed to see one of his hearers—a man whose mirth was of the heartiest but whose tongue could scathe—silently rise from his chair with a look of contempt and walk away. 'Everything mean or base,' wrote a friend, 'seemed to shrivel up in his presence.' Men came to realize that to be funny at the expense of decency in Wilson's presence was not wise, and their respect for his scruples in matters of good taste led some of them to form and guard their own. For he combined in a remarkable degree the qualities of constitutional reserve with absolute moral fearlessness.

He had always a very pleasant smile and a very expressive face which could, by a swift change of look, let it be known whether he approved or disapproved of a word or act, and this without uttering a syllable. He never obtruded himself, but he could never be overlooked.[1]

In the summer of 1885 his mother, a lady of various accomplishments which included scientific farming, took over and farmed the Crippetts, an estate situated within three miles of Cheltenham on a low spur of Leckhampton Hill above Shurdington. The home of the fox and the badger, and of birds and butterflies in endless profusion and variety, it was a perfect paradise for the young naturalist : and later in his youth and manhood it became to him the dearest place on earth.

It was then decided that he should enter Cheltenham College as a day-boy, before (as he said later) 'the compulsory games act came into force.' The rival claims of the day-school and boarding-school system, always debatable, are nowadays more than ever debated ; but it is clear that for a boy who knew as well as he did how to employ his leisure, the advantages which he would have gained as a boarder were more than balanced by

---

[1] Sir A. E. Shipley (*The Cornhill*, March 1913).

The Crippetts.
Leckhampton. 1900.
Ted Wilson.

THE CRIPPETTS

the opportunity of continuing uninterrupted during
term-time the lessons he was learning so rapidly
during the holidays from Nature, his real teacher.
Though a keen football-player, he found little joy
in cricket, which seemed to him a waste of time,
robbing him of the priceless summer afternoons
and long evenings which he could spend so much
more profitably.[1]

He entered the College in the winter term of
1886, under the regime of the Rev. Herbert Kynas-
ton, D.D., who reports of him before resigning,
'he ought to make a useful and hard-working
man.' In 1889 the reins of the College were
taken and tightened by the Rev. Herbert A. James,
D.D. (afterwards of Rugby and St. John's, Oxford),
who at the end of a year reports of him, 'I am
much pleased with his conduct in several particu-
lars.' He shared with the College in general a
great respect and affection for Dr. James, and in
later years kept in touch with him from time to
time. His future brother-in-law, Godfrey Rendall,
well remembers him at this time—'as a thin, lithe
schoolboy, with close-cut, wavy, dark-red hair, a
pair of unusually bright blue eyes, and a half-
amused, half-quizzical expression, often turning to
a merry smile.' [2]

His school reports show him to have been slightly
above the average in classics, but below it in
mathematics, a defect which handicapped him in
chemistry and physics, and proved a burden to

---

[1] Compare the last request of Captain Scott concerning
the education of his son : ' Teach the boy Natural History :
it is better than games.   They encourage it in some schools.'

[2] From his Memoir in *The Treasury*, April 1913.

him long afterwards when he had to learn how to take observations on the Polar Journey. But in spite of this, science was the study of which he had the ' best grasp ' in his schooldays ; and in this he obtained Honours in the Oxford and Cambridge Board Examinations. He won the school prize for drawing four years in succession, in his last two years that for geology, and in his last year those for the best collection of eggs, and butterflies and moths.

The Rev. Maurice Tanner was at that time President of the College Natural History Society, and Wilson was early appointed Secretary of the Ornithological Section. In the *Cheltonian* for March 1913 Mr. Tanner records that :

He was most conscientious, and faced much unpopularity by correcting certain irregularities which had grown up in the collection of birds' eggs. He was an enthusiastic and capable observer of the habits of birds, recording the arrivals and departure of the migratory species, and even when quite a boy had a singular gift of accurate and patient observation. He would take endless trouble to discover the nest of a rare bird, and would not give in till he found it. One of his early triumphs, not yet forgotten, was the finding of a Hawfinch's nest at the Crippetts. But he was no mere egg-collector, for he had the true scientist's love of knowledge for its own sake. What remains most in the recollection of those who knew him in these days is the freshness and interest which his intense love of Nature gave to his companionship. He had even then a kind of scientific reserve which prevented him from forming conclusions without long search and observation. There was an indescribable charm about him.

But his real interests lay outside school and school-life altogether and the hours of his freedom

were so precious that he stole them from his sleep.
During term in summer-time he would rise soon
after dawn, steal out of the house with a piece of
bread in his pocket, and away to his favourite
haunt—a coppice at the Crippetts or on Crickley
Hill—in order to note the budding of some particular wild flower, the state of the clouds and
weather, or the dates of the arrival and nesting
of migrant birds. One of his sisters recalls an
occasion of his return to Westal at breakfast-time
(but this was in the holidays) with two plovers'
eggs in his pocket : on arrival he found that the
chicks were on the point of hatching : without
waiting for breakfast he immediately walked the
three miles back, deposited them safely in the nest
he had taken them from—and so home again. A
touch very true to character this.

It was indeed during the holidays that he laid
the foundations of his own special education, dis-
ciplining his body to endure hardness by nights
spent on the bare ground under the open sky,
wrapped in a horse-rug, training his ears to distinguish the sounds and his eyes to mark the habits
of every little wild thing in wood and on wold,
as well as to observe and memorize the colours
of land and rock, tree and sky ; and committing
all the stores of his observation with fidelity and
exactness to systematic notes and sketches.

In his eighteenth year he was confirmed by Dr.
Ellicott, Bishop of Gloucester.

I remember I was prepared carefully for it in a class
with other boys, but I think I was always much more
at home with God in country rambles than in Church
matters, and I think I felt a confirmed *child* of God long

before the good Bishop laid his hands on me. I like the expression ' child of God ' immensely, for it was just as a very child that I was always speaking and praying to Him.

From January 1889 he began to keep a Journal, a practice suggested to him by reading Darwin's notes on *The Voyage of the Beagle*, which he kept up to the end of his life. During his schooldays each week was made to occupy a page, tabulated under the several days and subjects to include notes on temperature and wind, birds and insects, zoology and botany, and miscellaneous.

From these it can be gathered, *inter alia*, that he read Wallace's *Naturalist on the Amazon*, *The Malay Archipelago*, and *Darwinism* ; and developed an early appreciation of Kingsley ; that ' if you rub Kestrels' eggs when wet, the colour comes off ' ; that he tried Planchette, but ' it won't write for me ' : that ' on a memorable walk I met a certain Mabel Brown (aged 10)—the first person I really fell in love with ' : that, while given to trespassing, he always parted on good terms with the keepers. He notes the songs of birds :

Hedge Sparrow's song reminds one of musical chairs. Disconnected sentences.

Distinctly heard the agreeable notes of the Jay denied by Hewitson. They reminded me of a Peewit's cry and a Blackbird's low contented chuckle—Putty wit, ti-woo, two choo choo.

The Wood Warbler has a sibilant laugh like quick shrill prolonged Chiff-chaff.

His father and uncle had been brought up as boys to a sturdy self-education. With a little money in their pockets they were sent off for excursions afoot on the sole condition that they were to make

it last as long as possible and to bring back full
notes of all that they had done or seen.[1] Dr.
Wilson passed on this method of training to his son ;
and it was one which his son said later had taught
him more of lasting value than anything he had
ever learnt. In this way he made himself familiar
with nearly the whole of Wales during his holidays, and out-of-the-way parts of Pembrokeshire
and Snowdonia particularly, where he taught himself to climb.

Thus it is evident that while at school, apart
from a remarkable quickness of eye wedded to a
deftness of touch, Wilson showed no signs of mental
power much above the average. He was not
brilliant ; he did not shine at school. In fact he
never ' shone ' : he was like his own pictures in
this, that there were no ' high-lights ' about him ;
half-tones there were, and these of an extreme
delicacy. He was never conspicuous, but content
to be in the background, except when he could
be of use, and then as unobtrusively as possible.
He had that modesty which comes of a true sense
of proportion and is the hall-mark of a balanced
mind.

But the school of whose noble traditions he was
justly proud, and to whose record his own life
and death have added a new lustre, has fitly
honoured him. The magnificent life-size portrait
in the College Library by Hugh Riviere [2] (also
an old Cheltonian) shows him alert, sketch-book

---

[1] See *Life of Sir Charles Wilson*, pp. 5–6.

[2] The picture is composite. The portrait and background
are the work of Hugh Riviere, the dogs that of his father
Briton Riviere.

in hand, with sledge and dog-team on the sea-ice at the foot of the Great Ice Barrier ; his Antarctic sketches grace its walls ; the Light in the *Fortitude* Window of the Chapel shows him also in polar dress with his dog ' Stareek ' at his feet, the theme for the background being suggested by two of his best studies in colour on the Last Expedition—Mount Erebus, with a Lunar Halo crowning it above ; while underneath the window in the Old Boys' stalls a tablet to his memory is set next to that of his uncle, Sir Charles Wilson.   The statue of him executed by Lady Scott, given by the people of Cheltenham, stands in the Promenade. And the *Cheltonian* for March 1913 concludes its tribute to his memory with these words :

Of all Cheltenham boys whose life and death will be remembered with pride by Cheltenham boys and masters who knew or taught them, no one has left memories of a life more absolutely simple, gentle and honourable.

CHAPTER II

Caius College, Cambridge

Self-reverence, self-knowledge, self-control,
These three alone lead life to sovereign power.
TENNYSON.

IN October 1891 Wilson entered Caius College
as an Exhibitioner, and spent his first term
in rooms outside the College, at 4 Round
Church Street. His 'year,' we are told, had the
reputation of being turbulent as well as quarrel-
some, and Wilson was the trusted mediator in all
disputes. Dr. J. Stanley Gardiner (afterwards
Professor of Biology at Cambridge) thus recalls
his impressions after their first Hall together as
freshmen.

We adjourned for coffee, and endeavoured to show
off to one another as the heroes of football, cricket and
rowing. He was silent during our discussion, until he
was pointedly asked what he proposed to do. It was
his first trial as a man, and he replied that he intended
to work seven hours a day and also row, a position he
maintained all his years in Cambridge. That night he
made his mark in his year ; he showed he had a character, but he remained in many ways an irresponsible
boy during his undergraduate life, always respecting
himself, but always in the midst of whatever fun and
jollity that might be going, noisy among the noisiest. . . .
He was then a man of facts with a strong moral sense
to support him, but with little idea as to his future ;
the why and wherefore did not interest him. . . .

13

He immediately began rowing with zest ; its moral and physical demands on stamina, and the sheer thrill of the races, all appealed to him ; besides which, he was always very keen for the honour of his College. While training for the ' Lents Trials,' he wrote to his father :

It is all great fun, and though everyone at one time or another wishes he were well out of it, there's a fascination in keeping oneself at the treadmill. . . . How men can go through three years at Cambridge and not row is to me a marvel. [And to his mother]—Don't you fash yourself over my heart, because it's all right so far. You can't really mean that *no* race is worth hurting it.

In this event the second boat in which he was rowing succeeded in bumping the first, and so he got his colours for the ' Lents.' In subsequent years he stroked the Caius Senior Trials, finally securing his colours for the ' Mays ' in his third year. But he was never a conspicuous athlete, and his election to membership of the highly exclusive ' Shakespearian Society ' is, surprisingly enough, a tribute to his popularity among those who were. For like many other collegiate societies with literary titles, ' its exclusiveness did not take the line of confining itself to the more profound students of Elizabethan Drama in residence, but of closing its doors to all but the leading athletic lights of the time.'

Returning to College for his second term, by a happy coincidence his ' gyp ' proved to be a Sapper who had served under his uncle, Major-General Sir Charles Wilson, R.E., during the Nile Expedition ; and Wilson settled in the highest rooms over the Gate of Virtue where, says a friend, ' he had a veritable museum of skulls, birds' feet and claws, and miscellaneous bones, while the whole place was littered with chalk and pencil drawings.'

Carved in the stone below the mantelshelf the inscription now runs :

EDWARD ADRIAN WILSON WHO REACHED THE SOUTH POLE WITH CAPTAIN SCOTT IN 1912 LIVED IN THESE ROOMS FROM 1892 TO 1895

And the flag bearing the College arms, given to him by Mrs. Roberts, wife of the Master, and carried to the Pole, now occupies a niche above the dais in the College Hall.

For all his geniality there was about him, as all his contemporaries at College testify, a certain inaccessibility. He never sought friendship, either at that time or after ; men sought his ; and those to whom he gave it were chosen, on his side, with deliberation and judgment. Two of his fellow-students—Fletcher and Young—were among them, and with two others—Fraser and Charles—his friendship, begun at Cambridge and cemented at St. George's Hospital, continued through life. To them must be added Abercrombie, a friend of post-graduate days. To a great extent it may be said of him that ' all men counted with him, but none too much.' He had a way of studying people from a distance, reading them with his inner eyes as he read a landscape ; and among those whom he thus studied and appreciated were some commonly called eccentric, whom the majority either scorned or ignored. The loan of his excessively neat and accurate notes of lectures, clearly illustrated, was in frequent request, and he was as free in sharing his knowledge as his possessions.

E.W.A.   D

I knew Wilson intimately [writes Dr. Fraser], both at Cambridge and St. George's, and of all the men I have known he stands out by reason of the beauty of his character and the highness of his aims. As an undergraduate he lived a life of ascetic purity, but he was quick to make friends and saw the good in the wildest undergraduate, for his purity was of the quality of flame which need fear no contamination. With even the lighter-minded undergraduates he was immensely popular, for he possessed that certain passport to the College's heart—a vein of delightful humour. No one could meet him without being the better for it, and it falls to few men's lot to be so deeply loved by his friends. . . .

He was essentially a very just, tolerant, and extra-ordinarily strong man. He was utterly fearless and would condemn a man's action which was not pure and sound in the strongest possible way. He had a tremendous belief in his own powers ; there was nothing that he would not attempt to do, and yet he was the most beautifully modest man in the world. He was completely unselfish, and had no idea of self-advertisement nor of advancing himself except in his work. He was absolutely without any personal ambition, but was just intensely keen on doing the work he had in hand to the very best of his ability. His faith was the essence of his life ; his religious views were simple but very strongly held.

From the outset he clearly took his own line and meant to stick to it. Below the surface of his gaiety lay a deep seriousness, known only to his intimates, or revealed uncompromisingly whenever a right principle was impugned. He respected the principles of others, even if they conflicted with his own, but only if they were consistently and sincerely held. ' Each man,' he was fond of saying, ' is a law to himself.' And this uncompromising attitude to life was beginning to make itself felt not only at College but at home. An

idealistic habit of thought and a Spartan way of
living drove him in upon his own resources, and
when he found that his thoughts and interests were
not shared by the majority his sense of isolation
deepened and he shut up like a sensitive plant to
the touch.   By nature intensely nervous and highly
strung he steeled himself to self-mastery by the
deliberate exercise of his will.   He took out-of-the-
way means to acquaint himself with the experience
of pain, and resolutely set before himself that ideal
of Christian asceticism which was later to reach its
supreme test when he led the Winter Journey of
1911.

The standard which he set himself was too
severe, and the levels on which his mind habitually moved were too high, to find favour with the
merely pious.   Simple, direct, and sincere, he
was impatient of all that seemed to him second-
rate, or that savoured of compromise.   His comic
fits of earnestness which his mother had noted in
his babyhood no longer reacted in violent outbursts of temper when he was misunderstood, but
to a manner mildly cynical—even at times a trifle
contemptuous ; and the half-amused, half-quizzical
expression, often turning to a merry smile which a
friend had remarked in his boyhood, could also
assume on occasion a look of disgust which he was
at no pains to conceal.   And if there were two
vices which excited his disgust more than others
they were hypocrisy and injustice, in any shape or
form.   Indeed, the two qualities which probably
attracted him most in Captain Scott later on were
the latter's transparent sincerity and love of justice.
But there was also one human frailty which he

could never tolerate ; although his sympathies were sensitively quick and very easily touched, he detested self-pity. ' It's quite possible that even a child's worries,' he once wrote tersely to a victim of self-pity, ' are as hard to put up with for it, as yours are for you.'

Indeed, in any social atmosphere where conventionality, respectability and mediocrity prevailed, Wilson in his early twenties could not have been perhaps an altogether comfortable person to live with. A caustic tongue was a formidable weapon which could also become a dangerously unruly member, and this he sternly set himself to curb, but it took some little time ; he was ' Bill the Critic ' and even ' Bill the Cynic ' to a few of his comrades of the *Discovery* days, but he was ' Bill the Peacemaker ' to all without exception on the *Terra Nova* and ever after.

His deep affection for his home and every member of his home-circle remained unalterable all through his life, while his love for his father was always and especially ' most beautiful.' He could never bear to feel, or to be felt, out of love with anyone for long ; he was not blind to his own faults, and in the making of amends was always ready to meet the other more than half-way. This inherent humility is evinced by the following revealing words, written to one with whom he had felt for some time out of touch :

Write and tell me I am forgiven. I know I am proud, conceited, scornful, bitter and hard and insulting very often, and always selfish, but I don't like you to treat me as though I wasn't trying to do a bit better. The dog will out now and again, but he hasn't broken his chain yet.

GLOUCESTER CATHEDRAL

His Easter vacation of 1892 began with a crowded week, typical of many. He attempted to walk to London, his luggage consisting of a toothbrush and a clean collar ; but being overtaken by rain he dried himself in a waiting-room and proceeded by rail. His main object was to attend a course of addresses which his friend Canon Knox-Little was delivering in Kensington ; the remaining hours of every day were spent in the Zoo, the British Museum, the Natural History Museum, the National Gallery, Olympia, or Westminster Abbey. This vacation ended with a ' night out ' also typical of many. He slept out in the gorse on Leck-hampton Hill, walked to Cooper's Hill and through Birdlip woods to the Crippetts when the sun was rising, bathed, and went on to Westal for break-fast.

In the summer vacation he and his friend Young matriculated at the University of Göttingen. He could make himself understood in German, though he blames himself for not having applied himself more thoroughly to its grammar. His comments on the paintings and architecture of the cities visited *en route* reveal a considerable knowledge of art already acquired as well as æsthetic discern-ment and feeling. At Göttingen, after a severe climb of a very dirty tree, he succeeded in securing a young kite which he brought home to the Crip-petts, where for some time it was, to say the least (says his father), a troublesome pet. It subse-quently found a more permanent home in the Zoo.

But the Crippetts, which no other haunt ever displaced in his affections, was still his happiest hunting-ground.

To see Wilson at his best [wrote his friend John Fraser] one had to go and stay with him at the Crippetts. There he was really at home and in his natural place. He knew every stick and stone, every hedge and tree in the neighbourhood. To see him climb a tree was a revelation. I have always been, since a boy, very keen on birds, and my training is to make me observant, but I was like a child with Wilson. He would come to a hedge or a bush I had examined and show me nests which I had overlooked. I have seen him, when we were working a hedge, suddenly stop and then swoop down like a merlin hawk and produce a large grass-snake. I had not seen it : Wilson had seen it, and observed that it was not an adder—which were common in the neighbourhood— and had beaten the snake for quickness. He loved to spend nights in the woods and listen to all bird and animal life. He could tell you not only the species of every bird that sounded a note (and how difficult that is at night), but also the precise occupation at the moment of the bird that had uttered it. An old canal near Tewkesbury, overgrown with grass and bushes, was the place he loved best, and there every bush and tuft of grass revealed to him its secrets. He was tall and thin, rather like a thoroughbred horse, and walked with a long raking stride with his body slightly bent.

At Cambridge he seems to have combined together with a strict obedience to high principles a curious indifference to academic rules and regulations. For his respect for the former it will be sufficient to quote his own words (written later at Battersea).

Each man's conscience is a law to himself.—But no one lives up to his highest aspirations.—A law to oneself ! and therefore a very rigorous and exacting law (which one cannot humbug as one did the masters at school), for my present teacher is God Himself who has put the law in my heart with perfect liberty.

But his apparent ingenuousness in regard to the

latter may be gleaned from a letter to his father
after he had overstayed a vacation.

Jan. 21, '93. No unpleasantness whatever arose between the tutor and myself, for I told him I had had
orders from a sister not to leave home before she returned. So he asked me if she was Vice-Chancellor of
the University, and I told him she wasn't, and he seemed
quite satisfied and grinned. So I grinned and we passed
to the more interesting topic of rowing.

Still more from the following anecdote related
by Sir William Hardy.

There usually are in the Cam, and especially in the
Granta, a few trout, some of large size. In Wilson's time
there was a large and well-known trout some pounds in
weight which lived at the edge of the mill-race in the
pool below Grantchester Mill. Many people had tried
to catch this trout. Wilson was one of the keenest fisher-
men, and it occurred to him that the trout might be
caught in the very early morning.

One morning in the summer of 1893, he slipped out of
College, made his way to the pool and caught the trout.
It was on the Monday immediately after the May Races
and probably the head porter, Beckley, who would have
done anything for Wilson, let him out. At any rate
Wilson caught his fish and in the pride of the catch,
without thinking of consequences, he sent the fish as a
present to the then Master of Caius College, Dr. Ferrers.

The Master sent for Wilson to thank him for his hand-
some present. But the Master was a strict disciplinarian
of the old school and in the course of the conversation
Wilson told the story of how he had caught the trout.
The Master in his curious high-pitched squeaky voice
said :

' But, Mr. Wilson, you were out of College at three
o'clock in the morning ? '

' Yes,' replied Wilson.

' You had leave, no doubt ? '

' No,' said Wilson.

'Then I am afraid I must send you down.'

And sent down he was for the last few days, in spite of the intercession of the Senior Tutor, E. S. Roberts, who was himself Master after Ferrers' death.

At the end of May '94 he successfully passed the first part of his M.B. Exam., and wrote importunately to his father :

You certainly ought to pay me a visit before I go down, oughtn't you, Dad ? I should be so delighted if you could manage it. It costs very little to come up for the day, and though the journey is pretty long I think it will do you a lot of good to get a glimpse of undergrad days again. *Do* manage it.

[And again]—I blessed you for making me draw all those flowers and their parts ; you can't think how they helped me in the Botany. . . . You say you will come up when I take my degree, or at some indefinite future time. I think you had much better come up when the races are on, than the week after when I suppose I shall take my degree. Do manage it, Dad.

His father managed it ; had the satisfaction of seeing his son row in his College boat ; and of receiving the expressed wish of the Master that he should stay up for another year, because of the value of his influence in the College. The following week Wilson passed with First Class Honours in the Natural Science Tripos, Part I. The prize he chose was five volumes of Ruskin bound in blue calf. To his father he wrote on June 17, after taking his B.A. degree :

I am so very glad that I haven't disappointed you after my three years up here. You don't know how your letter delighted me ; to feel that you are proud of something I had done is enough for anyone. I had a line from Dr. James which made me very proud. . . . ' Butterflies and Bees ' is a picture in this year's Academy, and it just gives my idea of the six years' medical training. The first three are the butterflies up here, the last three are the bees in Hospital, and now the sooner I get there the better.

His own wishes were all for getting to grips with his Hospital work without delay.

I am afraid, Dad [he writes], I am quite set against taking the 2nd part of the Tripos. It will not help me in the F.R.C.S. ; I don't want to take to scientific work for itself ; I don't like it sufficiently. But what I *am* anxious to get on to is the practical part of Medicine and Surgery. I am certain I shall do better in it than I have done in anything so far.

In spite of this, however, his parents accepted the advice of the Master, which was strongly backed by the opinion of Sir Clifford Allbutt, that he should take Part II of the Tripos ; so he stayed up for a fourth year, and although unsuccessful it is probable (in his father's judgment) 'that his additional time at the University was an unmixed gain.'

During the Long Vacation he found time for teaching a class of ten in a Sunday School, and wrote to his mother :

My Sunday School boys are little beasts. I've got about the worst class—or rather, a class in the worst room, which is the top one. They are about 14. As they won't listen to a lesson, I only give them a quarter of an hour, and then read them Fowler's *Tales from the Birds*.

[And to his father]—You poured balm into my soul in your last letter because I had been thinking that I had spent too much time in general reading. I shall think so no longer, nor shall I be shy of taking up some time with my drawing.

His general reading was various. It included

the lives of many famous painters, and finding that
they all had to learn the technique of their art he
was anxious to attend evening classes at a School
of Art while working at his Hospital.   Yet he never
had time for this, and from first to last was a self-
taught artist.

He went in for Part II of the Natural Science
Tripos and the second M.B. Exam., close together
in the summer of '95, and failed in both—a great
disappointment, for ' I could have managed one
if I had left the other alone.'   But he had just
carried off the University prize for Diving, so it
may be supposed that the disappointment was
much mitigated.

Thus ended what he called the ' butterfly '
existence of his academic career, and the much
busier ' bee ' life of his medical training was at
hand : how much busier, and fraught with how
great consequences, neither he nor his parents
guessed.

CHAPTER III

St. George's Hospital and Life at Battersea

Be earnest, earnest, earnest,—mad, if thou wilt!
Do what thou dost as if the stake were heaven,
And that thy last deed ere the judgment-day.
When all's done nothing's done : there's rest above :
Below, let work be death if work be love!

KINGSLEY.

IN October 1895 Wilson was inexpensively lodged at 18 Denbigh Road, Westbourne Grove, but in June of the following year transferred his few belongings to a single room ('8s. a week and quite comfortable') at 23 Delamere Crescent, Paddington.

My rooms were in Delamere Crescent along the canal —or rather my room was ; it looked over acres of chimney-pots and a Plane tree, all of which I drew most accurately because I was reading Ruskin on truth in drawing being the main thing to aim at, and I was so pleased when I thought these chimney-pots made what I thought was a picture : there was even a corner of brickwork in front close to my window, and I copied each brick.

I spent part of each day at the Zoo drawing ; and had the happiest time there, but in a strange solitary way, hunting in Hyde Park for weeds and mushrooms to draw. I had no meal in my room except breakfast of tea, toast, and watercress, so I got to know all the tea-shops and restaurants in Westbourne Grove, and exactly how much you could get for your money at each of them, and the regular customers and the cats and the waitresses ;

25

one of the last I remember now, she had a nice face and used to forage for me and tell me when the meat was high.

'Ted's financial arrangements (says his father) were at all times peculiar, and he took special pleasure in doing on as little as possible. "My principle," he said, "is to have as little money in hand as possible, for if I have any I spend it." '

His financial arrangements were in fact much more peculiar than his father supposed. '8s. a week and quite comfortable' speaks for itself (even in pre-war days), and requires no further comment ; but his habits of life as a medical student were frugal in the extreme. After the 'breakfast' already described he would walk back and forth from his lodgings to Hospital (always allowing himself a little extra time for such a breath and a sight of the country as a saunter through Hyde Park afforded) and lunch on hot potatoes and coffee, or some equally meagre fare, at a street-stall. Denying himself every luxury, except that of tobacco, he found it next to impossible to resist appeals for help in cases of genuine distress : he could seldom pass a flower-seller or a pavement-artist, for a fellow-feeling makes us wondrous kind.

Life in the slums of Battersea later on, though better adapted to personal comfort than his Paddington lodgings, 'seems' (he confessed) 'to run away with all my money. I used rarely to pawn anything—now my watch and chain are in durance vile. It is true that the watch won't go, so it is more useful in than out.'

Mrs. Leighton-Hopkins recalls an occasion when, happening to be kneeling behind him in church,

she was horrified to see that the soles of his boots
were worn through to the socks. Yet it was his
' to keep the eye clear by a sort of personal alacrity
and cleanliness ' : his linen was always spotless and
his clothes, if old and worn, scrupulously neat :
even in the Antarctic his dress was conspicuous
among the others' for its tidiness.

Practise neatness [he would say]. It is a good thing,
and all one with general restraint and patience and
godliness. To be neat you must never be impatient, and
to be really tidy you must never be in a needless hurry
or bustle.

There was indeed a perfection of refinement in
his person and manner, as well as a delicacy, precision, and deftness in every thing he touched,
whether a patient's bandage, a dried leaf, or a
bird's wing.

The inner current of his life was setting in a
course of which his parents were unaware, but a
few extracts from a long correspondence with his
mother at this time may serve to indicate the
direction it was taking.

Everyone is too much afraid or too selfish to be
' quixotic ' even in little things. Everyone lives by a
rule of thumb—by the laws of Society, or the laws of
the land, or the laws of the Church, or what not ; whereas no one is bound by anything but the law of his own
conscience.

One must not throw over responsibilities which one
has undertaken, that's a certainty. If one finds one has
made a mistake one must live it through, even if it is
life-long. . . . I am quite convinced that everyone
should follow his own conscience so long as it does not
interfere with any responsibility previously undertaken.
If we find it does, we have made an error and we must
just take the consequences.

I wish we could go shares in one another's energy. I have much more than I can do with in this hen-coop. I would swap it for some of your pain, my dear old Mother, but that is easier said than done.

One gets one's ideas from within and one wants no proofs, and so one has none to give to another. Conviction is above abstract reasoning ; I never feel that I have suffered for any of my sins half enough, so that I should feel in no way surprised or disappointed by any bodily ailment that happened to me, such as losing a hand or getting Consumption. . . .

At the beginning of May an epidemic of small-pox was raging in Gloucester. Wilson, being then at home, packed his bag as if for London, and having without his parents' knowledge secured admission to the Isolation Hospital, spent a day there ' seeing every type in every stage,' and then walked to Churchdown where he lay out on the hill to disinfect before continuing his journey.

In September he was beginning his Midwifery Course, with little sleep and long hours in the slums, relieved by the constant companionship of his friend John Fraser with whom he used to spend hours with some chocolate and rolls on Wimbledon Common in what he called ' one of God's ditches,' watching the nightingales, night-jars, and other birds.

But the strain of a year's work at high pressure on short commons could not but tell : though he had tried to tone himself up by long walks to Oxford and elsewhere, the effort had resulted in acute tonsillitis ; and in October Dr. Rolleston, under whom he was working, recommended his returning home for another week as he appeared run down in health : ' I need hardly say I am not ill,' he wrote, ' all I want is a decent atmosphere for a bit.' And this warning of physical overstrain led to a decision to make a change in his mode of life. His Journal for November 5, '96, has this entry :

> Packed everything into a four-wheeler and came down to live with the Leighton-Hopkins' at Caius House, Battersea Square. This change will open my eyes to another phase of life which I think will have a good deal of interest. . . . Living here in Battersea is really a good healthy change for me, as I hate Society, and here I shall have to learn to put up with a certain amount every day.

So he wrote the day after his arrival at the Mission House, and afterwards in retrospect : ' The Warden and his wife were real parents to me in their kindness.'

But social gatherings were pain and grief to Wilson. His heart was in the wilds, or with the dreams and deeds of men. There was nothing gregarious in his nature. The nervousness of his disposition was accentuated by the high tension of the life he was leading, with its long working hours and late nights : ' Alternations of abject misery, almost suicidal,' (so he afterwards expressed it) ' with feelings of extraordinary freedom and happiness.' This neurosis was so acute at times that it had a physical reaction of a painful kind necessitating the use of a sedative whenever he had an unusually trying social ordeal to undergo ; and this he administered to himself with the judicious caution with which he would have treated a patient, and was able to abandon without the slightest effort.

He smoked, however, to excess, and many were the resolves he made unavailingly to break himself of the habit. At intervals, for periods often of weeks and even of months, he gave it up; he would, for instance, at the beginning of Lent fling his pipe away in Crippetts woods, but always remembered when Lent was over where to find it. After many severe struggles with himself he did eventually give up tobacco in 1900, though he had been a 'vicious smoker,' deeply inhaling the smoke of pipes and even of cigars; and after a year's trial of abstinence declared that there was no doubt that his general health was much the better for it.

Several pages of his Battersea Diary devoted to this subject show how seriously he sought a scientific as well as a common-sense basis for his principles when they clashed with his inclinations, and they stand as the record of a battle that he fought with himself and nobly won. But not indeed at once: after a six-years' total abstention from tobacco he returned to his pipe again for a few months when living on the moors of Scotland, and only finally abandoned it in 1908, after which the craving entirely left him, so that he was able to watch Scott and Oates enjoy their cigarettes at the South Pole with perfect equanimity.

For Christmas 1896 he took the place of a married man at the Hospital 'that he may go home and play with the children.' His only wants for the season's gifts, when asked to state them, were 'medical and surgical books, and any small contribution towards the purchase of an ophthalmoscope.'

On February 9, 1897, he heard Nansen speak.[1]

A tall powerful fair-haired man ; good sense of humour, and a good touch of pathos now and again, but something makes one doubt if it is always genuine, e.g. when deploring the necessity for shooting their two last dogs, Johannsen shot his and he shot Johannsen's. There was a photo shown of the latter walking off with a string to the dog to do it. The pathos goes if this photo was taken at the time, but perhaps it was not.

Perhaps a reminiscence of this was in his mind when, six years later returning with Scott and Shackleton from the ' Farthest South,' he had to perform the same sad duty, and made afterwards one of the most moving of his sketches—' The Last of the Dogs.'

Feb. 18th. (To an 'At Home' at his uncle Sir Charles Wilson's.)

Aunt Olivia clapped her hands when I came in, really a little embarrassing in a drawing-room full of strangers. I almost wished I had my hair brushed up to look like Nansen, but I had had it cut that very afternoon to show a bit of collar.

He never missed his Sunday evening's walk from Battersea to Paddington (4½ miles each way) to hear a sermon from the Rev. T. H. Passmore whom he describes as ' the little, fluent, hook-nosed, don't-care-a-damn man—as sound a Christian as I have ever heard.'

And he enjoyed his walks to and from the Hospital through Battersea Park and along the Thames—

---

[1] ' Yesterday I was pleasantly astonished to find that Wilson had some notes on Nansen's " Farthest North," giving extracts of his sledge-weights, &c., and these may be of great use in calculating our own weights.'—Scott, *Voyage of the Discovery*, I, 306.

where one sees gulls and yellow wagtails and even carrion
crows, just enough to remind one that the world isn't
all made up of bricks and mortar and stinking wood
pavement. . . . One of the days on which the river
looks really beautiful—absolutely still water with a
brilliant reflexion close at hand, fading further off into
a mist which was lit up by a real Spring sunshine on
the S. side, and thicker and deeper on the North.
London has a beauty of its own at sunset, which you
don't see elsewhere. It's the smoke that does it. Crossing the river as I do now when the sun is going down
is a new treat every day. . . . I feel in London like a
soda-water bottle in an oven.

For exercise in the winters he played Rugby
football for his Hospital, sustaining a ' hæmatoma '
—' a name which makes me proud, the Footballer's
or Lunatic's ear.' And in the summers he rowed
in its Four-oar. Any other hours that he could
spare were spent in the Zoo, to draw and study
birds ; or at the Natural History Museum ; or
at various Art and Picture Galleries, at one of
which he remarks, ' There are some good pictures
there, but I am certain that with practice I could
put more character in than some of them had.'
But it was at the National Gallery that he laid the
foundations of his own special skill, being, as he
said, ' smitten to distraction with Turner's drawings.' Ruskin and Turner may be said indeed
to have been his only teachers.

He was under no illusion in regard either to his
capacities or his limitations. He trusted to his
mother wit in medicine as in art. As an example
of the former :

Confidence in Diagnosis as in Billiards comes and goes
early, and the stage has to be passed through when you
think you can get to the bottom of every disease you

HYDE PARK CORNER.
From the top of St. George's Hospital.

come across. I am very hopeful about it though, because
I feel my eyes are quicker to spot things than other
people's, and it's chiefly a matter of observing and keeping your common senses awake.

He noticeably preferred clinical work in the
wards and study in the Hospital museum to attend-
ance at lectures. One day, Dr. Whipham gave
him a ' queer brain ' to draw quite unexpectedly,
and it had to be done at once.

The conditions were not the best possible. They fished
out an old paint-box, some throat brushes, and some
shiny foolscap, and I had to do it then and there before
it was put into spirit. I hope it will be good enough
for the Hospital Museum. . . . The brain was quite
appreciated, but even more were some sketches I did
of the Staff during lectures which they say must be
exhibited at our Graphic meeting next year.

The authorities recognized the value to medical
science of this combination of artistic skill and
anatomical knowledge, if employed in pathological
drawing ; but to Wilson himself it had an
immediate practical advantage, in that the guinea
fee ' enabled me to redeem my valuables from
sundry pawnbrokers.' Drs. Rolleston,[1] Ogle,
Shield and Latham all made use of his services in
this way, the first-named especially, for whom his
great regard ' both as a doctor and as a man ' was
ripening into friendship, and who now asked him
to illustrate his book on *The Diseases of the Liver.*

To return to his life at Battersea. Caius Mission
was in the midst of a large slum area, and immediately after his arrival he undertook to conduct the
children's service in the mission room on Sunday

---

[1] Afterwards Sir Humphry Rolleston, Bt., Regius Professor
of Medicine at Cambridge.

. . . I am mad to leave town and feel as fit as a horse.
I think Mowgli felt so in the time of the Spring running.
The fitter I feel the more I swear.

Having spent the day before his examination,
May 3, '97, ' with the birds and beasts of Madingley
woods' rather than with books, he finished his
papers ' feeling confident that I was through.' He
was. He had crammed two years' reading into
fifteen months. Meanwhile he could afford to shed
some of the grime and grind of London in Crippetts woods by night as well as day, watching the
birds ; and on returning to London made friends
with a fellow-traveller : each took to the other but
parted without learning each other's names :

' Ships that pass in the night' [this is a phrase that
he was fond of using]—not the first instance lately ; and
if you can't touch pitch without being defiled I am certain that it's more true that you can't meet a sound
man or woman without being the better for it.

At this point in his career it nearly came to pass
that equatorial Africa and not the Antarctic should
be his destiny. He had been reading much about
foreign missions, especially in Africa. Now, having
attended a meeting of South London Missioners
in Rochester (May 15), he obtained an introduction
to the Bishop of Zanzibar.

With him I had a long talk ; a big man, bald-headed
with an enormous red beard turning white. He was
very kind and spoke very straight, sitting over a fire in
his gaiters with a thick great-coat on, and this a swelter-
ing hot June day without a breath of air. The dear old
chap gave me his blessing when I left, holding my hand
in his for a long time ; there was no humbug in him,
and I think he saw little in me. I spoke very freely and
thought of calling him ' my lord ' after leaving the house ;

everyone calls him ' my lord,' but I haven't felt inclined
to ; I shouldn't feel myself if I called anyone ' my
lord.' . . .

He introduced me to Oswald Browne, one of the
Medical Board. He went to the point at once. I felt
rather like an out-patient. He said, what you propose
to do is to take a big step. It means that you throw
up the chance of a comfortable home practice and the
society of all the people you know and the chance of
making any money at all, to go and work in an unhealthy
tropical climate for the rest of your life. What on earth
leads you to do it ? You must have some reason.—
Well, I wasn't going to talk piety within hearing of an
afternoon-party crowd, so I told him I saw what he
was driving at—that he wanted to know whether I was
interested at all in the work as Mission work—and I
told him I was and should be ready to give any spare
time I had to it ; in fact, put my time in the hands of
the Mission.

That satisfied him and he changed his manner a bit.
They have to be cunning in taking medical men—very
few volunteer, and all have hitherto wanted salaries,
and what is more got them. . . . But beyond all that
I feel that it is the duty of everyone to nurse that
inclination till it grows up into a full-fledged feeling of
purpose.

In reply to parental objections a long and somewhat argumentative correspondence followed. In
the end he agreed to postpone the idea indefinitely
until he had qualified as a doctor, when ' Jim
(his younger brother, preparing for ordination) and
I might go out together, and I could treat his
fever while he teaches the Catechism ' ! The idea
continued, nevertheless, to colour his thoughts for
some while after.

Meanwhile his work in the slums of Battersea
was making more and more demands upon his
time. Though he loved the children and they

him, his descriptions of them are often tinged with a whimsical humour that might lead a stranger in reading them to suppose otherwise. A home-letter of July 11 is a typical instance of this.

Children's Service 11 a.m. which I took, while Bobby (Dr. Roberts, Master of Caius) read the Lessons. Bible classes 3 to 4, most excellent for learning to keep the temper ; everything conspired to tear one's hair out this afternoon. The room is too trying. It is a converted Battersea shop with the wall broken down so as to throw shop and back parlour into a longish low room with a window at the far end into which the sun pours. The heat was trying because you can't get a draught through and the window has been shut all the morning. The floor is of deal boards, the furniture naked wood forms and chairs and trestle-tables. The room is excellent for sound, having a resonance of its own, so that a book dropping makes you screw up your eyes and clench your teeth till the vibrations die away. Well, all the boys like to keep things going, so they wear iron sole-protectors and upset anything within reach to see how you take it. They are about 10 in a class and they have younger brothers in the street outside. The street is divided from this sounding-box sort of a room by a window boarded up inside about 8 ft. up, and of course the shop door. The door has a key-hole through which the younger brothers watch their elders and criticize their work, or else they deliver funny but imaginary messages from ' our Mother,' or they will fibble and scrabble till they get something to drop through the key-hole into the shop, then there's a rush to see what has appeared. Inside all this time, besides things falling about, and the French blindman's buff game at guessing who the last person was that squeaked a message through the key-hole, one will be asleep after a big Sunday dinner, another pro-tecting sweets in his pocket from his neighbour with his mouth full, another will be reading ' Scraps ' folded up quite small in the palm of his hand, two more perhaps preparing an empty form's downfall with their feet, and if things begin to flag a bit outside, two or three will

want to set them going again and will ask if they can
go and send Moule Nipper and young Tringham away
from the key-hole outside. All the while I am telling
them how nice it is to be like Christ and how soon they
will get to the ' jungle book ' if they'll only be a little
quieter, and the hokey-pokey man has settled his barrow
close outside the shop window and someone is scrambling
up the boarding outside to see how we are getting on
inside, and a Band of Church Army or perhaps the
Green Foresters or the Oddfellows with a local drum and
fife band come down the street, and then I thank God
for a respite and wonder why I haven't filled the room
with dead little Battersea boys ; but the hymn comes
always at last and the dismissal prayer when we thank
God for ' the help He has given us in our work this day.'
This is a sample of a stuffy bad day for me and the boys
and I must say I am glad they are not always quite so
bad ; and though they don't see what help God has
given them this day, I do, for without it I almost think
anybody's patience might have given a bit. The *tout
ensemble* is really sometimes very thick.

A week later he was with his friend Charles in
Brittany. He was enchanted with the Cathedral
at Rouen, and among other studies made there
is one of it and of the Great Clock Tower. On
his birthday they were in the heart of the Roumare
Forest when—

To crown all the wild cry of a buzzard suddenly came ·
to us. We crept along towards it and then the bird
sailed up and settled on a tree not 20 yards away right
against the sky, and there it sat and gave out its weird
cry. Splendid wings and a splendid bird that will be
still in my mind's eye when most of the rest of this
trip is all forgotten. I don't know why, but the voice
and the bearing of a bird such as this strikes deeper
into my heart than anything else I know. There is a
fierce wild independence about them and a beauty in
their eyes and in their shape and a symmetry about
their strength which gives the lie to convention and

civilization. As a fat duck or a barn-door fowl compares
with one of these, so does the work of our hands compare with the work of God.—Sounds like rot but I think
it's all right.

He returned with just enough money for the
price of ' two cups of tea and a penny steamer
to Battersea,' and having arrived at the Mission
House ' sat up with Fraser, a man after my own
heart, and Dr. A. M. Knight (Dean of Caius),
with whom we discussed many things puzzling to
us both.'

But he was sensitively reticent on the subject of
his religious convictions, and during these years
he confided his deepest thoughts to a diary : and
while he would probably have modified them in
later years as his experience deepened he would
in equal probability never have recast them, for
they had entered into the structure of his soul.
The Quaker element, whether inherited or inherent,
was strong in him, and his spiritual perceptions
were too alive and aware to be permanently confined within the limits of any orthodoxy. Thus,
every doctrine which the Church presented had
to be hammered out on the anvil of his own personal experience before he accepted its validity.
Then it entered into the fibres of his whole being
as a living truth to be acted upon, as something
which would shape character and determine conduct. Theories as such never interested him :
ideals must become real, thoughts must become
deeds, or he had little use for them. His faith
was the very substance of his life. As a St. George's
friend well expressed it, ' For Wilson religion was
a divine life, not a divine science ; and embodied

A STREET IN ROUEN

personalities and examples, not philosophical systems or doctrinal formulas. He sought and cared little for originality, but greatly and entirely for truth.' To use his own words :

Every bit of truth that comes into a man's heart burns in him and forces its way out, either in his actions or in his words. Truth is like a lighted lamp in that it cannot be hidden away in the darkness because it carries its own light.

During his two years in Battersea he paraphrased in his own language, and annotated without reference to any commentary, nearly the whole of the New Testament. He did this deliberately, as the prelude to each day's hard work, to set himself a standard to live by. His annotations upon the Gospels show a directness, a simplicity, an unerring intuition to seize the essential meaning, and an uncompromising challenge to himself especially, very remarkable in a man of his years. Always in the background of his mind is the antithesis which the Gospels make between the will of the flesh and of the spirit, between darkness and light, between this life and the Life Eternal. He sums up the conversation with Nicodemus, for example, thus : ' Ours is a double life, distinct though united. Our body lives and our spirit lives : each must be born.' And he is emphatic that the one can only develop *at the expense* of the other.

His paraphrase of the Epistles is even more remarkable. Especially is this so in the difficult passages of St. Paul, and most notably of all in his reading of the Epistle to the Romans. This last, under the title of ' Paulinism Simplified,' might with advantage be addressed to students

(not to say professors) of theology. The involved
language of the apostle is reduced quite naturally
in short concise sentences to the simplest and most
lucid terms, as though he already knew without
hesitation St. Paul's method and could read his
meaning at a glance. These meditations conclude
with a characteristically happy touch—' Dear good
old saint, we Gentiles are very grateful.'

Much might be written here of the content of
his faith in relation to the concepts he derived
from life, and the ethical values he set upon them ;
yet more of his faith in its most real bearing—
its touch upon his personal life. Sufficient to say
that he held with an unalterable conviction that
there is no situation in human life, however apparently uncongenial, that cannot be made, if God
be in the heart, into a thing of perfect joy. That
in order to attain this ultimate perfection one must
live through every experience and learn to love
all persons ; that the love particular should lead
up to the love universal ; that the worth of life
is not to be measured by its results in achievement or success, but solely by the motive of heart
and effort of will ; that the value of experience
depends not so much upon its variety or duration
as upon its intensity ; and that by one single
whole-hearted concentrated effort a brief life might
attain a level that ages of ordinary development
would fall short of, so that a man who lives his
life thus ' having become perfect in a little while
fulfils long years.'

These are big words, and who shall say whether
this man's character was the result of his faith, or
whether his faith was the result of his character ?

But the broad fact remains that among those who knew him one said that 'there was from him a radiation of goodness which left an impression deep and lasting,' and another that 'every life he touched was made better and happier for that touch.' The fact remains too that in the hardships and emergencies of polar travel, perhaps the most arduous and exacting that the human spirit can endure, this man was always unruffled and self-possessed : it was upon him that all his comrades (men of diverse persuasions) most often leant, and one of them (Pennell) confessed to Mrs. Wilson, 'I never thought the Christ-life possible as an ideal till I saw it in your husband.'

Beyond his Hospital and Mission work he was now constantly attending Guild meetings and controversial debates at Caius House, while in the autumn he followed a course of lectures for three months at the Western Fever Hospital. He had, moreover, been part-illustrating with the author, Charles E. Walker, a book on fishing-flies entitled *Old Flies in New Dresses*.

[To his father.]—If you see in my letters to Mother too much time given to drawing, Guild meetings, Mission business, and things of that sort, you must remember that all one's recreation in Town lies in such things. If one works continually one wants more holidays ; if one works moderately with other interests thrown in one doesn't find holidays necessary. I am as fresh for my work every time now as I was months ago.

In spite of this optimism, however, his account of himself a month later, in early December, is—

not over robust, no rude country health down our way ; a little anæmic, a little thin, a little nervous, but wide awake—is the hallmark of the dwellers in big towns, and one soon gotten by all who live in them.

At Christmas he came home looking, his parents thought, delicate and worn. One date in this vacation is worth recording, for it is one that he had good reason never to forget. On New Year's Day 1898 he began reading the *Life of St. Francis of Assisi* written by his friend, Canon Knox-Little, and just published. Next year the Temple Classics published an English translation of the *Fioretti*, and he at once procured a copy. Writing to Miss Souper later from Davos he says :

I don't know whether you have ever been bitten by that man's character as I have, and indeed I think it is the best after Christ's. I admire the man more than anyone else I ever heard of, and that's a thing no one can do without trying to follow him. I despair sometimes of ever seeing my way to it, yet I always feel that the method and the opportunity will turn up when it's time.

Before the end of the month he was back at his work in London. His health was now rapidly failing : however willing the spirit, flesh and blood could no longer sustain the strain to which he was subjecting them. His work went on as usual, though during the illness of the Warden double duty fell upon him at the Mission. He undertook the responsibility of all the services at the Mission on Sundays and on weekday evenings, and at the Caius debates of the chair to which he had been elected. His letters home became brief and infrequent, every minute of every day not spent in actual work is conscientiously logged in his diary under ' idle chatter ' or ' pottered ' : reaching the Hospital punctually at 10 on foot, working hard

all day, lunching on biscuits and milk, walking
back to dinner at 6, ' talking, praying and singing in a positive reek of Battersea children ' till
8, and reading in bed up to anything between 2
to 3.30 each night. Towards the end of this month
and through February he began to develop a temperature, pains and giddiness, intermittently but
increasingly ; yet he stuck to his work as usual
both in the Hospital and at the Mission. For
three weeks he was working at high pressure with
a temperature of anything between 100° and 103°
His practice of midnight reading had been continued for many months. How his early morning
hours before breakfast were spent has been already
told.

On March 1 he went for examination and advice
to Dr. Rolleston, to be told that he was suffering
from pulmonary tuberculosis and should go to
Davos next month. Even then he was unwilling
to acknowledge the gravity of his illness and wrote
to his mother on March 2 :

I am no bad invalid but up and about, and I have
some business to do before I come home. It's fresh air
and a bit of the country that will put me straight. I
have got me a bit soot-sodden.

Meanwhile it seemed that destiny was already
determined on a renewal of the conversation commenced so late one spring evening and too soon
interrupted. By one of those coincidences which
mould events Miss Souper, in entire ignorance of
any connection of the Wilsons with Cheltenham,
had accepted the post of Matron to a Preparatory
School for boys there. Hearing of this early in
January through Mrs. Leighton-Hopkins, Wilson

had written to his parents asking them to ' be
kind ' to her. Now, after a week in bed under
strict orders (painting a narcissus, and reading
Kipling—' the best tonic for any sickness '), he
broke bounds once : this was on the occasion of
her first visit to Westal.

But his deepest feelings he still felt no human
being on earth could ever share, and his Battersea
diary ends with a veritable cry of the heart.

Westal, March 10, 1898.

If there was one whom I could trust and love and be
so bound up with that he or she could share with me
and understand my joys and my love, and my passion for
beauty, for colour, for form, for pure joy in nature,—if
he or she could enter into my thoughts and feel with
me,—if my sorrow, my pain, my doubts, my unspoken
thoughts and hopes and fancies and longings—my life
and my love—if only—

If I could find such a one, shouldn't I bring every joy,
every delight, every pain, every sorrow, every passion,
every love to be shared and to open the whole before
that one : I know that I should : but there exists not
the person on earth with whom lies the power of even
to a small extent feeling with me in one of the smallest
of my joys. Now and again one can truly say that one
has felt with another, in joy or pain, in love or sorrow.
But it is only now and again, and for years the heart
hungers in between.—Why hungers ?

CHAPTER IV

Norway and Switzerland

Purity, constancy, control of self—
. . . . .
Loving all solitudes, and shunning noise
Of foolish crowds, endeavours resolute
To reach perception of the Utmost Soul.
SIR EDWIN ARNOLD : *The Song Celestial.*

HIS departure for Davos was postponed by
an unexpected offer of recuperation in
Norway. An introduction through his
friends, Canon and Mrs. Knox-Little, to Mr. and
Mrs. Rice led to an invitation from them to spend
the summer at their home in Horstadt, Brönö,
Bindalen ; after a consultation with Dr. Rolleston,
who agreed, his departure was fixed for May 30 ;
and within a week he was rambling and bird's-
nesting in the far north of Norway—

Where one feels as if it is sunrise always : and where
no one worries about anyone else : no one is ever waited
on at a meal, and things are not kept hot for one. It's
Liberty Hall to the ground. I never realized such
freedom. Mrs. Rice is a most delightful hostess, taking
an interest in everything one says or finds.

And he found in his hosts not only that perfect
hospitality which allows a guest to entertain himself, but also similarity of tastes in a love of the
wild, while Mr. Rice and he vied with each other

as to the number and variety of the patches on
their rent garments, for a ramble was never the
same to either unless it also entailed a scramble.
His best hours for sketching and for collecting in
this northern twilight were from dinner to dawn :
he slept in the afternoons, set off alone after dinner,
and returned to bed at 2 or 3 a.m.

The series of letters which he wrote home to his
father in diary form are confined mainly to the
observations of a bird-lover and are often of great
interest, dealing with birds such as the Hooded
Crow, the Ryper, the Merganser, the Dipper, the
Ringed Dotterel, the nests of which he found and
describes, though he sought in vain for the nest
of the Arctic Jay. It will be seen that his ' birdy
excursions ' were not unattended with difficulties.

The whole place is so big that one has to walk and
scramble and wander miles between each find. But one
feels that if one only keeps on with it one is bound to
come across something. Stiff pegs of branches are always
jabbing into your shins and ankle bones, your face is
netted in a spider's web every few yards and you sweat
like a pig under the boiling sun. Thick moss fills up
the crevices between the boulders of rock and lets you
into secret places when you least expect it ; fir branches
take pieces out of your shirt, for I leave my coat at home
and wander in shirt sleeves. Lichen and dry twigs and
dust find their ways under all your clothing and so on—
but I want to get a Goshawk, eggs or young, and the
free rambling in unlimited forest is just grand. . . .

But his sketches were produced under far greater
tests of endurance. Wrapped to the eyes in scarves
and in a cloud of tobacco smoke, his fingers swollen
with insect-bites, he contrived nevertheless some
most exquisite miniatures of landscape ; they are
little gems of colour, and though his style after-

wards developed in breadth, these brilliant studies already display unmistakable genius.

Sunsets which get all the mountains flaming in yellow and red and gold, with contrasting greys and purples in their shadows, the red trunks of the Scotch firs blaze out like rods of fire, and the greens of the Spruces in the light all become orange and red. Then the snow patches become rose and blue in the shadow, and the sky tones up from a yellow into very light green and blue, and then in a few minutes when you wonder what is coming next it all goes out, and you are left with sober greys and greens and mosquitoes. It takes a lot of yellow paint, a cast-iron resolution and a power of tobacco to sit and sketch. . . .

One has to take one's chance what with rain and clegs and mosquitoes, and no room of one's own to draw in. The mosquitoes are of 2 kinds, one large and one small ; they raise red bumps on your face and hands ; one finger looks like a sausage. But they are worst on the legs, hardly a speck on the stocking hasn't got its bite and they look like German sausages. Clegs are worse than mosquitoes ; they are big horseflies which leave a speck of blood upon the bite like a cairn on a mountain when it swells up. The bite is like a drawing-pin and itches like the devil. I use a clothes brush for the itching and then hazeline. I have tried vaseline and turps and the cleanings of a foul pipe rubbed all over my stocking, but there is nothing like a clothes brush for real happiness. . . .

In reply to inquiries from home about the state of his health, he had written on July 3 :

About my blooming self all I have to say is that I am as fit as a dog, the amount I eat is astonishing. I only wish you were all as free from bodily troubles as I am. . . .

But a letter from Mrs. Rice, written many years afterwards, tells a different tale :

He suffered nearly every night from dry Pleurisy,

though he was never laid up with it. [She says also]—
We certainly entertained an angel unawares. At that
time he was slim in build, very active and keen about
everything, always cheerful and ready to do anything for
anybody. Our river was full of salmon and trout, but
he was no fisherman. His whole heart and soul were
given to Ornithology and Botany. He had a charming
voice, manner, and smile, with a keen sense of humour.
We met him after his return from the Antarctic, and when
he told us of the (to him) glamour of the expedition, I
asked him to tell me some of the drawbacks. He said :
' I can't think of any ! '

In mid-August he returned from Norway, and
he spent the autumn at the Crippetts, for which
he had longed, as his letters tell, even while in
Norway.

I have got more joy from that place [he wrote after-
wards] and learnt more too of things worth knowing
than I have in any of my rambles . . . in the early morn-
ings especially when I had the wood entirely to myself
at 4 or 5. Cold it was, and I used to wrap up well in a
cloak and light my pipe and watch the sunbeams
gradually lighting up the different corners of the wood,
and sitting like an old stump one was never noticed
. . . with *Modern Painters* and the New Testament and a
good deal of pain, but I was most intensely happy. For
one thing I thought that the end of life was within
measurable distance anyhow, and that alone brings
extraordinary peace of mind.

From here some of his best landscape pencil-
sketches were made : of distant Gloucester in the
setting of the Severn valley, and of Cheltenham
below backed by the Malvern Hills. Some fine
studies of the interior of Gloucester Cathedral, to
which he walked back and forth, were also at this
time given to his friends.

But examination proved that the tubercular mis-

chief in his lungs had been checked only, by no
means cured, by his visit to Norway ; and it was
decided that he should go to Davos as previously
arranged, and undergo the regular routine of treatment there through the winter. To so vital a
temperament as his the enforced idleness of life in
a sanatorium was almost unendurable :

The conversation is all about bacilli and hearts and
weights and expectoration, so that one hardly dare clear
one's throat without feeling that one has said something
tuberculous ; still more, I think, the want of a smoke
begets a desire to bite everybody and run away.

He tried to regard the life as a penance ; yet
as events proved, if his medical adviser gave him
an inch he took an ell. The truth is that foresee-
ing no useful future, and believing his illness to
be without permanent remedy, and refusing to
entertain hopes of the new-found happiness that
were now awakening but which he resolutely hid
in his own heart, he had little care whether he
lived or died. The beginning of his correspondence with Miss Souper, however, dates from Davos.

In late October he was on his way and ' fairly
fell in love with the South of France, with its vine-
yards all crimson and orange, and poplars all
golden spatterwork, and beech forests orange and
brown, with deep blue-green patches of fir-treees.'
But the journey through the Alps induced in him
an alternation of moods, his spirits rising in sympathy with the bright colours on lake and vine-
yard in sunshine, and sinking again as the sun
sank amid the pines in a dismal mist. The climax
of depression was reached when he alighted on
the platform at Davos Platz,

all cold and white and ghastly, stone-grey, slate-grey, and stucco—nothing but *pensions* and balconies. But the Victoria 'bus was waiting for us, the man Charles was a friend at sight, the rooms were warm, tea was brought to the bedroom, and to crown all a letter from O.— and that a long one.

For his own part he had never dared to offer or hoped to receive more than friendship from the friend who wrote it, and his Davos Journal reflects the period of his intensest introspection : it was a period however to which he always looked back as the most important in his life. The day after arrival, his Journal has this entry :

Very, very beautiful, with everything just draped in snow, the sun quickly clearing it off where it could reach it. There is something that suggests tenderness and love in the way in which these clouds, heavy grey rolling masses laughing up at the sun above, softly fold themselves right round a mountain peak.[1] For a whole day long they will remain there with the mountain top buried in their embrace, and then at sunset the clouds will clear, the moon break through, and the mountain stand again above—but how changed, how much more white and clean, smiling up to heaven with a heart renewed. What have they to say to each other, these God's creations ? Why cannot we as they come closer heart to heart, to brighten our purity and cleanse ourselves that each may be more spotless ? Yes, yes, we can. God give us sufficient strength, for we too are thy creations.

Meanwhile he found it hard indeed to curb his restlessness. When after a fortnight's trial of ' vegetation ' he had lost weight and was allowed to take ' a little exercise ' he seems to have regarded himself as a prisoner on reprieve.

---

[1] ' Snow Clouds on Tinzenhorn ' : a pencil-sketch given to Miss Souper.

Eato. Davos. March 1893.

DAVOS

Nov. 15. Started off at once up the Dischma valley.
I must have got up to nearly 8,000 feet above sea-level ;
got very breathless at times and had to sit and gasp, my
head felt like bursting with the pulsation in it ; pulse
168 per minute, but a few minutes' rest lowered it to
120. Extraordinary pains in the chest, shoulders, ribs
and back, as though rheumatic all through,—these went
off on the lower levels. For some hours also pleuritic
pain in left lung ; might possibly have been heart, but
was worse at inspirations. The views along the valley
were very grand. . . . Collected many bits of plant—
crinkleberries, blueberries, cranberries, saxifrage aizoides
in flower, several rock-fern. I heard a Gt. Spotted Wood-
pecker rattling in the fir-wood, three times distinctly ;
struck me as funny, because I thought it was a breeding-
season trick.

Nov. 16. Started after breakfast up the Fluela Pass
till a mile beyond Tschuggen. Started climbing up snow
and boulders at 12.30, and at 3 began the last and steepest
slope of snow on bare rock, a pure climb with teeth and
nails on the rock and sometimes snow up to the waist.
Still by 4 I was astride of the peak I was aiming at, and
certainly it was a grand stretch of snowy alps. . . . I
ate my last bit of brown bread and butter and started
down, heels and elbows well in at each step for the first
ten feet or so, and then a slide down for another ten,
and a catch in deeper snow which checked me and
nearly threw me forward, but not quite. The snow
slope ran down so steeply for a couple of hundred yards
that in some places I couldn't see where I was ; it ran
between ugly black rocks too steep for the snow to hold
on. I saw the pace the snow went down as I shifted it,
and at the bottom was a level terrace heaped up with
boulders as big as carts. So the care with which I felt
my heels hold at each step was phenomenal, but useless,
for a few yards lower the snow slid with me on the rock,
and in a few seconds the pace took my breath away.
For twenty or thirty yards I kept my balance with my
elbows, and all I said or thought was ' You must keep
your head and go feet first, but you must keep your
head.' Then my heels caught in something, and I shot
out head first, sliding, rolling, and bouncing clean into

the air ; and all at such a giddy pace and in such a
cloud of snow and with one bump after another that I
hadn't time to think at all.   When the first bang came I
realized that it was a bad accident ; when the second
came I was fairly stunned, though conscious enough to
think that a third would do the trick.   But the third
slam never came, for within ten yards of the boulders I
found myself held up by elbows and knees dug into deep
snow, and then I did indeed wonder and thank God.
And my cap came slowly sliding down with a tuft of
campanula in it.   A walk of eight miles home.   It was
an experience worth having—once.

The only reference to this escapade in his letters
home is as follows : ' I have been up from 7 to
8 thousand feet in deep snow.   One day I crossed
some bears' footprints, and another I put up
ptarmigan.'   But to Miss Souper he wrote :

On Monday Huggard allowed me to try my own
method—taking exercise : and I have.   Two days I have
been out in the mountains.   I was so pleased with myself
when he unchained me that I walked six miles along
the high road after supper in pitch darkness, except for
stars. . . .   Now for my ' disgusted ' face : if you saw
it really you would say ' disgusting,' for I have scraped
the skin off it sliding down a frozen snow slope ; such a
beastly mess all over the place.   I put up two white
ptarmigan at the bottom as a reward for slipping, quite
sufficient to make it worth while.

The next morning, however, he was out and
about as usual ' walking off the bruises,' and the
day after that was away up and over the mountains
again.

During the winter he lost weight again, and in
appearance at this time was so frail that a fellow-
patient remarked years afterwards that the greatest
miracle he ever heard of was that Wilson should
have reached the South Pole.   Even tobogganing

was denied him : ' I came down a mile run this morning in a blinding snowstorm ; it was exhilarating, and I have been in a glow for hours since ' ; but it sent his temperature up. Skating had the same effect, and he writes disconsolately to his father :

I am convinced that the sitting still and stuffing and lying out system of cure does kill some people as surely as it cures others. The killing part about it is the lack of occupation, nothing but idle loafing, terribly depressing and demoralizing. My most violent exercise is ten minutes' walk to the Belvedere, then a good rest of two hours—and a ten minutes' walk back. In the afternoons I generally look at my skates. The only thing I miss is a perambulator, to be let down the toboggan runs on a string.

When at the end of January the prohibition on skating was removed ' after five weeks' total abstinence,' he immediately spent between three and four hours daily on the Lake. And when in the spring the ban on tobacco was lifted he shamelessly confesses ' Smoked all day ! ' It was a wearisome period of waiting, but was relieved by companionships that came to him unsought. Because he had the rare gift of allowing himself to be made a friend of he found, with a kind of surprised humility, that his fellows even in Davos instinctively turned to him for advice, and leant upon him in their difficulties.

Even here I have my duties. I would do them, but never overdo them, lest I bore the people who want help. . . . Thank God for the assurance that I am wanted.

He was, in fact, laying here the foundations of an active mysticism. It was to prove the key to that selfless reliability which so constantly sustained and inspired his comrades in the South, who, though unaware of its origin, noted in him ' some mysterious force that triumphed, some faith that upheld ' at all times of stress and emergency. From a physical aspect also his life in Davos was a preparation, for the conditions of his treatment were rigorous. He would sit in his fireless room writing long letters to his home folk and to Miss Souper while the ink froze in the bottle. The following sentences, from his letters to her, are a forcible expression of his practical philosophy :

Look at life carelessly. The only things worth being disappointed in or worrying about are in ourselves, not in externals. Take life as it comes and do what lies straight in front of you. It's only real carelessness about one's own will, and absolute hope and confidence in God's, that can teach one to believe that whatever is, is best. Don't you think this is the key to happiness in an apparently spoilt and disappointing life ?

His Journal also reveals an interesting contrast. A love of freshness and colour was in his blood, but a cold and white expanse unrelieved by rock or verdure depressed him. In February he wrote :

Only yesterday we were rejoicing in the first signs of Spring. To-day we woke up to a new winter and five inches of snow. Awful, awful, I cannot abide the snow. [And later]—A deadly black sunless cheerless day, on which merely to be alive and to have to pass it is a curse and a punishment. A patch in my left lung has been waking up the last few days, giving me touches of pleurisy and a trace of grey sputum. But I got a letter from O., so my left lung may go and bury itself.

His lungs appear to have responded to this summary mental treatment, for with the arrival of

spring he was out in the woods all day revelling
in the birds and flowers, and filling a portfolio
with pencil-sketches of scenery. He left for home
in May with a favourable medical report, which,
however, stipulated a sedentary life and recommended pathological drawing for occupation. But
his medical advisers did not know their patient,
as the following extract from a letter to Miss
Souper shows.

I can't bear people who always take for granted that
one's main object is to save up one's health and strength,
eyesight and what not, for when one is sixty. How on
earth can they tell whether one is going to reach thirty ?
I think it's better to wear a thing while it's good and
new, patching the odd corners as they wear out, instead
of putting it away carefully year after year till at last
the moths get in, and you find it's no good when at last
you think you will wear it.

Immediately on arrival at the Crippetts, freed
at last from medical restrictions, he wrote to his
sister like a schoolboy :

It's time for sketching ; you had better come soon ;
we will do some this month. I have only done black
and white so far, except flowers, beasts and devils. Once
or twice I have seen heaven ; I painted a primrose there.
Upon my soul, the glory of God in Nature has never
been so continuously before me as it is now, and no
one to tell of it ! Sometimes I feel full to overflowing
with it. Oh, the joy of tobacco, and life—and ill-health,
and how far above them Death, the door to Love and
Eternity !

Yet his family found him more reserved than
usual, and he spoke little of his ailments or of
future hopes and aims. His mother evidently felt
this, for there is an entry in her journal of this
date—

We know people in various ways ; some are so transparent, Ted is not : some so ordinary, he is not : some
trust us with their hearts, he does not : some tell us of
their hopes and fears, their joys and sorrows, and make
us know them ; alas, he does not to me do this either.

His intentions of at once resuming Hospital work
received an unexpected but most pleasant check
in an invitation from his true friends in Norway
to spend another summer with them there.   Nothing could have been better timed, for he was
in fact still far from fit for work, and the chance
of a second peep into that northern wonderland
was irresistible.   Before midsummer he was in the
North again, and spent several nights in a *saeter*
(mountain hut) with the rare northern birds, a
reindeer bull, and one Johann 'a birdy Norwegian,'
for companions, watching the sun set and rise
again over a world of woods and lakes and mountains while fishing for brown trout.

The lake is over a mile long, and its edges are loaded
with water-lilies yellow and white, and these twinkle like
glow-worms all along the ripple with reflections.   It
seemed sinful to row amongst them.   In the woods an
owl was calling, occasionally one hears a blackcock or
away at a farmstead a dog, and beyond these nothing
but the rising of the trout.   All night long from nine till
two is one long sunset, sunrise, glow, and afterglow, all
rolled into one blaze of colour and light at every point
of the compass.   The river blazes with the sky, the snow
is crimson, the mountains and forests purple and gold
and green, and the sky fairly goes mad.

How, he asks himself, can one recapture and
retain the memory of such scenes ?   'It's as though
someone said, This is for you only—learn what
you can from it.'   But he longs to be able to com-
municate it to others, and to one especially, who

can appreciate and understand. And the only way
possible is by means of paper, paints, and brush :
all too inadequate.

Last night there were showers of rain flying about,
and a rainbow, and the whole of heaven was a rosy
orange blaze, and one of the mountains caught the light
and was flooded into a brilliant scarlet haze.—I covered
seven bits of paper with red and orange and purple
paint, but oh ! they're so ghastly and insufficient, and
yet I couldn't tear them up because they are all one has
to help one's memory. You and P. [his sister] could
worship well under a sky like that, like true Quakers.

Once while sketching in the woods at 2 a.m.
he disturbed a sparrow-hawk's nest. He sat quite
still, while the hen-bird swooped at his head ten
times in quick succession, finally knocking his cap
off. He climbed the tree, took one of the four
fluffy white fledgelings from the nest, and brought
it home. ' It's a most fascinating little beast and
eats like an alderman.' When the bird found its
wings he gave it jesses and a leash, and brought
it up ' in the way approved by falconers.' But,
in an unguarded moment, it fell a prey to one of
Mr. Rice's eagle-owls.

The tragedy of the sparrow-hawk led him to
reflect on ' birds' sorrows—keen but short-lived.'
It led him to a further reflection : why, averse
as he is to predatory habits, such as field-sports,
in man, does he so much prefer the wild birds
of prey—hawks, owls, buzzards and their tribe—
to game-birds such as grouse ? Why do creatures
like stoats and foxes fascinate him more than
rabbits ? The only reason he can find is that he
' likes them in much the same way as he likes

Esau better than Jacob.' But it is their superior
grace, suppleness and swiftness, ' their fierce wild
independence,' that really appeal to him. The
problem of 'Nature red in tooth and claw' he
leaves unresolved.

He spent two rainy days in ' making portraits '
of the changing expressions of eagle-owls in an
outhouse. These were afterwards pronounced by
Thorburn as very fine studies. Before leaving
Norway he made a descent of a vertical cliff by
rope to a buzzard's eyrie, and secured one of
the young birds. With infinite pains he brought
it safely back with him to England ; for, having
cut his ankle deeply on a rock, he was a crippled
traveller, and then an unwilling prisoner for some
time at Westal, where he and the buzzard improved
acquaintance until he could walk. It eventually
found a home, together with his kite from Ger-
many, in the London Zoo.

The Buzzard [he wrote] is a delightful old beast ;
came into the dining-room while I was at supper and
put his foot into a plate of sliced tomatoes. Then he
went to sleep on my knee. . . . I went to Crippetts
Wood for church, and sang hymns with the owls.

From letters to O. F. S. from Norway.

There are things and many things that are apparently
only for the few : things which have to do with the long
and mysterious history of life, where the wilderness of
Nature holds its own, have also, all of them, something
to tell of the power and method of God. . . . I have
made an idol of Nature, and until a few years ago I
thought that man classed with his artificially reared cows
and pigs and tame sheep, as a sort of set-off to the real
beauty of all natural things, lest earth should be too
much like heaven. . . . All my religious ideas are

Young Eagle Owls.
    Horstad, Norway.
July. 1899-

STUDIES OF EAGLE OWLS

founded on the principle of evolution driven to its logical
conclusion. . . .

I so long that you may come to work in the wards of a
big Hospital, for in sickness everyone is far more natural,
and a mere look is enough to tell you of something in
common. Nothing is more extraordinary, I think, than the
feeling one has of loving people at first sight, and without
a word being spoken. *You* know what I mean by love
in this way. If you and I could love everyone we meet
as we love each other, and the same with everyone else,
that would be more like the coming of God's Kingdom
on earth. We ought to love one another much better
than we do. . . . Love everything into which God has
put life : and God made nothing dead. There is only
less life in a stone than in a bud, and both have a life
of their own, and both took their life from God.

Can anything be more perfect or more beautiful than
such a love ? No jealous exclusion of everybody else,
which is really only selfishness, but a more perfect love
for the one whom rightly or wrongly we think most
worthy of it and as much as we can give of the same love
to everybody else. . . . Human nature is jealous and
selfish, and it's just this that we have to keep well in
hand. . . . What is right for one may still be wrong
for another, but each of us must act on what we are
convinced is the Truth.

No sooner had he returned to work, early in
October, to his rooms in Delamere Crescent, than
he developed a temperature and cough which
compelled him to return to Cheltenham, as the
atmosphere of London was considered definitely
prejudicial to his health. But on October 19 he
was engaged to be married to Miss Souper, and
from that day he dated not only the beginning of
his recovery but also the real happiness of his life.

CHAPTER V

From Life at Stanmore to Marriage

To watch the corn grow, and the blossoms set; to draw
hard breath over ploughshare or spade; to read, to think,
to love, to hope, to pray,—these are the things that make
men happy.

RUSKIN.

WILSON now settled down in earnest to
work for the final of his M.B. degree,
having two months in which to make
good the ground that he had lost in eighteen.
With medical promise of restored health, given
time and care, he set forth in high spirits with
the help of his future wife to find lodgings near
the bird-haunted common of Stanmore in Middle-
sex, and in the first week of November was happily
settled in rooms at Loscombe Lodge.

At last he had found the will to live again, and with
a new sense of responsibility for health wrote home :

I am not sound yet, I know. . . . I could break down
again if I took many liberties, and God knows I don't
wish to. I am afraid when I came back at the beginning of October to Delamere Terrace that I cared as
little about getting well as I cared about being ill, and
that wasn't much. Now things are different : but one
cannot live well, be out much, get some exercise every
day, do only a few hours in the Hospital each week, be
in bed at 11 every night, *and* be working hard for an
exam. at the same time.

He soon made the acquaintance of Mrs. Brightwen, a naturalist authoress and ' a very sweet old lady,' who gave him the free run of her estate on Stanmore Common which had been a bird-sanctuary for forty years.

> There are cots up in the woods [he wrote] where the Brown Owls breed, coot and moorhen in the ponds as well as herons, sometimes gulls and tern. The estate is surrounded by a furze, bracken and beech-tree common, full of streams and boggy bits, where there are magpies, jays, kestrels, sparrow-hawks, nut-hatches, tree-creepers, and all three woodpeckers. No country to be sneezed at and 500 feet above sea-level, and only 10 miles from Hyde Park Corner as the crow flies.

Early in December he went up to Cambridge for his examination, staying in the intervals and over Christmas with his future relations at Hilton. After excusing himself for not having come straight home he continues :

> Not many people know their fiancée for three years and get engaged many months before they present themselves to their relations-in-law for approval. Mrs. Souper wrote me such a very nice letter to say that everyone of them weren't sick, but rather pleased.

He never expected to pass, and the fact that he did so after eighteen months' rustication is a remarkable testimony to the retentiveness of his memory and his powers of concentration. His unhoped-for success provoked the following *jeu d'esprit* of December 22 :

> This is a home-letter for you all, ALL at Westal, married or single, maiden ladies or aunts, insects or Buzzard Eagles. It is meant to be a letter such as may well be written by a demented monomaniac recovering from general Paralysis of the insane. As a monomaniac on Physic and the allied sciences I have been found not wanting. I am admitted into the comparatively select

circle of amateur and other druggists. The prospect of immediate admission to the degree of M.B. is the Christmas present which I propose to proffer for your acceptance. It has cost a mint of money, but will produce such consequences in aiding Nature to abet only the survival of the very fittest that I am glad to join that select company to the dismay of their Pyrixities Bacillus Tuberculosis and Staphylococcus Pyogenes Aureus. . . . There is no doubt whatever that anyone with a first-class university degree in Arts and another in Medicine, with no knowledge of his work, can do more good towards balancing Nature and Civilization than any person in his right mind. Therefore let all now at home take me at my own valuation, and realize that for a cheap and easy solution of the difficult problems of life, they have a near relative and a dear friend in a ginger-headed copper-knob named Ted, M.B., who will do the trick in sublime and blissful ignorance for the very lowest fees, till he has made a name. When he has made a name the fees will begin to expand in proportion as his knowledge begins to dwindle, when he will in all probability be dropped by his nearest relatives like a hot potato, and taken up in turn as a shining light by first-class experts in rare mental diseases and allied conditions, or by a second-rate policeman as something else.

Anyone who is keen on Christmas presents may choose anything they like up to fifteen or twenty shillings, but O. and I are both blowed if we pay for them, because we neither of us have any money to spare. I have hung on like grim death to my railway fare and a little over, so I shall spend anything anyone may send me on Clifford Allbutt's six volumes, on a microscope, on a case for hypodermic injection, and any small sum that may be left over on some furniture for our house, because we must have a good piano.

On his return to Stanmore to prepare his thesis for the degree [1] he devoted all his spare time to

---

[1] The subject which he chose for his thesis was 'Yellow Atrophy of the Liver,' on two cases of which rare disease his father was able to supply him with ample notes.

drawing as the safest course for a livelihood, till
his health should be sufficiently established to take
up Hospital appointments. His friend, C. E.
Walker, had asked him to illustrate for *Land and
Water* of which he was now Editor, and he had
Dr. Rolleston's introduction to the *Lancet* for pathological drawing. Through Dr. Philip L. Sclater,
then President of the Zoological Society, he was
given every facility for drawing in the Gardens
and for studying in the Library of the Society.
But he heartily disliked the idea of selling his pictures, especially of birds, ' because it seems like
selling a bit of oneself which isn't even one's own
to sell.'

My little bird-pictures are just visible proofs of my
love for them, and attempts to praise God and bring
others to love Him through His works, and that's why I
love to give them all away and hate to sell them. I
can't believe God has given me such an intense absorbing
love for drawing unless it was to be used in some way.

Do you think I am right in keeping the prices of my
beloved little bird-pictures down as low as possible to
give the poorer people a chance ? I just would love to
make them see and feel and interest themselves a little
in such things. They would get to know God through
His works and life would become a different thing to
them.

If only one could knock out the dealer and sell them
to those who want them for what they are, for as much
as they would choose to give !

At an annual meeting of the British Ornithologists' Union he met among other distinguished
bird-lovers of that day Bowdler Sharpe, Head of
the Ornithological Section of the S.K. Museum,
with whom his future work brought him into
closer touch, Selous of Africa, and most notably

of all, the bird-artists Thorburn and Lodge, both of whom invited him to see their work, and at the same time very appreciatively criticized his own.   A little later he was asked by Mr. Rice to accompany him to the house of a Mr. Hammond in Kent, then an octogenarian, whose beautiful studies of birds, made when past the age of seventy, excited his most enthusiastic admiration.   This was a rare privilege, for Mr. Hammond never exhibited his pictures or showed them to any but a select few, and they were dispersed after his death.

Twenty volumes containing water-colour portraits of 360 British Birds *in their surroundings*, the most perfect little pictures imaginable . . . the utmost refinement, truth and exactness, and yet with the breadth of Nature herself, and no trace of carelessness or affected impressionist style ; everything there to the dead leaves and worm-casts on the seashore ; all true to Nature and copied lovingly from her, but also with her freedom and openness . . . altogether one of the best things I have seen in my life ; but I feel as though I should never want to touch a pencil or brush again.

As regards his own methods he knew his special qualification to be intimate knowledge of his subjects, and wrote thus on the question to his father :

I have begun as you suggested some of these birds in pencil, but naturally one longs for colour. To say that because one can draw in pencil one shouldn't draw in colour sounds like saying that because one can drive a single horse one shouldn't drive a pair.

You may say, which is quite true, that one must be taught how to put paint on but I have always believed that by sticking to one's own mother-wit one may eventually succeed.

Only give me the time and I don't despair of producing something, because I have got the results of nearly 20 years' study of birds and plants and beasts to start on, and, as you allow, some idea of light and shade. What I feel I want now is knowledge and experience in paints, and it is just that that I am trying to get hold of. . . .

And lastly I believe that I could persuade a section of the public that my pencil-drawings and even some of the sketches were worth more than the dreadful things one sees exhibited, well reviewed, *and sold* for 8 and 10 guineas.

Though the offer of a course of study at an art school was suggested to him from home, he set himself to acquire the technique of painting un-aided, for he felt it a point of honour to impose no further financial burden on his father. However, the time thus lost in self-tuition was gained in the development of a completely original style. His letters to Miss Souper from Stanmore enlarge on this subject.

The more quietly and privately one lives with God's own gifts, the more one fits oneself for helping others to see them. That's one thing I have always felt God meant me for—to show his glorious Beauty to others who haven't had the opportunity of finding out the things that are so wonderfully beautiful in the most common country. My pictures are the realization of little things that have been treasured up in my mind, little traits of character picked up crumb by crumb in fields and by hedgerows, at last pieced together and put into the form of something living.—The realization of every happy day I have spent on the hills is in the pic-ture of a stoat I chanced to see ; in the snake's, in that little head and one eye is all the fascinating quickness and supple gracefulness of all the snakes I have known, and I have never lost a chance of trying to know them better ; the whole concentrated beauty of that glorious Norwegian forest at midnight is what I see in the picture of the sparrow-hawk's nest. . . .

I spent an hour at the water-colour Exhibit in Picca-dilly . . . dreadful stuffed birds ! There were plenty of flowers, nicely done, but then they merely want a faithful copyist—anyone can do that ; but *why* don't they open their eyes to birds which are much more subtly beautiful than flowers ?   No one would think of painting preserved flowers—why on earth do they paint preserved birds ?

I tried a shop in Regent Street.   A young man with well-pomaded curly hair and a very smart frock-coat came to me.   I asked if I might show some drawings ; he said he would *look* at them, and turned over the leaves as you might a *Whitaker's Almanac*, and said, ' No use whatever for that sort of thing,' and walked away. I am not disappointed because it's exactly what I expected, but I think it's useless to repeat it.

Visitors to his rooms were surprised by their strangely decorative appearance.

There isn't a picture without a branch of willow or hazel or alder or fir or birch over it.   There are bunches of last year's dead bracken, dock, and rushes stuck into various crevices, there's a glass-covered box on the wall with the Swallow-tail chrysalises, pots of water with sprouting chestnuts and young sycamores, branches of thorn, beech and oak, with the old leaves on, and a map of South Africa stuck on the wall with seccotine.

The Boer War was then in progress, and his brother Bernard was at the front.   His own sentiments as to its motives and methods, though unpopular at the time, are those commonly held to-day.

Now that I know what the duties of a soldier are in war I would sooner shoot myself than anyone else by a long, long way.   I simply could not do it.   The very thought of it now is a ghastly nightmare to me, chiefly the result of a very realistic account of our sinful— though as things are, necessary—cruelty over that bombardment of Kronje in the Modder.   It made me cry like a baby and I threw away the paper in perfect disgust.

A nation should be judged on exactly the same ground

as an individual. As a nation we have the vilest of sins which everyone extols as the glories of Imperialism. *One day* all this part of our history will be looked upon in its proper light.

More and more his impatience of all that is merely popular, conventional and respectable in the world's standards was taking settled shape.

Sad as it is to find so many lies in life, it is an undoubted joy to see the whole farce in its proper colours. Thank God for mistrust of accepted authority, for splendid quixotic carelessness. A big name is no authority, unless governed by the Holy Spirit. . . . Ruskin I look upon almost as an apostle of Christ, but who else ? very, very few. Perhaps Kingsley, perhaps Carlyle ; it's all a matter of personal judgment. Kingsley I believe in, but I do not think he was as spiritually-minded a man as Ruskin : Carlyle is splendidly true, but I think he was rather profoundly influenced by himself.

His impatience of the same adventitious qualities in formal religious observance finds expression in a letter written when alone in Mrs. Brightwen's estate on a fine spring Sunday morning.

I think of the good, honest, religious folk who are just now putting themselves away from sunlight, from fresh air, from the songs of joy and gladness, from all the wonder of the Spring's awakening that fills my heart with gratitude, away from all that God has laid out so lavishly to inspire our hearts with love and worship for Him—into a dark and stuffy building made with our own hands upholstered with cloth and tapestry, decked out with dust and fading cut flowers, the crude vulgarity of stained-glass windows and brass candlesticks, and a ludicrous brass image of an eagle. Here, in the heart and love and life of Nature, and with Christ by my side, I cannot bring myself to go to church, when the whole creation calls me to worship God in such infinitely more beautiful and inspiring light and colour and form and sound. Not a single thing out here but suggests love and peace and joy and gratitude, every single thing is true, lovable, and full of virtue and praise —it *is* better than the best Church service, there *can* be no doubt about it.

His sense of the value of time was equivalent to most persons' sense of the value of money. For money he had never had concern except to do with as little of it as possible, but time was a free and sacred gift to be spent up to the last minute of every day. Though he himself lived three days to most men's one, the thought was never absent from his mind of the great host of private or public servants in houses, factories, shops, offices, who do the world's drudgery behind the scenes of life.

What a huge responsibility we who employ servants in any way incur by doing so . . . they are giving us time to ourselves to use as we like, usefully or wastefully, busily or idly. In no sense does our paying them alter the case—it is purely a matter of time, not money. . . . Each one of them is doing a little of my drudgery and thereby giving me time for other work. *They are all fulfilling their side of the bargain ;* they are at drudgery day after day from morning to night ; and the question comes to me *whether I am fulfilling my part of the bargain* also day after day from morning to night. Cooks, house-maids, bootboys, gardeners, labourers, milkmen, dustmen, postmen, clerks, agents—in hundreds and hundreds— who have given their lives to save time for the few ; and one by one we, the few, will be brought face to face with them and asked what we have done with our lives, and the time they gave us, to make the world better. How awful it will be if we find that there are practically none whom we have helped, and all we can do will be to answer for ourselves—so many hours or days or months I spent playing golf, or hockey or billiards ; so many years while you were cooking my meals I was eating them, and so on. . . . Is this the best that I can do with their time ? Am I getting good enough out of this

book to warrant my getting others to do my drudgery
while I read it? Does the writing of this letter, the
painting of this picture, the good of this walk or ride
or conversation, warrant my using their time for it?
If not, I am not fulfilling my side of the bargain, and I
shall be responsible to them for the time they have
given me.

Even more Franciscan in its feeling is his hold
on that ascetic mysticism which was now the firm
guiding principle of his life. He wrote much of
life's purposes and of the perfecting power of pain,
accepting it in his own case as a valuable check
to self-confidence and worldly success and ambition.

This I know is God's own Truth, that pain and trouble
and trials and sorrows and disappointments are either
one thing or another. To all who love God they are
love tokens from Him. To all who do not love God
and do not want to love Him they are merely a nuisance.
Every single pain that we feel is known to God because
it is the most loving and the most pathetic touch of
His hand.

The glory of man is that in his poor human life and
body can be expressed all the attributes of God.

A sentence that I harped on years ago, and one that
used to comfort me—so well—was this, ' What I do thou
knowest not now, but thou shalt know hereafter.' That
saying has always been a perfect treasure to me ; I
have never been able to get along without it.

A happy life is not built up of tours abroad and
pleasant holidays, but of little clumps of violets noticed
by the roadside, hidden away almost so that only those
can see them who have God's peace and love in their
hearts ; in one long continuous chain of little joys ; little
whispers from the spiritual world ; little gleams of sunshine on our daily work. . . . So long as I have stuck
to Nature and the New Testament I have only got
happier and happier every day.

Finally, the principles on which he acted were
associated in his mind with the thought of the

ending of his life, to which he had long looked
forward with a strange intensity.

Our knowledge of what can happen is very limited,
and we understand precious little of what everyone is
bound to allow *does* happen. . . . I have myself no
doubt that the dead are with us somehow, I believe
even that they can influence our lives. . . . It is no
sin to long to die, the sin is in the failure to submit our
wills to God to keep us here as long as He wishes. . . .
Rise above your difficulties—be sorry for *them* through
whom your difficulties come to you. In refusing to be
put out or annoyed, you are taking God's hand in yours,
and once you feel God's hand, or the hand of anyone who
loves good, in yours—let pity take the place of irritation,
let silence take the place of a hasty answer, let the longing to suffer in ever so small a way take the place of a
longing to rest. Overcome evil with good. . . . Charity
suffereth long and is kind, especially to the unkind.

On June 7 his thesis had been accepted, his
degree conferred, and he had left Stanmore for
Cheltenham. He was still far from fit, and still
undecided about his future.

But only a week previously a brief letter from
Dr. Sclater had turned his thoughts in a totally
different direction. This was to tell him that a
junior surgeon and zoologist was required for the
National Antarctic Expedition to leave England
in July 1901—a similar post as botanist having
been held by Sir Joseph Hooker in the last Antarctic Expedition in 1840—would it be in his line?
Wilson appears to have replied that he felt unqualified for the post, for on June 1 Dr. Sclater
wrote again : ' I am on the Committee that makes
the appointments, and my opinion is that you
would be a suitable person for the post.' A further
letter on June 15 told him that the post was not

yet filled and advised him to see Professor Poulton
of Oxford, the leading member on the biological
sub-committee. This was backed by a letter from
Professor Poulton himself suggesting an early date
for the interview. The interview was very favourable, and Sir Charles Wilson now interested himself in bringing the application to the notice of
Sir Clements Markham, President of the Royal
Geographical Society, the promoter and ' Father '
of the Expedition. On October 28 Sir Clements
wrote :

My dear Wilson,—
     I am sure that your nephew's remarkable artistic talent
alone makes him a great acquisition to the Expedition.
It is very desirable that he should see the Commander of
the Expedition as soon as he is well enough. Will you tell
him to write to Captain R. F. Scott, R.N., 80 Queen's
Road, Chelsea—asking him to make an appointment to
see him.
Ever yours sincerely,
Clements R. Markham.

Meanwhile Wilson, who had taken but little part
in these negotiations, had been spending the best
and as it proved the last of his summer holidays
with his future wife at the Crippetts, and August
found him working at Cheltenham Hospital as
' locum tenens.'
     It was on September 14 that he drew, from a
small photograph of the Della Robbia statue at
Perugia lent to him by a friend, the picture of St.
Francis of Assisi which he gave to Miss Souper,
and which is here reproduced. Though the figure
is copied, the face of the saint is entirely his own
conception. After several attempts which were re-
jected this one was finally evolved. ' It came,' he

wrote, ' with an expression that somehow satisfies
me.' In that expression the reader may catch
glimpses of all that St. Francis meant to one of
his truest disciples. Recently occasion was found
to take the picture to a well-known art-dealer to
be remounted. In returning it a question was
asked as to the name of the artist.—' Why do you
wish to know ? '—' Because it is quite remarkable.
I have examined it through a magnifying-glass and
I have never seen such intricate pencil-work. The
naked eye unaided cannot see the full expression
in the eyes. Whoever drew it must have possessed
extraordinarily keen eyesight.'

On September 20 he was appointed Junior House
Surgeon at Cheltenham, but a pricked finger during a post-mortem three weeks later resulted in
blood-poisoning and an abscess in the axilla, which
became so serious that it obliged him to resign.
For some weeks he was in intense pain, and Miss
Souper came down to Cheltenham to nurse him.
An operation was only partially successful, and
his prospects of joining the Expedition seemed
more remote than ever.

On November 22, with his arm in a sling, he
went to London to see Captain Scott, to whom he
fully explained the nature of his illness. Scott
definitely offered him the appointment provided
that his health continued satisfactory, and this
although there were now many candidates for the
post, among them G. Barrett Hamilton, whose work
on *British Mammals* Wilson afterwards illustrated.

The trouble in his axilla recurred in December,
but he said nothing about it until Christmas was
over. Then he underwent a second operation,

ST. FRANCIS OF ASSISI

and presented himself with his arm still in a sling before the Medical Board at the Admiralty on January 4.[1] The doctors dismissed the local trouble, but told him that he must report again for final examination on July 13. When he did so he was passed as sound, and was actually leaving the room when his conscience smote him. He returned, and told the Medical Board of his old tubercular trouble. On re-examination his lungs, though devoid of any active disease, showed traces of old scars, and the Board reported unfavourably to the Antarctic Committee. Scott, however, was by this time determined to take him if he would come at his own risk, and on Wilson's agreeing, confirmed the appointment in spite of the adverse medical report.

I think [he wrote] I am intended to go. If I had tried to get it I should have had many doubts, but it seems given me to do. If the climate suits me I shall come back more fit for work than ever, whereas if it doesn't I think there's no fear of my coming back at all. I quite realize that it is kill or cure, and have made up my mind it shall be cure.

His future wife took the same view, and relieved him of a great part of his work in preparing details

---

[1] On January 7 he was elected F.Z.S., and this introduced him on pleasant terms to many men of kindred tastes, among them Dr. Dresser.

' His eagles' and hawks' eggs made my mouth water. He has spent, he says, 46 years travelling in every corner of Europe getting a complete collection. But better than all his eggs and what he too values most, is a beautiful collection of Wolff's drawings and studies of birds. Oh, what a collection ! Words are quite out of it. Still, as I told him, Hammond's were better.'

of the medical and scientific lists. The important
question had arisen as to whether the marriage
should take place before the Expedition started,
but the couple concerned had long since made up
their minds. The wedding was arranged to take
place at Hilton where the bride's father, the Rev.
F. A. Souper (formerly Headmaster of Bradfield
College) was Vicar, on July 16, only three days
after his interview at the Admiralty. 'I am as
happy,' he wrote to his friend Fraser, 'as it is
given to mortals ever to be on this earth.'

To fit himself for his Antarctic duties, he began
at once his work on *Whales and Dolphins* in rooms
at Pinner, took lessons in taxidermy at the Zoo,
and began working with Hodgson (biologist to the
Expedition) at Borchgrevink's collections at the
Natural History Museum. Amongst other things
he was writing an illustrated paper on Seals for
the British Museum, and designing at Scott's request a crest for the *Discovery* crockery and paper.

Final farewells were made to a house full of
guests at Westal, and on August 5 he embarked
on the *Discovery* at Southsea.

His mother's entry in her diary at this time
describes him as 'a body so frail and delicate, a
noble soul and spiritual.' Such a man might well
seem to the outward eye as the last to undertake
the rigours of exploration in the Antarctic. And
yet he was to prove, as Scott said, 'The life and
soul of the party, the organizer of all amusements,
the always good-tempered and cheerful one, the ingenious person who could get round all difficulties.'

CHAPTER VI

The ' Discovery ' Expedition

THE VOYAGE OUT

Wilson will do great things some day. He has quite the keenest intellect on board, and a marvellous capacity for work. You know his artistic talent, but you would be surprised at the speed with which he works and the indefatigable manner in which he is always at it. He is called to see and sketch the sunrise. He is on the spot when a new bird is seen. The next moment he is at a microscope sketching. He has fallen at once into ship life, helps with every job that may be on hand, doctors the men, keeps an eye on the ventilation of the ship, runs the wine as caterer, is great friends with all the young lieutenants, and in fact is an excellent fellow all round.

Letter to Sir Clements Markham from Captain Scott.

ON August 6, 1901, the *Discovery* weighed anchor and the last farewells were made : ' We watched the tug full of relations out of sight. I had my Zeiss glasses and saw O. to the end . . . and was happy all the same, for my pride in her pluck and determination to be bright to the last . . .' and the *Discovery* was under way in a head wind and a roughish sea, bound via the Cape and New Zealand for the Southern Seas and whatever lay beyond.

The objects of the Expedition were at once geographical and scientific, since although two former expeditions had touched the fringe of the Continent

77

neither had succeeded in penetrating beyond its coast. Ross had indeed in a remarkable voyage been the first to sight and chart the Great Ice Barrier in 1842 ; Borchgrevink in 1896 had even wintered at its northernmost extremity, Cape Adare : but no attempt had been made upon the interior, so that until the *Discovery* Expedition the mystery that hung over the Barrier was still veiled, and the Antarctic remained in fact as in name the *terra australis nondum cognita* of early geographers.

The night watches were kept in rotation by Barne, Shackleton, and Royds ; and Wilson loved to spend the hours till midnight on the bridge with one or other of them, as a refreshment after long hours of stuffy work below deck ; remarking of Shackleton on watch, ' he knows nearly every bit of poetry that has ever been written and is always ready to quote it.'

On the morning of the 15th, a little before sunrise, they made Madeira, and he set to work at once with paints and brush on a sketch of the Pique Port. He was thrilled with the luxuriant flora and brilliant bird and insect life of this semi-tropical island, and hearing a ' wild-voiced Black-cap in full song was like a breath of good old Crippetts back again.' So many quaint and picturesque objects ' wanted drawing ' that he made a second journey in grilling heat afoot into the Upper Town, and was still busy sketching the Harbour when the ship got under way.

The sight of a shoal of Bonito in pursuit of the small flying-fish, ' pale silvery green,' moved him to offer a bottle of champagne for one of the former fresh-killed to paint, ' brilliant peacock blue and green and purple, like fiery arrows in the water.' When in the latitude of Cape Verde, he reports that the theory of an estuarine submarine flow from West African rivers after heavy rain-storms inland is confirmed by the discoloration of the sea, by the appearance of storm-driven land birds on deck, and of fresh-water algæ in the tow-nets. Thereafter the reading of the xanthometer, an instrument designed to estimate the colour of the sea in various waters, was committed to him as having the most trained eyesight on board.

On August 28 he wrote :

. . . It's a blessed thing we get so much heavy work, because none of us need ever feel the want of exercise at all. The Captain turns to with all of us and shirks nothing, not even the dirtiest work. Royds works well and has most of the work on the ship itself to do. Shackle and Barne and I are a trio, and one is never dirtier than the other two, and all three as a rule are filthy. We three generally sleep down aft the poop in moonlight as bright as day, except when driven below by rain. Hodgson is always on the go. I think that Shackleton has so far done more hard work than anyone on board.

South of the Line the harvest of the tow-nets yielded rare larval forms of molluscs and crustaceans—

funny little hobgoblins, many of them wonderfully beautiful. Murray [1] gets me to draw their portraits in every imaginable position. . . . My paint-box has been upset more times than I can say, and this in the Tropics where most of the paints are semi-fluid and all get swamped in pasty vermilion, makes it hard to know where you are.

---

[1] Mr. George Murray, F.R.S., was appointed temporary Director of the Scientific Staff till arrival at the Cape.

Everything wanders if it isn't chained up. Every single
thing that isn't fixed or wedged in is on the floor in the
morning—ink, red and black, candle grease, medicines,
soapy slops, all get mixed up from time to time with
everything in the cabin, but it's a dear comfortable little
corner all the same, full of happy recollections and nice
faces, and one dearer than all . . . a happy little hovel
where I wouldn't alter anything for whole worlds if I
could help it.

On September 13 they put in at South Trinidad,
an island which had never before been scientifically
explored, the best account of it hitherto being that
by Knight in *The Cruise of the ' Falcon.'* Wilson
began at sunrise to sketch its precipitous and in-
hospitable coast.

Strange, weird, blighted island is South Trinidad. . . .
There is not a single beast on four legs on it. . . . Thousands of white bleached tree-trunks everywhere, and not
one living tree of the kind to be seen. Knight found
them all dead as we did 20 years ago, and yet within
the memory of man the island was covered with this
dense forest, and no one knows what the tree was or
what killed them off.

The island was

alive with birds that knew no fear, and with myriads
of quick scrabbling shore-crabs that were the prey of
fish ; and land-crabs, large fat bloated anæmic-looking
beasts with staring black eyes, sat in every hole and corner
of the whole island and just slowly looked at one. We
fed them on potted meat and cheese and chocolate, and
they ate it all slowly and deliberately without ever taking
their eyes off us. There was something horribly uncanny about these slow things ; one didn't know a bit
how old they were ; they might have been there since
the island came up.

Scott, always at heart a scientist, had organized
his preparations for the examination of the island

with care, and the results, illustrated by Wilson's
sketches, were collected by Mr. Murray and written up by him, for a report which he read before
the Royal Geographical Society on his return.
Wilson had secured a petrel unknown to the British
Museum, which was provisionally named after him
—*Æstralata Wilsoni.*[1]

Arrived at Cape Town on October 3, a dash
was made for the post-bag. Mails had gone astray,
and many long-expected letters from wives at home
were missing, ' I was lucky for I had about ten,
but then mine's a special sort of wife.'

The voyage to New Zealand was relatively un-
eventful save for one occurrence of the broaching-
to of the ship in heavy following seas, and for a
detour south to the fringe of the pack-ice. On
October 27, when on the bridge with Barne who
was helmsman, Scott joined them and was discussing where best to dry the wardroom carpet when

an enormous wave broke right over the ship. We all
three hung on to the stanchions and rails and were
swept clean off our feet. We were simply deluged, and
I burst out laughing at the Skipper who was gasping
for breath. He had been nearly a minute under water.
The whole of the upper deck was afloat. The water
had flooded the magnetic house ; laboratories, fo'c'sle
and wardroom ; galley filled with steam, winter clothes
just brought up from the hold for distribution all
swamped, and they call this a dry ship ! . . .

Painting a bird which is swinging through 30° every few
seconds is trying, things won't stay as you put them. Your
water is hung on a hook, your paper pinned to a board,
and you hold your paint-box ; you yourself are wedged

---

[1] Not to be confused with the commoner small Wilson's
Petrel. But see page 201.

into the bunk cupboard and kept there by a boot on the chest of drawers opposite. You put your paint-box down to settle a wing for the thirtieth time, and down it rattles and the paints go all over the cabin. . . . However, nothing breaks because nearly everything breakable was broken long ago. . . . For deck work I have made a bad-weather sketching box to hang round my neck, and can sketch comfortably in it even when it rains and blows a gale and spray comes all over one ; the paper keeps comparatively dry. The Skipper thinks it's an excellent plan, and we use it for a barrel organ in our impromptu theatricals on the bridge. . . .

(Sunday) Morning service as usual with interruptions. Scamp, our Aberdeen terrier, tried to enter Church when Koettlitz seized him by the tail and flung him out. Scamp gave tongue in a high-pitched voice and in three minutes pelted in again, having got past Koettlitz, and was silently applauded by the blue-jackets who beamed upon him. . . .

At dinner we had an immense argument on the Ethics of Sport, and I was practically unsupported in arguing that it was a relic of barbarity which was certainly fated to die out in time in any civilized nation, an end to be devoutly hoped for. As I expected I found myself in a hornets' nest. The young naval officer hasn't thought much about such things. Only the Captain had ever realized that the question of sport had another side to it.

Nov. 15. (First sight of pack-ice in latitude 60°.) The sky was grey with snow falling, the breakers were white on a dark grey sea, and the ice only had its whiteness broken with the most exquisitely shaded blues and greens, pure blue, cobalt, and pale emerald, and every mixture in between them. I never saw more perfect colour or toning in all Nature. . . . I couldn't leave the upper deck ; from early morning till 11 p.m., many of us remained spell-bound, though it was more beautiful than ever in the dusk when sea and sky alike were white and the pack faded into the near distance with no horizon ; a wonderful waste of beauty.

Nov. 22. (Macquarie Islands.) I told the Pilot I would give him a bottle of liqueur if he could persuade the Skipper to allow us to land here for collecting. Off he

went like a shot and soon came up and told me he wanted
the liqueur. Up came the Skipper and down came
the sails.

Here Wilson first made acquaintance with the
Penguin at close quarters, the bird on all the
species of whose tribe he afterwards became an
unrivalled authority. He went ashore with Scott
and Barne, and entering a deserted hut they found
an almost perfect collection of bird-skins, well dried,
sexed and numbered, evidently a year or two old,
and among them ' 4 or 5 Landrails of a kind of
which no museum in Europe possesses a specimen,
except Rothschild, and he only one,' besides other
rarities. No vestige could be found of the collector,
though they hopefully searched every bunk for a
corpse, but in vain ! So they left the collection
intact, and, turning their attention to the living
species, saw how the King Penguin protects its
egg from the mud in which it roosts by resting it
between the insteps of its feet and its lappet.

I carried one some distance by the neck at arm's
length, and Shackleton seeing the egg drop told the men
that all you had to do to get a penguin to lay was to
throttle it and the egg would drop out.

He regretted, as always, the necessity in the
interests of science of butchering these innocent
birds, but returned to the ship with a collection
of nearly every species which the island produced.
Three hours ashore was all too short for what he
would have done, most of all to find the Albatrosses'
nesting-places on the higher summits of the island.
Bird-skinning then proceeded under difficulties in
very heavy seas, with Skelton, Hodgson, and Seaman Cross as his pupils.

Wilson had already formed his opinion of Scott, and in view of all that was to come of their close co-operation later, his first impressions of him written in a letter home just before they sighted the ice-pack, are not without interest :

He is a most capable man in every way and has a really well-balanced head on his shoulders. I admire him immensely, all but his temper. He is quick-tempered and very impatient, but he is a really nice fellow, very generous and ready to help us all in every way, and to do everything he can to ensure us the full merit of all we do. He is thoughtful for each individual and does little kindnesses which show it. He is ready to listen to everyone too, and joins heartily in all the humbug that goes on. I have a great admiration for him, and he is in no Service rut but is always anxious to see both sides of every question, and I have never known him to be unfair. One of the best points about him too is that he is very definite about everything ; nothing is left vague or indeterminate. In every argument he goes straight for the main point, and always knows exactly what he is driving at. There will be no fear of our wandering about aimlessly in the Southern regions.

In the same letter he could tell his parents that he had already put on more weight ($1\frac{1}{2}$ stone) than anyone else on board and was ' habitually held up as an example of the excellence of our provisions.' He depreciated his capacity either as a zoologist or as an artist, ' in nothing am I professionally expert,' and was equally unimpressed with the proficiency of his colleagues on the scientific staff :

With the single exception of Hodgson we are all intensely ignorant of anything but the elementary knowledge of our several jobs. I certainly am no ornithologist, as my knowledge of the technical side of the business is nil.

This self-depreciatory opinion, however, was by

no means shared by the experts to whom the results of his work were afterwards submitted.

On November 24, Scott, than whom few commanders of expeditions have more keenly felt the personal responsibility for the welfare of their subordinates, wrote to Mrs. Wilson as follows :

There is one thing your husband will not have told you, and that is what a fine fellow we all think him. His intellect and ability will one day win him a great name, of this I feel sure. We admire such qualities, as well as the artistic talent which goes far to cheer our monotony ; but his kindness, loyalty, good temper, and fine feelings are possessions which go beyond the word admiration and can be simply said to have endeared him to us all. How truly grateful I am to have such a man with me, and how much it lightens my responsibilities for the general well-being, it would be difficult to express, so I hope you will find some comfort in knowing that we shall look after such an invaluable messmate to the best of our ability when he is not looking after us.

P.S.—I nearly forgot the most important item of all, viz. that he is in the most ' rampagious ' health and seems to thrive on hardships. His appetite and waist measurements play an important part in our little stock of homemade jokes.

True to schedule at midnight on November 28 the ship was anchored in Lyttelton Harbour, New Zealand ; and a busy fortnight ensued of some anxiety for Scott in the work of storage, refitting the ship from the severe buffeting she had received in the ' forties,' and in an only partially effectual endeavour to repair a leak. For Wilson the inevitable round of social festivities, of which he had had a surfeit at the Cape, was happily relieved by the necessity of cleaning his bird-skins against time, and he got off with no more than a couple of official dinners, and a reception by the Maories.

At Dunedin Scott loaded the ship with every ounce of coal she could carry, and on Christmas Eve she steamed out of Port Chalmers, Wilson writing in high spirits—

Now—neck or nothing—we are fairly started, thank God : and by His grace we shall do something worth the doing before we sight New Zealand and civilization again.

From the outset fortune favoured the adventurers, and it seemed as if the sea-gods smiled upon their enterprise. In striking contrast to the disasters that befell them in these regions nine years later, this voyage was unimpeded either by gales or by delay in the pack, and within a week the *Discovery* was through the floes and in the open water of the Ross Sea.

Wilson was seldom below deck—now with Skelton capturing sea-birds by means of long weighted streamers of strong thread afloat in the wind, then sketching and skinning them as fast as they were caught, and again helping Hodgson to sift the ever-new treasures of the tow-nets ; now on a floe securing the Weddell, the Crab-eater, and the rarer Ross seal ; then bathed in blood from head to foot flensing the skins of blubber ; now assisting to ' water ship ' with loads of hummocked ice ; even rousing Scott at night to stop the ship for the capture of a sea-leopard, ' though the Skipper hates the sight of our butcher's shop.' [1]

He was with Royds on the bridge a little after midnight on the morning of January 8, when the

---

[1] ' All his life Scott suffered extreme nausea from the sight of blood ; even in the *Discovery* days to get used to " seeing red " he had to force himself to watch Dr. Wilson skinning his specimens.'—Sir James Barrie.

Antarctic coast was first sighted, 'immense snow-peaks rolled up in a mass of golden clouds and flooded with golden sunlight.' These were the high peaks of the Admiralty Range that fringe the coast of Victoria Land, and were distinguishable at a distance of 100 miles. The course was set for Robertson Bay and in twenty-seven hours a landing was effected at Cape Adare.

Bernacchi, who had wintered on this spot with Borchgrevink's expedition in 1896, led them to the hut still standing, and to Hanson's grave 1,000 feet above. Wilson and Shackleton went inshore together, investigating the Adélie Penguin rookeries, and securing with some difficulty one of the eggs of the Wilson's Petrel from the rock crevices in which they breed.

From this point onwards they steamed southwards along the coast through heavy pack, and Wilson commenced his series of panoramic sketches of the mountain ranges which were afterwards reproduced by the Royal Society and are entirely unique in the annals of polar exploration. He gave a standing order to be called by the watch whenever any land stood out clearly, and the midnight sun made his task as easy by night as by day. Not content with pen and pencil sketches only, he made many beautiful studies in colour of some of the loftier peaks such as Minto, Sabine, Herschell, Monteagle, and Melbourne.

For three days and nights a gale obliged them to shelter in the lee of Coulman Island at the entrance to Lady Newnes Bay,[1]

---

[1] Sir George Newnes was the promoter of Borchgrevink's expedition.

an amazingly beautiful sight, hemmed in on all sides
with vertical cliffs of ice of 100 to 150 feet ; and from
the edge of these ran smooth limitless fields of glistening
snow many miles back to the shining mountain ranges,
pure white with the faintest shadows of prussian blue.
. . . An eternal peace that could never be disturbed
seemed to hang in the cold clear air ; I shall never
forget it.

While engaged in seal-hunting here (' I had to
superintend this beastly butcher's work, a duty
much against the grain ') he found himself with
Ferrar and two of the seamen, Cross and Weller,
adrift on an ice-floe. Here, lightly clad for the
heavy work of skinning and hauling, they were
marooned for five hours, but although

there were 14 degrees of frost, the sun kept our bodies
pretty warm, and we ran races and chased penguins.
. . . Happily there was sun and no wind or we should
have had a bad time indeed.

The incident is related by Scott as follows :

Although the sun had been shining brightly all night,
the temperature had been down to 18°, and afar off I
could see four disconsolate figures tramping about to
keep themselves warm on a detached floe not more than
fifteen yards across. When at length our wanderers
scrambled over the side, it was very evident they had a
big grievance, and it was only after some hot cocoa that
they could talk of their experiences with ease. They
had been obliged to keep constantly on the move, and
when they thought of smoking to relieve the monotony
of the situation, the smokers found they had pipes and
tobacco but no match. It was whilst they were dismally
discussing the fact that Dr. Wilson, a non-smoker, came
nobly to the rescue and succeeded in producing fire
with a small pocket magnifying-glass, a fact which shows
not only the resource of the officer, but the power of
the midnight sun in these latitudes.

It is characteristic of Scott that he makes no
allusion to the 'winged words' with which he
addressed the officer of the watch ; and of Wilson
that his diary contains no allusion to the tobacco
incident.

To Wilson and Shackleton from the crow's-nest
of the *Discovery* was granted on January 19 their
first sight of Mount Erebus far to the southward,
the giant volcano of the Antarctic, with his smoking crater towering 13,000 feet above the sea.
Then crossing McMurdo Sound, and steaming now
eastwards by Ross Island they made Cape Crozier
under the slopes of Mount Terror on January 22.

A long low but heavy swell broke on the shore with
an appalling force, but a collection of 6 to 8 stranded
icebergs into the midst of which we rowed produced a
lee. They were all sea-worn and weather-worn, with
enormous gulf-like caves and arches and tunnels into
which the swell broke in thunder. No words can describe their blues and greens, and lights and shadows.
Sometimes when on the shady side of an iceberg one
would see the sun's light come through an archway with
an unsurpassable green light. It was a scene one can
never forget.

Even more impressive was his first full view of
the Great Ice Barrier, gained after a steep climb
with Scott and Royds to the highest of the volcanic
cones above these cliffs. From this point the great
ice plain could be seen with long undulations
stretching southwards into infinity whilst ' the Barrier edge, in shadow, looked like a long narrowing
black ribbon as it ran with slight windings to the
eastern horizon.' (Scott.)

It was viewed by Scott with the eyes of a physi-
cist and a surveyor who was even more intent upon

unravelling its mystery than on navigating the ship along its course. It was viewed by Wilson with the eyes of an artist, and never since have its many aspects been traced—its caves and fissures, calved bergs, sudden inlets, the wind-blown snow-drifts on its summits—with a more faithful or a defter hand.

Scott was a writer : with leisure for application he might have become a writer of the first rank ; and although in his preface to his book he modestly apologizes for his ' literary inexperience,' the hand of the born craftsman is evident throughout in his lucid, chiselled phrases. Wilson was not a writer, but he was an artist whose inward purity could reflect and transcribe those frail pure tones with a rare blend of delicacy and strength. Never before or since have the qualities of two such men, each supplementing the other, combined to present such a picture of those frozen wastes.

Hoping to attain the eastward extremity of the Great Ice Barrier, Scott ran on under ice-cliffs varying from 70 to 280 feet as far as the 150th parallel of longitude, till the pack barred further progress when he reluctantly decided to return to McMurdo Sound. *En route* he made a balloon ascent from the Bight, afterwards named the Bay of Whales. He had already formed the opinion that the Great Ice Barrier was a floating shelf of ice, which later study confirmed.

The last half of the month of February was actively spent in erecting the hut at Hut Point below Observation Hill on Ross Island, and in general in securing winter quarters on the ship against ' freezing in.'

CHAPTER VII

The ' Discovery ' Expedition (continued)

THE FIRST WINTER

In the midst of these vast ice-solitudes and under the frowning desolation of the hills, the ship, the huts, the busy figures passing to and fro, and the various evidences of human activity are extraordinarily impressive. How strange it all seems ! For countless ages the great sombre mountains about us have loomed through the gloomy polar night with never an eye to mark their grandeur, and for countless ages the wind-swept snow has drifted over these great deserts with never a footprint to break its white surface ; for one brief moment the eternal solitude is broken by a hive of human insects ; for one brief moment they settle, eat, sleep, trample, and gaze, and then they must be gone, and all must be surrendered again to the desolation of the ages.

Scott's Journal, July 18, 1902.

THE ship being now, though somewhat insecurely, anchored at the ice-foot in Arrival Bay, Wilson's first ten days ashore were spent in local exploration, ski-running, and testing the use of crampons on the ice-slopes. But on February 19 he was sent with Shackleton and Ferrar to reconnoitre White Island, and observe whatever land lay beyond it to the South, thus undertaking the first sledge-journey proper ever made in the Antarctic : a journey of only four days, but remarkable for the way in which mettle compensated for inexperience.

On February 19 the trio started from ' the Gap '
(between Crater Hill and Observation Hill) ¹ to
which they had previously hauled their ' pram '
(Norwegian skiff), in case of meeting open water.

Unused to the visibility of the Antarctic, they
underestimated the distance of their objective by
half, and pulled for twelve hours at a stretch till
the point of exhaustion was reached ; ignorant of
the dangers of sledging in a blizzard they pushed
on despite it ' heads down and pulling all we knew
against wind and snow at the rate of a mile an
hour,' and suffered from frost-bite in consequence
when they camped, ' hanging on like grim death
to the tent pole to prevent the whole bag of tricks
going to blazes ' ; nursing each other's frozen ears
and fingers back to life in the tent they got their
foot-gear off, ' the ski-boots frozen to the socks so
that both came off in one ' ; novices as yet in the
use of Nansen's cooker they made a sorry mess of
their pemmican, and regardless of hours confused
breakfast with dinner ; and when Wilson was
seized with cramp ' the other two were bricks to
me : they dressed me first and put me on the floor,
and sat on me while they dressed each other.'
When at length they attained the summit of White
Island, 2,700 feet, at midnight—

As far as the eye could see was a level ice-plain, the
true Great Barrier surface, and no Antarctic Continent

---

¹ It is perhaps necessary to say here that these landmarks,
and those to be mentioned hereafter, were named by Scott.
Ross, whose name is given to the island which he discovered,
had named after his two ships the two great volcanoes upon
it, Erebus and Terror, the one active, the other extinct. He
had named the mountain peaks of Victoria Land, McMurdo
Bay, Cape Crozier and the Great Ice Barrier.

'MUSHROOM' ICE

Feb. 1902.   Fractured mounds of blue ice on the NW side of White Island.   4 ft to 5 ft high.

ICE-MOUNDS

at all. On the west the coast-line ran in a series of
promontories formed by splendid mountain ranges, and
beyond them all was the setting sun just dipping below
the horizon. Shackle took bearings and angles and I
made a sketch, though we were nearly frozen in doing it.

They continued their explorations round the
island,

in a minglement of Barrier and glacier ice . . . to a
bay full of strange mounds some 6 or 8 feet high of very
deep blue ice with star-shaped fractures, raised probably
by water pressure underneath, also heaps of crystals of
magnesium salts on the flat ice.[1]

On February 22 they made a great march for
home, leaving their pram at a point below the
Barrier Edge where it abuts on the southern slopes
of Crater Hill ; and it has been called Pram Point
ever since.

Meanwhile another larger party had been dispatched in the direction of Cape Crozier under
Royds, and on March 10 Wilson, having taken a
day out in bitter weather to a distant seal-rookery
to sketch, discerned a ' black dot far away towards
Mount Erebus which could be nothing but the sledge-
party or part of it returning, but they were more
than a day's journey off.' With this news he
returned to the ship : it was not credited, but the
next day confirmed it.

The tragic fate that befell this, the second sledge
party, has been told at length by Scott. It was the
occasion of the death of Seaman Vince, who,
losing his footing on an ice-cliff, shot past his
horrified companions into the sea ; and of the loss

---

[1] The true origin of these ice-mounds with their deposits
of Mirabilite (natural Glauber salts) was discovered by Prof.
Debenham, a geologist of Scott's Last Expedition.

in a blizzard of Barne and three seamen. In less
than half an hour after Wild's report of the disaster
at 8.30 p.m. a volunteer party which included
Wilson was over the ship's side and had disappeared
nto the blinding drift. They found Barne and
two of the seamen and continued their search for
the third till 2 a.m. After dressing the frost-bites
of his patients the next morning Wilson, in charge
of another party, set out in a forlorn attempt to
find the still-missing seaman, Hare. Two officers
and five men quickly succumbed to frost-bites and
were sent back, while Wilson with Bernacchi and
Seaman Cross continued the search for five hours,
but in vain.

The miraculous return of Hare alone and
unaided, the following day, was regarded by all
as an escape as providential as it was inexplicable.

I shall never forget the effect it had on some of us,
notably on the Skipper, who looked as though he thought
the dead was really walking in. I felt much the same,
but as I was the only doctor on board I had to begin
and bustle about. . . . Imagine our amazement when
we found he hadn't even a superficial touch of frost-
bite. However I decided to run no risk with him after
this, and put him in blankets in the magnetic observatory
at a temp. of 17° F. and lit a lamp there which gradually
raised the temp. to freezing-point, when I allowed him
to go to his bunk in the sick bay. We took turns to sit
up with him. I kept him on a low diet though he was
ravenously hungry. He slept the whole day. The next
day, apart from some aching pains, he was as well as ever.

Thus far their experience had been dearly bought
indeed, and the sick bay was full of patients. One
of these was the steward, Mr. Ford, who had broken
a leg while ski-ing : and after thirty years his

personal recollections of Wilson, as a man and a doctor, remain the most vivid of his life.

Dr. Wilson combined with an essential manliness a sweetness of character unusual amongst men. Full of constant thoughtfulness for others, always sensitive to their peculiarities, never harsh to their weaknesses ; temperamentally nervous himself, yet always setting an example of the highest courage ; he was the bravest and most unselfish man I have ever known. The way he nursed and washed and fed me when I was ill will never be forgotten.

In spite of the lateness of the season, Scott was determined on a final effort before the winter closed in.

This journey [wrote Wilson] is calculated to last three weeks and its object is to establish a depot of provisions on the farthest point of land due south from here, as a preparation for the big Southern Sledge Journey next year.

The start was made on March 31, with dog-teams, but on April 2 Scott decided that neither men nor dogs could sledge continuously in such low temperatures and persistent drift, and, depoting their provisions on the Barrier ice, they turned back the following day. It was their first experience of a three-man sleeping-bag and some idea of its discomforts can be gathered from Wilson's account of it on this journey :

I slept again in the middle and had a very good night. We none of us thought we had slept at all, but from listening to the others snoring we knew that everyone else had. So close are we packed that no one can turn without waking the others, for our bodies are jammed in tight, and every crevice of the bag-opening closed over by flaps of reindeer-skin with loops and toggles. One breathes 19 to the dozen to begin with for an hour or two till one gets used to partial asphyxiation : a crack left open or a hole in the skin lets in the cold air like a knife, forming a cake of ice round the aperture inside the bag. . . . Your only chance of keeping warm is to lie still. There is half an inch of rime coating the inside of the tent, the result of the evening's cooking, and this drops on your face and melts there and runs where it chooses, for you can't possibly get a hand up or wipe it with anything if you could. Reindeer-skin hairs tickle your nose and face and get into your mouth, and you can't do anything but move your head, which brings the ring of ice on your Balaclava round your mouth in close contact with warmer skin, so that it melts and runs down your neck. . . . One is in a chaotic state of dampness at night when one gets warm. In the morning one puts on frozen socks, frozen mitts, and frozen boots stuffed with frozen damp grass and rime, and one suffers a good deal from painfully cold feet until everything is packed up again and strapped on the sledges, and one is off to warm up to the work of a beast of burden. There's a fascination about it all, but it can't be considered comfort. . . . The burberry suit of overalls which one wears from crown to heel is wet and frozen so that every movement makes it crackle like a suit of armour, and one must stand rigidly still to hear one's neighbour speak.

Now with the closing in of the long winter night the little party made shift to beguile the passage of the dark hours. The day's routine of seven hours was quickly sped : officers and men were fully occupied in the special tasks allotted to them, but how to employ an equal number of leisure hours was a problem that called for inventiveness and resource. The pianola was in constant use except when Royds, the only musician, played from the great composers (Wilson delighted in such music— Chopin especially—and constantly refers to Royds' playing with gratitude), or when concerts were arranged at which these two friends invariably sang duets. Another source of entertainment was the weekly debate, more often amusing than instructive, when men argued heatedly upon subjects of which they had little or no knowledge. The following was an amusing exception.

After dinner a Tennyson *v.* Browning competition which resulted from a discussion as to their respective merits yesterday. Shackle upheld Browning and Bernacchi Tennyson. Each had to choose a passage from his own author on various subjects such as Love, Science, Philosophy, Wit, Art, Beauty. They read these out to us and we voted. Tennyson won by several votes.

With reference to the day's routine of work Scott wrote :

It would be difficult to say who is the most diligent, but perhaps the palm would be given to Wilson, who is always at work ; every rough sketch made since we started is reproduced in an enlarged and detailed form until we now possess a splendid pictorial representation of the whole coast-line of Victoria Land. Wilson starts his day early by an examination of the breakfast food ; his next business is to see to the ventilation of the living-spaces, which he does so thoroughly that when we come to breakfast there is no complaint about the freshness of the air, though occasionally people appear in fur mitts as a mute protest against the temperature. He next takes the eight o'clock meteorological observations, and after the men are told off for the work of the day his business takes him to the superintendence of those who are detailed for bird-skinning and who carry on this work in the main hut. Under his direction a few of the men, and especially Cross, have become quite expert taxidermists, and the collection of prepared skins is gradually growing. The rest of his day is devoted to working up sketches and zoological notes, making those delightful drawings for the *South Polar Times*, without which that publication would lose its excellence, and performing a hundred and one kindly offices for all on board. He and Shackleton generally journey together to the top of Crater Hill, a height of 950 feet, each day, and return with a record of the temperature at our second outlying station.

The editorship of the letterpress of the *S.P.T.* was in the capable hands of Shackleton during the first winter, and of Bernacchi in the second. With the passage of time the point of its topical allusions is dimmed, but the charm of its illustrations is still enduring. It attracted the interest of so many friends of the Expedition on its return that 250 copies were printed by Messrs. Smith, Elder & Co., for private circulation in exact facsimile from the original. Wilson took as much pains with the illustrations of this obscure periodical as with any of his more serious studies. He always feared that his Antarctic paintings, by far the majority of which were made in the winter under artificial light, would not bear close scrutiny in the light of day ; but when the sun returned their colouring was seen to be as true in tone as his daylight sketches had been. As the winter advanced he found so much close work under acetylene gas a severe tax upon his sight. ' I only hope my eyes will hold out,' or words to similar effect, frequently recur in his Journal.

Shackle and I arranged the ' Editor's Office ' in one of the holds. We built up all the cases to form a small passage and room at one end, with cases for seats and for the table of his typewriter. It is lit by candle lamps, and Shackle has fixed a rope to the door which enables him to open or shut it from the other end of the hold according to whether he wants a visitor to come in or remain outside. It's a select office, and strangers with no business are not admitted as a rule.

But the secret of his inspiration, in his art, in his

they sleep in the winter, and for how
many hours a day, is a problem full
of interest. Now and again as we
walk among the Weddell's Seals
we find a Crab-eater, seldom
more than one or two, asleep
with the rest.

When we were in the pack
ice these were our daily
food, for we saw
some every day, and
often ate them. Here they are a
rarity, and an interesting
one, as they have hitherto
been considered the peculiar
property of the pack ice.
The "Southern Cross" expedition
found one on the Great Ice
Barrier, and we saw several
as we sailed along it, but
here we have them still
farther South, and
prospect of our
from time to

there seems every
seeing them
time during the winter
and perhaps even some-
-thing of their family
arrangements in the Spring.
I think the
general admiration of our
party is divided somewhat
between the Crab-eater and Ross'
Seal. We have had but few opportunities
of getting to know the latter, though
both are very interesting. No one has
ever met with Ross' Seal except in the
pack ice, and possibly his coat would
be found to vary much if seen at
other seasons of the year,
but he has only been seen
in summer when all have
had a roughish hair

Sea Leopard
chasing Emperor Penguins

E. a. W.

A PAGE FROM THE *SOUTH POLAR TIMES*

work, and in those many kindly offices, came from
a source none guessed.

[To his wife]— . . . The little that I have done,
it's all for you, and that is why I never do less than I
know how. But if I ever do make a mistake or anyone
comes to grief at my hands, you at any rate will know
that it will not be for want of care or trouble, and God
will know that too. . . . The world is not so forgiving.

When help was needed in other departments
than his own he was always ready to postpone
whatever work he had in hand to give it, and it
was with the excuse that he was bound to be up
betimes in any case to inspect the milk and superintend the ventilation, that he volunteered to take
the extra meteorological observation regularly at
8 a.m. Of all the scientific exigencies of the
Expedition this, the special care of Royds, was the
most important as well as the most severe in
execution. Throughout the winter each officer
was detailed in rotation to take the nightly readings
of the various recording instruments. In a blizzard
this journey of 100 yards to and from the screen
was sometimes made perforce on hands and knees
in a whirling drift almost too thick to breathe in,
the slack of the guide-rope buried under compact
snow, the hurricane-lamp not proof against the
wind, entailing as much danger of getting lost as a
walk of as many miles in normal weather ; and
Wilson does not disguise in letters to his wife the
awesome and terrifying nature of this experience
for him on occasion. 'When I have to get out of
my warm bunk and go on deck at 4 a.m. I often
wish everything wasn't so dark and that everyone
wasn't asleep.'

But he rejoiced in the fact that he could stand these rigours as well as any :

Strange, isn't it ? After being considered an invalid and unfit for much work, I feel so alive and strong. This cold agrees with me so wonderfully, and I can stand it rather better than most of the party.

With the desolation of that snowy wilderness, of stark rock and icy crag, all round him, he turns his thoughts at Easter to

the beautiful Spring with all its freshness and green and colour ; I think of the primroses turning up at Birdlip, and last year when I brought some roots home to you. I think still more of the celandine's bright green, crisp and juicy, and the yellow star in the hedgerows ; and the feathery willows of Crippetts wood, and the squirrels and the wood-anemones ; and then again of the winter aconite and the crocuses in that little side-path from the park on the way to your school playground. And yet there is no sadness in all these thoughts, only a longing hope and belief that I shall enjoy them again with you, my one dear Love.

. . . I would so like to come to you, just for a little bit of the old happy times we have had together, but still it *will* come, or something far far better, though that is quite impossible to imagine and for once beyond hope.

And with this an equally intense longing to share with her the exquisite colours of mountain, ice and sky :

. . . And I would to God I could lay it all before you . . . utterly impossible to represent with my poor paints and poorer skill in using them, and yet I try ; and God knows how I long to do as much as I can that others may share the joy I find in feasting my eyes on the colours of this wonderful place, and the vastness of it all. Shackleton, Ferrar and I were actually the first men who ever saw that red glow on the southern side of Erebus and Terror. . . . ' The works of the Lord *are* great and very worthy to be praised and had in honour ' ; I don't think you and I will ever get tired of praising them, but I do wish you could see them.

It was in the language of the Psalms indeed that he found the truest expression of his sense of awe amidst these scenes of desolate grandeur, but there was another sentence of mystical meaning that also rose repeatedly to his mind with an ever-fresh significance. ' The hidden things of God are understood and seen clearly in things created.'

This work of Antarctic exploration is very different from the work I had planned for myself some years ago. And yet I do honestly believe that God's will is being worked out for us in what we are doing, and though it may seem to some rather more ' worldly ' and ' scientific ' than ' spiritual,' yet there *is* a spiritual work to be done here. And as for its main object, the acquisition of knowledge pure and simple, surely God means us to find out all we can of his works, and to work out our own salvation, realizing that all things that have to do with our spiritual development ' are understood and clearly seen in things created,' and if it is right to search out his works in one corner of his Creation, it is right for some of us to go to the ends of the earth to search out others.

As if to reflect the solitude without there fell on him a solitariness of spirit which none of his companions guessed, for no cabins were more resorted to by all and sundry than were his and Shackleton's. But the right to enter one's private sanctum and ' sport one's oak,' the inviolable privilege of college life, was impossible on shipboard where no privacy is recognized ; and there was no one among his messmates to whom he could open his soul as he could to his old friends at Cambridge, so that he thought often with regret of Fraser, and Charles, and Abercrombie, and of all the difference that the companionship of one of them would have meant to him here. Though Royds in one way, and Scott in another, came nearest him in understanding, yet with neither of them could he exchange those ideas on the deep things of life which were always in the background of his mind. Only in the early morning or in the night-hours when the others were absorbed in games was that solitariness lifted, and he could commune in spirit with the one who knew and loved him best and most.

I get an hour to myself as a rule before breakfast when I am quite alone, and then I sometimes pray, sometimes read your letters, and sometimes write to you, often a little bit of each, and I feel it is all communion with God.

The thing I miss most is the feeling you have given me more than anyone else on earth, I mean the quick understanding of me that your love gives you, you *read* me . . . you understand what I mean.

From the outset he had insisted on making his own bunk, tidying his own cabin, and fetching his own water from the galley ; when sent out with a party of seamen he had made a point of sharing his special rations with them, and of very literally working *with* them, instead of merely overseeing their work ; finally, he tried to be a nurse as well as a doctor to his patients.

It is so difficult [he wrote to his wife] to get decent cleanliness anywhere, and I am afraid the sick get a very uncomfortable time indeed. Women know by instinct how to nurse ; I'm afraid I am a very bad hand at it. I wish I had you here to help me, you are so very quick to grasp what is wanted and how it should be done.

In the wardroom it was not always easy. In a small community of men of diverse temperaments confined in such close proximity, with the best will in the world to preserve harmonious relations good-natured banter might easily lapse into acerbity. Wilson saw that if he was to help others in this respect he must first look to his own armour.

[To his wife]—I am more thankful than I can say for having been brought to this life because it is such an education. But God knows it is just about as much as I can stand at times, and there is absolutely no escape. I have never had my temper so tried as it is every day now, but I don't intend to give way. . . . It's a hard school down here, but I wouldn't have missed it for worlds. . . .

He had long recognized criticism of others as his own principal failing, and his readiness for repartee had been a snare to him. He could always ' give as good as he got ' and better ; he could never suffer a fool gladly ; and he accused himself of having been often sarcastic, cutting, and contemptuous, when he might have been a peacemaker.

I want to tell you what an immense help that little remark of your Father's has been to me. You told me your Father had said I was a ' peacemaker.' What made him think so I can't guess, but I determined I would try to be one, for I had never thought about the matter before ; and indeed a little bit of peace-making is wanted here and there in this community of men, some of whom are not inclined to live peaceably with one another. We have had *very* few rows, but friction is continual between some parties, and your Father's remark has helped me to do something at any rate to smooth things over sometimes. That this is so, and that his remark and good opinion have been a great help to me, let him know if you think fit. I think he would be glad.

The secret of his influence lay in a self-discipline that was as habitual as most men's habits are, an inner culture of mind and heart and will that gave his life a poise, so that he could not be untrue either to himself or his fellow-men.

As the winter drew on his cabin became a more and more frequent rendezvous for mirthful meetings as well as for confidential talks. Shackleton, eager, impulsive, inquiring, with whom his relations hitherto had been those merely of good fellowship at work and play, now came to him with doubts and questionings of faith and morals, mixed with a tangle of theological perplexities ; to be met with the reply that faith in Christ was not primarily a matter of doctrinal or intellectual belief, but a way of life, a following, an allegiance.

[To his wife]—Shackleton's conversation is sparkling and witty to a high degree. He has a wonderful memory, and has an amazing treasure of most interesting anecdote. That and his quick wit and keen humour are his strong points at table.

He is still my best friend, but I have a great admiration for Royds' character, a most simple, honest, lovable soul, full of high feeling for all that is good. He doesn't think deeply but has a strong, simple, childlike faith, and sticks to it through thick and thin. He is a marvel of patience as a rule, though it is a ' Service ' patience, which takes any amount of snubbing from superiors, is very considerate to inferiors, but very hasty and stern sometimes with his equals. He has an extraordinary amount of sentimental feeling for a man, full of music and artistic tastes, and yet a manly powerful chap, and an excellent sailor.

The Captain and I understand one another better than anyone else on the ship, I think. He has adopted every one of my suggestions. It's a great help to have one's ideas appreciated by a man who is always trying new and knacky things on his own. . . . Only once

have we got on religious subjects, but I soon found that
his ideas are as settled in one direction as mine are in
another, and our only agreement was that we differed.

There came a day in midwinter, June 12, when
Scott called him into his cabin for an unexpected
consultation on practical details of the various
sledging parties for the summer, and on calculations
of weights and rations for the Southern Journey.
After outlining these plans in detail he told Wilson
of his early decision that he should accompany him
on the Southern Journey. The only remaining
point on which he wished to consult him was the
advisability of taking a third. Since Nansen's
journey of thirteen months' duration with Johansen,
the old methods of Arctic travelling with many
men and a train of sledges had been abandoned in
favour of the fewest possible, and Scott wished to
limit his polar effort to the minimum of two.
Wilson was as astonished as he was delighted, but
maintained that a third man was necessary in the
event of one falling sick. Scott at first demurred,
but ultimately agreed. His choice in favour of
Shackleton was prompted not by his own wishes,
but by what he believed to be Wilson's. It proved
to be an unfortunate choice ; for Shackleton's
physique and constitution were not as strong as
they became later. His system already showed
traces of that bronchial and cardiac weakness
which, though allayed in middle life sufficiently to
enable him to make his heroic journeys, was to
cause his death twenty years later. Wilson kept
his misgivings to himself, being as glad for his
friend's sake as for his own, but his private observations on the point are not without interest.

I feel more equal to it than I feel for Shackleton ; for some reason I don't think he is fitted for the job. The Captain is strong and hard as a bull-dog, but Shackleton hasn't the legs that the job wants ; he is so keen to go, however, that he will carry it through. . . . They call it the ' Sentimental Journey ' because in a debate yesterday I said that when Polar exploration became possible to any form of motor transport or flying machine its attraction to most people would be finished, and would interest an entirely different mind. I was glad that the Captain and Shackleton both agreed.

With the return of the sun, as early as the first week in September Scott launched a series of ' spring ' sledging journeys. On the first of these he took Wilson and Shackleton for a short trial trip to the north over the sea-ice along the edges of the Glacier Tongue, mainly with a view to testing the dogs ;—' we took two pullers and two ' sooners ' as they are called. Why ? because they'd sooner do anything than pull.' On the second journey Barne took the place of Wilson who needed the time to complete his work on seals. Of the various other journeys that were made was one the report of which thrilled Wilson more than any other ; even the imminent adventure of the Southern Journey paled beside it. This was Skelton's discovery of the Emperor Penguin Rookery below the cliffs of Cape Crozier. He felt that the claims of zoological research were far more pressing for him than pure geographical exploration, and having begged, but in vain, for a few days to hunt for Emperors before starting for the South, wrote in his Journal regretfully :

I am afraid this long southern journey is taking me right away from my proper sphere of work to monotonous

hard pulling over an icy desert where we shall see neither
beast nor bird, nor life of any kind, nor land, and nothing whatever to sketch. . . . Anyhow it is *the* journey
and I cannot but be glad I was chosen for it.

[To his wife]— . . . If anything happens to me so
that you can't see me again in this life, and you want
to hear about me from those who do get home, will you
please make a point of seeing the Captain and Royds
in preference to anyone else. . . .

Do not be cast down, *kind Lady mine.* Don't give way
to despair. . . . There will be nothing for you to be
ashamed of in me, my wife, and the thought of meeting
you eventually will keep me cheerful and, I pray God,
more unselfish, to the end. . . . God keep you.

CHAPTER VIII

The 'Discovery' Expedition (continued)

FARTHEST SOUTH

> I count life just a stuff
> To try the soul's strength on—educe the man.
>   BROWNING.

REFERENCE to Scott's ability as a writer has already been made, but seldom was his 'sledging-pencil' used with more telling effect than on this journey. He naturally enough put the best possible complexion on a feat of endurance which taxed physical and moral stamina to the utmost limit. But, reading 'between the lines,' one perceives that this was nothing but a voluntary sentence of three months' hard labour, in which extreme discomfort was the only relief to excessive toil, and toil the only mitigation of discomfort. It is this pitting of the last resources of human energy against stern circumstance that constitutes the 'fascination' of polar exploration.

Each of the three men engaged in this hard struggle was an idealist, but with attributes and attitudes of mind widely divergent.

Shackleton—ambitious, romantic, impetuous, essentially an adventurer ; with dreams of the day when he, too, should be a leader.

Scott—temperamental, purposeful, his mind always busy, bent ever on attainment, impatient of delay ; with a fundamental nobility underlying all his surface complexities.

Wilson—doctor and counsellor to both, serenely steadfast, vigilant, single-minded and regardless of self; his knightly spirit unfailingly responsive to the keen temper of his will.

Some hint of these qualities, expressed in action, is perhaps unconsciously reflected in the picture Scott gives of them at work with the dog-teams :

> Shackleton in front, with harness slung over his shoulder, was bent forward with his whole weight on the trace ; in spite of his breathless work, now and again he would raise and half-turn his head in an effort to cheer on the team. . . . Behind these, again, came myself with the whip, giving forth one long string of threats and occasionally bringing the lash down with a crack on the snow. . . . On the opposite side of the leading sledge was Wilson, pulling away in grim silence.

The heart-breaking necessity of driving the dogs to the last ounce of their strength gave to the three their acutest misery—Scott especially was painfully sensitive to the sufferings of animals—and their distress was doubled when they realized that the premature failure of the dogs was due to their food (Norwegian stock-fish) having been tainted by its passage through the Tropics.

The view southward and eastward from the summit of White Island had revealed nothing to Shackleton and Wilson but the level ice of the Great Barrier, bounded by a high mountain chain to the west : nothing was yet known of what might lie beyond their field of vision to the south. Perhaps land ; perhaps open water ; perhaps a continuation of the ice-field. The object of the Southern Journey was to discover which. The course was therefore set under the lee of the mountain ranges which follow the 160th parallel, rising in altitude from upwards of 9,000 to 12,300 feet in the region of the Polar Plateau.

With only their wit and their courage to stead them, as they plodded on across a white desert uncharted and untrod ever before by any of the human race, these men experienced their foretaste only of what Antarctic travel could mean : as they bent over the traces, the train of their sledges sliding, dragging, checking, glissading behind them ; sometimes under clear skies, sometimes through snow-drift, sometimes through patches of dense fog, sometimes ankle-deep in soft snow—' the heel of the advanced foot never planted beyond the toe of the other ' ; sometimes up and over long, low undulations, or through sastrugi (ice-crested snow-waves that stubbed the foot through the soft finnesko), or again with easy glide along hard wind-swept surfaces ; sometimes delayed by blizzards, the approach of which was heralded by Wilson's rheumatic pains —' a very effective though unwilling barometer ' ; relaying their sledges (i.e. covering thrice the distance of mileage made good) ' for one-and-thirty awful days ' ; sunburnt and frost-bitten simultaneously, and with the ever-pressing pangs of hunger which only their dreams could delusively assuage.

Dreams of ball-suppers—but one shouts at waiters who won't bring a plate of anything ; or one finds the beef is only ashes ; or a pot of honey has been poured out on a sawdusty floor—one very rarely gets a feed in one's sleep. Occasionally one does ; one night I ate the whole of a large cake in the hall at Westal, and was horribly ashamed when I realized it had been put there to go in for drawing-room tea, and everyone was asking where it had gone.   These dreams are very vivid—I remember them now, though it is two months ago.   One night Sir David Gill, at the Cape, was examining me in divinity, and I told him I had only just come back from the farthest South and was frightfully hungry, so he got a huge roast sirloin and insisted on filling me up before he examined me.

On Christmas Day they had a clear and cloud-less sky, a good sledging surface, a respite to the weary dogs, a long march, and then supper for once without stint ; and the three travellers, full-fed for the first time for weeks, turned into their cosy bags and slept with the torpor of repletion.   For once their nightly reading of Darwin's *Origin of Species*, the only book taken on this journey, was ' given the go-by.'

Five more days of travel brought them to their last outward camp, almost within sight, had they known it, of the gateway to the Polar Plateau, which Shackleton was destined to enter and name six years later.   The mountain ranges increased in grandeur with each day's march, but for the best part of three days an attack of acute snow-blindness compelled Wilson to pull in the dark.   A week previously Scott had written :

Wilson is the most indefatigable person.   When it is fine and clear at the end of our fatiguing days he will spend two or three hours seated in the door of the tent, sketching every detail of the splendid mountainous coast-scene to the west.   His sketches are most astonishingly accurate : I have tested his proportions by actual angular measurement and found them correct.   If the fine weather continues we shall at least have a unique record of this coast-line.   But these long hours in the glare are very bad for the eyes ; we have all suffered a good deal from snow-blindness of late, though we generally march with goggles, but Wilson gets the worst bouts, and I fear it is mainly due to his sketching.

Now, under entry December 26, he wrote :

Poor Wilson has had an attack of snow-blindness, in comparison with which our former attacks may be considered as nothing . . . it is distressing enough to see, knowing that one can do nothing to help.

27th. Last night Wilson got some sleep, and this morning he was better : all day he has been pulling alongside the sledges with his eyes completely covered.

28th. Wilson, in spite of his recent experiences, refuses to give in ; whatever is left unsketched, and however his eyes may suffer, this last part must be done.

Wilson's own account is as follows :

26th. Woke at 5 and made a sketch, using the right eye only. . . . The Captain decided we should camp for lunch, as the pain got worse and worse. I have never had such pain in the eye before—could not lie still in my bag—dropping in cocaine from time to time. We tried ice, and zinc solution as well. . . .

27th. The Captain and Shackle did everything for me —nothing could have been nicer than the way I was treated. . . . From start to finish I went blindfold, pulling on ski ; luckily the surface was smooth, and I only fell twice. I had the strangest thoughts or daydreams as I went along. Sometimes I was in beech-woods ; sometimes in fir-woods ; sometimes in Birdlip woods—all connected in my mind with the hot sun ; and the swish-swish of the ski was as though brushing through dead leaves, or cranberry undergrowth, or heather, or juicy bluebells—could almost see and smell them. It was delightful.

28th. Marched again the whole day with both eyes blindfold, as I want to be able to sketch this new range, the biggest we have met with and the farthest south we shall see. . . . My left eye still quite useless, but I got a sketch of the whole grand sight with one eye.

On the 30th he was recovered sufficiently to take on the cooking again, an important duty in which he was the most expeditious ; and on this day they pitched their southernmost camp, in lat. 82° 16′, a dense fog in high ridges of ice-pressure preventing a full day's march.

Here, following the traditions of the Arctic pioneers, they flew their sledging-flags ; each man's flag embroidered by hands at home with his own crest, coat of arms, and motto.

Later in the day Scott took Wilson some distance farther on ski, and charted the limit of the mountain-chain visible southwards at 83° lat. In honour to his companions he named the most distant Cape after Wilson, and the Inlet beside it after Shackleton.[1]

On the last day of the year they made their final effort. This was a determined but ineffectual attempt to cross a heavily crevassed region of pressure ridges for the purpose of obtaining rock specimens from the face of the red and black cliffs to the west. For Wilson at least, in default of any life to sketch, the delineation of new land or a geological find was of much more moment than a record-breaking journey.

With lightened loads and a following wind which frequently allowed of sledging under sail, the return journey was accomplished, in spite of bad weather and bad surfaces, with a speed that exceeded their hopes ; but all three men were now much enfeebled,

---

[1] It is characteristic of Scott that he named no geographical feature after himself, nor is there to this day any conspicuous landmark in the ' Ross Dependency ' named after that great explorer.

and the dogs still more so, for they could no longer pull. The butcher's sickening task of killing them one by one to feed the remainder was undertaken by Wilson ' with his usual self-sacrifice ' (says Scott) throughout : his picture ' the Last of the Dogs ' is more suggestive of his own feelings than any words.

During the first week of the outward journey Shackleton had been troubled by a persistent cough ; a fortnight after the commencement of their return it recurred with more serious symptoms—hæmorrhage and breathlessness. Snow-blindness and scurvy also afflicted him, and his condition during the closing stages was critical. Only his own indomitable pluck and the gallantry of his companions carried him through.

It was in those last long laps of the journey, when Shackleton, forbidden despite his protests to pull or to work at all, reluctantly made his own pace ahead or behind on ski, that Wilson (as he said afterwards) ' had it out with Scott.' There were still some points of difference between them which each had wished to settle ; and on their long marches side by side, out of earshot of their companion, they exchanged in perfect amicability a volley of home-truths which so effectually cleared the air that the basis of an understanding was reached and the links of a lasting friendship forged, on which their death together on their second journey set its imperishable seal. By those who knew them both the nature of these personal duologues can be guessed : for days together they were followed by ' long spells of conversation, with long spells of silence, on every subject imaginable. The Captain is indeed a most interesting talker

once he starts.' As one who also knew him
intimately has written, 'It wanted an understanding man to appreciate Scott quickly : to
others knowledge came with experience.' [1] Wilson
was determined to understand him, and having
done so, he came to love and honour him with
unswerving loyalty. And it was remarked of Scott
how that ever after this journey, on meeting Wilson
or when his name was mentioned, his face would
light up with that spontaneous radiant smile that
always bespoke his happiness and his deep affection.

Their desperate anxiety to bring Shackleton to
the ship alive, at whatever cost to themselves,
determined them to push on if necessary through
blizzards, and Scott wrote :

Wilson has suffered from lameness for many a day.
Each morning he has vainly attempted to disguise a
limp, and his set face has shown me that there is much to
be gone through before the first stiffness wears off. . . .
With Wilson, who at one time had shown the least
signs of scurvy, the disease had increased very rapidly
towards the end. This final collapse showed the grim
determination which alone must have upheld him during
the last marches.

But hunger was their worst enemy, and when
they reached their depot four days from home they
fell upon the provisions there with appetites so
wolfish that ' explosion seemed imminent ', and the
orgy resulted in a nocturnal procession round and
round the tent in their efforts to allay its pains.

Their arrival was greeted by the welcome sight
of the relief ship, the *Morning*, but instead of cele-
brations and congratulations each man longed for

---

[1] For the most perceptive character-sketch of Scott, see *The
Worst Journey in the World*, vol. I, 200–3, by A. Cherry-Garrard.

his bunk ; and Wilson for nothing so much as ' a long quiet yarn with Charles Royds about things in general, and about his second visit to the Emperor Penguin Rookery most particularly.' Of all his comrades on the ship, none had missed his company more keenly than Royds, and among the many letters of their friendly regard for him dispatched by the *Morning*, his must be quoted.

Your old husband is just one of the best and I missed him awfully during the long journey South and *was* so awfully glad to get him back aboard again. All during the winter I used to do drawing every Sunday under his able supervision. Life on board here would have been very different for me without him. . . .

Scott wrote as follows :

It isn't a kindness but a pleasure to write about your husband, therefore I do it again. I know he will tell you of our Southern trip, and my comments will be understood. We had some trying times, and if such come my way again I hope I may have such a man as your husband by me. . . . I have scarcely a doubt about the capability of us all to stand another winter, and I am quite sure your husband will. . . . I feel confident he will get home safe and in better health than when he started, and I trust it may comfort you in your disappointment to know how well he is and how much we all esteem him.

CHAPTER IX

The ' Discovery ' Expedition (continued)

THE SECOND WINTER

The heavens declare the glory of God, and the firmament showeth his handiwork.—*Psalms*.

BUT the reaction after three months' tension of nerve and will had told and, though released from his cabin after ten days, his sprained knee kept Wilson a prisoner to the ship for six weeks, while his rheumatic pains continued till well into the winter—' a nice clean discomfort, not an illness, which needn't worry other people.'

He employed this time of comparative inactivity in working up pen and ink panoramic sketches of the Victoria Land coast-line, and of the Southern Journey's mountain ranges (over a hundred feet of paper in all) ; and in carefully inspecting and labelling his collection of upwards of forty seal-skins and ninety bird-skins.

He writes with (for him) an almost passionate and pathetic longing for the chance of spending a season (' a year would not be too long ') frozen in in the pack-ice of the Ross Sea to study the bird and marine life there, so much more prolific than on the edge of the Antarctic ; but when the impossibility of freeing the *Discovery* from her winter prison was past doubt, his hopes all centred about the Emperor Penguin Rookery at Cape Crozier.

I have come to the conclusion [he writes in his Journal] that the eggs must be laid in the middle of August. They are incubated then for at least seven weeks, and the chicks are taken up northward on the floating ice at the end of October. So I am going to Cape Crozier where they breed, with Charles Royds, on about Sept. 8th, to get some eggs, and come back by Sept. 21st. Then I hope to go again on Oct. 10th, to catch the chicks there, and find out how and when they go north—whether in down or in feather ; also to see the arrival of the Adélie Penguins at the beginning of November. . . . Then once more I intend to go—starting about Dec. 12th, and remaining there as long as I am allowed to watch and sketch and collect the Adélie Penguins. . . .

He had more work to get through in the second winter than in the first, and now that Shackleton was invalided home he took his daily excursions to Crater Hill and elsewhere alone, refusing all company : as he wrote to his wife—'first because I want to sketch and one cannot keep others waiting about in these temperatures, and secondly because it is the only time I get to myself to be alone with God and you.' The patience required for sketching in the Antarctic calls for as much fortitude, to say the least, as any of the rougher activities of life in those regions.

Went up Crater Hill to make some sketches. One has to be pretty rapid over it. I started by getting my hands practically frozen in putting on my crampons—a matter of three minutes ; the pain in bringing them back in warm gloves makes you dance first on one foot and then on the other, because there's nothing else to do. I repeated the proceeding three times in sketching with my right hand. There is nothing to fear if you stop when you can no longer feel the pencil, then put on

warm gloves and you soon feel something else for 5 to
10 minutes. The softest B is as hard and gritty as an
H, and makes the same sort of mark. . . . My eyes
have been in a sorry state all day from sketching with
sun-glare, streaming with water and very painful from
time to time. Sketching in the Antarctic is not all joy,
for apart from the fact that your fingers are all thumbs
and you don't know what or where they are till they
warm up again, you can only sketch when your eyes stop
running—one eye at a time through a narrow slit in
snow-goggles.

It was a wonderful night with clear moonlight, the
sort of Arctic night one reads of in books. Sounds
carried an immense distance ; the stillness was almost
uncanny, one could imagine oneself on a dead planet,—
that we were standing, not on the earth, but on the
moon's surface ; everything was so still and cold and
dead and unearthly, with an absolute silence which one
felt as broken by nothing but wild Nature's storms since
the beginning of the world.

His eye-memory for colour was remarkable ; he
had always assiduously trained it ; but the conditions under which he now worked, demanding the
utmost rapidity, developed it still more. His
method was to make rapid pencil-sketches in the
open, supplemented with copious notes of colour-
effects for greater accuracy, and then to work them
up immediately by lamp-light in his cabin. But
now the supply of paraffin was exhausted, and
the stock of candles had fallen so low that he was
at first obliged to paint under acetylene gas in
the crowded wardroom, and finding this too difficult he contrived, with the assistance of Cross, to
make candles for use in his cabin from the remains
of tallow mixed with blubber.[1] He was also re-

---

[1] Some fragments of these candles can be seen among his
Antarctic relics in the Cheltenham Museum.

reading his old friend and teacher Ruskin, and
wrote to his wife :

Where his high teaching comes in contact with the
general low standards of public life it is too suggestive
of an attempt to hew timber with a hollow-ground, high-
tempered razor. . . . I see how right all his fundamental principles are, but they could not be reduced to
present-day politics and political economy except at the
cost of upheaval and revolution which would disjoint
everything, and the only thing that seems to carry any
hope with it is the leavening principle. Hope seems to
me to lie in the fact that there are always, in every
generation, men like Ruskin, who can see to the root of
things, and are not afraid to acknowledge and make
clear to everyone the ruts they are living in. . . . Only
I believe he would have done as much good, even more
perhaps, if he had stuck to principles instead of trying to
apply them to politics. He could then have supplied
the leaven which would have gone to work, quietly,
surely, and unrecognized, instead of putting people's
backs up by telling them that they wanted leavening
and he was going to do it. . . .

Ruskin's conception of what is due in worship
and in service to the Creator of all life from His
creatures, was intensely shared by him, and drew
from him the following reflections :

Why in the name of all that is holy were we always
taught to fear God ? It is an idea that still hangs in
my mind that if I don't fear Him enough something
terrible will happen some day—and that is the sort of
Ogre one is expected to ' worship and glorify ' . . . an
unapproachable Being to be addressed by the repetition
of high-sounding and eloquent phrases full of a rather
pompous grandeur. . . . I think I want a more familiar
God whom I can turn to at any minute of the day without fear, rather than a Being who must be approached
with extra special language on one's knees, or by priests
in splendid vestments. . . . It is everything not only

to reverence Him but to love Him, and to feel that
you know Him so well that you can even enjoy fun with
Him.

Can one kneel to God from any sense that He will
be pleased to hear us confess that we are worms, and
how merciful He is to let us live ? . . . Surely no simile
is more perfect than that God is the Father of us who
are His children, His own children, just as Christ was
His own Child. To what does one kneel in one's daily
prayers ? . . . some remembrance or anticipation of the
utter joy of being loved by you—before your photograph.
. . . I can kneel to a life such as St. Francis led—
before his picture. . . . I kneel in the same way before
a Crucifix, and before any thought or memory of Christ
and his life. I feel inclined to kneel before anything
that goes to my heart as being very beautiful, and the
more humble and lowly and unasserting it is the more
I feel inclined to kneel before it as representing to me
the presence of something very near to God and very
holy. It is this feeling which has in the old days again
and again led me to kneel and kiss a flower in the woods,
or in a hedgerow. . . .

By the end of the second winter he had completed a portfolio of some 200 coloured sketches
of Antarctic scenery, some dozen of which were
reproduced in the *Voyage of the 'Discovery'*. Of his
many word-pictures one is specially noteworthy for
its use of science to find a chromatic parallel.

In the North at noon there was a splendid sunrise
with a heavy bank of cloud arranged for all the world
like wavy hair, and wherever the sunlight caught those
waves and curls it was broken into the most delicate
opal mother-o'-pearl tints ; all colours of the rainbow,
pale rose, pure lilac, emerald green, lemon yellow, and
fiery red—blending but with no apparent arrangement,
so that a wisp of cloud standing like a stray curl in the
blue sky would be lit by pink and brilliant lilac, and
then would begin to shine at one end with a light that
can only be compared with the light you see in a vacuum

tube with a current sparkling through it, or perhaps the colour is more exactly what you get with incandescent barium. It seems far-fetched to go into chemical details to describe a sky, but neither lilac nor amethyst describe the colour I have spoken of as lilac, but the light of incandescent potassium does exactly. One can describe the yellows more easily, because all our ideas of light vary from white to yellow and orange ; but for red I like to refer to strontium, though a rose-pink describes a certain light chiefly perhaps because one so often sees light shining through a petal of the commonest form of rose.

If a dozen rainbows were broken up and scattered in wavy ribands and flecks of curl and fleecy forms to float against a background of dull grey, it would be something like the beautiful appearance of this cloud colouring. Erebus's smoke was rising in a straight column for some thousands of feet, showing three distinct curls from separate vents.

The results of his observations of the sky, made during this winter, were embodied in a volume published by the Royal Society—entitled *Album of Photographs and Sketches* (National Antarctic Expedition) which he was asked to arrange and edit.[1] The excellent photographs therein were mainly those taken by Skelton. Of his own many studies of atmospheric phenomena—such as earth-shadows ; mock moons and lunar haloes ; the fire-glow and the wind-vane of Erebus ; cirrus and stratus clouds and fog-bows, it contained a small but representative selection, concluding with a series of eight studies of the Aurora Australis. As with other scenic effects, his description of the latter, though too long to quote in full, is at once scientific and artistic.

---

[1] To the volume entitled *Meteorology* he also contributed a valuable note on Solar and Cloud Phenomena, with sketches.

AURORA AUSTRALIS

The colour of almost all the auroral displays which were observed in McMurdo Sound was a pale golden straw tint. Very occasionally there were observed also traces of rose and greenish light. In this sketch is shown the birth of an auroral arc. When first it appeared on the horizon as a glow of pale straw-coloured light, or as a row of upright beams, there may have been no trace of light in the whole heaven other than the stars ; and yet as one watched, imperceptibly the curtain rose, one arc above another, glowing here and fading there, but always up and upward with lengthening beams, and increasing brightness. . . .

The uppermost of these arcs might then begin to break and wave and fold into a curtain, gradually rising to the zenith, where it occasionally culminated in a corona of radiating beams or folding streamers. . . .

As the curtain appears to fold in one direction it is waved out of sight in another, while the varying intensity of the vertical beams of light which compose it, now brilliant, now vanishing altogether, now stealthily appearing or disappearing imperceptibly, gives the onlooker a strange feeling of expectation and bewilderment, to which is added the conviction that the whole is very beautiful, but quite impossible to represent on paper.

The form of corona here shown was the production of a rising series of arcs which followed one another upward from the horizon, slowly changing, folding, evanescing first here, then there, till overhead, though for a few moments only, the form of a crown appeared and passed rapidly, but with a strange appearance of deliberation, out of sight.

As the winter drew on his hopes rose at the prospect of home-coming, and he began to speculate on plans for future work and livelihood. He could not look forward with any great enthusiasm to life as a general medical practitioner. His friend John Fraser's estimate is probably correct—namely, that his bent was not for general medical practice, but that had he lived he could have made a name in independent medical research.

Medicine and Surgery [he wrote to his wife] form a
work that one should either give up one's whole and
undivided attention to from the first, or else leave strictly
alone in practice : and I'm afraid I have done neither,
for I have squandered my energies over various hobbies
instead of making my profession my one object in life.

But his real genius lay elsewhere ; and though
it is as an explorer and an artist that he is known,
it is as a naturalist in all its branches, but especially in ornithology, that he would have been recognized had he lived to finish his work.

His faithful henchman, Seaman Cross, had made
for him, from the German silver of old sledge-
runners, models of a sledge and ski to match it,
mounted on a piece of ship's teak ; and the model
of a pram from the same material as a reminder
of Norway. These were always among his cherished
souvenirs.

They are a really pretty piece of work that anyone
would admire. Cross still declares that he is going to
leave the Navy and come and be my coachman, and
live at the doctor's lodge ! Lodgings, I told him, more
likely, if he came to live with the doctor.

The published work of Seton Thompson, whom
he describes as ' my ideal writer,' stirred his ambition to give to the world an illustrated account
of his own zoological researches.

I get crazy sometimes in thinking what Seton Thompson
would make in the way of the most fascinating stories
and pictures out of many things that I have seen and
he never has. . . . I can't see how else I could have
got any knowledge or love of God except through all
these wild things that I loved instinctively, and without a
love for God I can't imagine either loving you or being
loved by you.

But he still depreciated his artistic ability.

I want to write, and I want to draw, only I want to
spend a year or two at least in *learning* how to draw,
because the more I draw and sketch the more hopeless
I feel about ever being anything more than an amateur
and a dabbler. . . .   I not only have never been taught,
but I have never, even once, *seen* anyone at work who
knew how to do things. . . .   I shall always hope to get
this training some day, for in painting I am quite sure
it is never too late to learn.   One has only to think of
that dear old Mr. Hammond whom Mr. Rice took me
to see in Kent ; he started painting when he was 70,
and I have never seen anything to equal his birds, and
rarely anything to equal his landscapes. . . .   What
would I not give for a few years at a good art school !

He thought also with longing of what fields for
specialization would be offered by the wild life
that he already knew in Norway, and how much
he could discover in South Trinidad, the Mac-
quaries, the Aucklands, and the Falklands ; of
what a field, too, of another kind Switzerland would
offer, and of how he could meet initial expenses
by translating German scientific works into English,
and by lecturing in both languages in the sanatoria
there on the fauna, local colour, and rigours of
the Antarctic.

I can't help thinking that my experience would be
very encouraging to many others who begin life by
catching phthisis.   It shows that it in no way unfits one
for roughing it in very trying conditions.   Lectures would
be a great boon to the unfortunates at Davos, and any
entertainments they can attend are welcome.

Meanwhile, living through the winter with a
community where ' even the most innocent remark
on whatever subject is turned into a jest and made
ludicrous,' sometimes jarred on a nature so finely

sensitive and considerate as his. One of his companions (Hodgson) was but expressing the feeling of them all when he wrote :

Billy he was, and Billy I think he always will be in the minds of us all. Only three know the inner history of the Southern Sledge Journey, but it was pretty broadly whispered that Wilson was the backbone of that trip which but for him would have been briefer. He was a born naturalist—one that no amount of training would make. Duty with him covered everything. Whatever he conceived to be his duty was first and foremost, and always done regardless of cost to himself. Only on one occasion did I see him with his ' monkey up,' difficulties being put in the way of his proper work. I think he was more or less the confidant of us all. He would intervene with most satisfactory results if any discussion arose and things showed a sign of getting warm. I have never met with a man so universally admired and respected in every way.

The same feeling on the part of the men before the mast is best expressed in the words of the burly and great-hearted seaman who was his right-hand man throughout the Expedition. Mr. Jacob Cross, chief petty-officer R.N. retired, says :

Dr. Wilson was a gentleman. He was straight and he was thorough—right through. The sort of life we had to lead down there brings out the man. A man has to look after himself in the Antarctic, or he goes under. The doctor could take care of himself as well as the best, but he also took care of others. He had great consideration for others, and he was always grateful for the least thing one did for him. At sea he would give a hand to brace round in a storm or in bitter weather with the seamen whose job it was. I never saw him excited—he was always cool and calm and collected. He was always the same ; and the same to everyone. Many and long were the talks I had with him in his cabin in the winters. One came to him instinctively. One could

talk to him on any subject whatever, or about oneself—
he understood. After our seal-hunt in Sept. '03, they
used to call us the 'Blood and Guts Brigade.' He
would join in any joke that was going, although he was
naturally a quiet man. I never heard anyone on the
ship say a word against the doctor. He was the sort
of man one would give one's life for willingly.

At length, on September 7, came the long-expected
day for departure for Cape Crozier.[1] The party
consisted of Royds and Wilson, with four men from
the after-deck, all on ski, with two sledges, and
two three-men sleeping-bags. The discomforts were
many ; weather was thick and foggy, temperatures
very low, surfaces furrowed or crevassed ; nights
worst of all, with little sleep and much dampness.
'Yet we are a most jovial party, full of humbug
over every discomfort.' On the 12th they reached
the ' Knoll—a low-lying parasitic cone of Terror,
with a well-marked crater,' and pitched camp ' on
a wind-swept plain of snow narrowing in front to
the cliffs of Cape Crozier, between tremendous
pressure ridges and the névé and glacier slopes of
Terror.' Away to the north Ross Sea was a plain
of ice to the horizon.
They found about a thousand Emperors clustered
in their Rookery at the base of the ice-cliffs, but
to their dismay found also that the eggs were

---

[1] Wilson's official Report of these journeys is contained in
the volume, which he also edited, entitled *Zoology* (National
Antarctic Expedition), Vol II. This was printed by the
British Museum. It is still the classic on the subject of
Antarctic birds and mammals, and is delightful reading
even to the layman. For readers who are unable to procure
this volume, a briefer and more popular account is to be
found in Appendix II to Scott's *Voyage of the ' Discovery.'*

already incubated and ready to hatch, or were
frozen addled as a result of a second incubation
after the birds' flight from a sudden ice-fall. The
chicks themselves were already well grown, and
but little smaller than those which Skelton had
found a month later in the previous year. Wilson
had to be content with the collection of fifteen
dead chicks and eight unbroken eggs. But he had
learned much of the habits of the Emperor Penguin,
and had besides greatly improved his knowledge
of the glaciation and geology of Cape Crozier.
Two live chickens were brought back to the ship,
and these were tenderly nursed by Seaman Cross
on the way, who fed them on masticated seal-meat,
and in a temperature of 'sixty below' sacrificed his
sleeping-jacket to keep them warm. One of them
suffered an early demise, but its fellow survived
long enough to keep the ship's company entertained for several weeks.

He is a regular caution, frightfully wayward and
obstinate, and very vicious, losing his temper and grizzling
in the most human fashion, pecking as hard as possible
if he isn't allowed to do exactly as he wishes. He has
me out of bed regularly twice every night, chirruping
in the most ear-piercing way till I feed him. He likes
sitting up late to look at the candle, and gets frightfully
angry—struggling and chirruping in his box if I put
him to bed early. He is covered with the softest grey
down, and his head is made of black and white velvet in
beautiful contrast. Only his figure is shockingly alder-
manic. . . .

With Seamen Cross and Whitfield, he started
again for the Rookery on October 12. Travelling
was even more difficult on account of soft snow
and frequent subsidences, necessitating some re-

laying, so that the journey took two days longer than before. On arrival the bay-ice was seen to be still unbroken, with no sign of cracks or open water ; and the same colony of Emperors were in view under the ice-cliffs. The living chicks were still in down : the dead were estimated at 77 per cent.

The chick is the desired of all, and every adult makes a rush for it ; but the chick can run and dodge, and evidently has no wish at all to be nursed and messed about. So the chase becomes lively until at last an old Emperor falls over the chick and immediately shoves it under its lappet with its beak ; a perfect football scrimmage ensuing with the fighting and shoving of six or eight other birds trying to hustle the winner off its prize.

The next day they visited the Adélie Penguin Rookery, 5 miles distant, to affix the cylinder containing Captain Scott's record to the Post for information for the relief ship ; and, delighted at finding some two dozen Adélies preparing their nests of stones, promised themselves another visit in a week's time for a ' fresh egg feast.' Here Wilson collected a bagful of morainic rubble for Ferrar to analyse ; and here he revived his recollections of two years ago at the point where with Scott and Royds he had ascended the cliff for his first view of the Great Barrier, remarking ' We know more of it now.'

It was not long before the weather began to show signs of an ominous change, and at the same time he observed ' large companies of Emperors going out on the new sea-ice in single file.' The blizzard broke on the 22nd, and continued for

ten days, during seven of which they were im-
prisoned in their sleeping-bags : Wilson beguiling
these long hours of cold wet misery by re-reading
Tennyson's 'Maud,' an old favourite of Caius
days, the feeling and phrasing of which now
touched him with a deeper significance than
formerly. At intervals during the lulls of the
blizzard they emerged to watch the continued
migration of the Emperors, and on the first of
these occasions were amazed to behold the Ross
Sea open water, with a long line of white pack-
ice just visible on the horizon. Large floes were
floating northwards, bearing the Emperors upon
them as upon rafts, in dozens or scores. For six
days the migration continued till less than half
the colony appeared to be left behind.

Wilson's Journal entry for the 29th must be
given verbatim.

Between 8 and 11 a.m. the wind gradually dropped
and there was less drift, so we started off with the wind
at our backs to the Adélie Rookery. It looked terribly
stormy all round, but we were getting desperate with
the continued bad weather, and we badly wanted our
feed of fresh eggs. It was now ten days since the birds
had arrived there, and when we reached the brow of
the hill overlooking this immense rookery, there they
were—in tens of thousands—the whole valley and sur-
rounding hills were alive with them, each at its own
nest with a mate sitting tight on the nest. Whitfield
turned to Cross and said, 'What say, Jumper ! Eggs or
no eggs ? ' 'Eggs,' says Cross ; and then, 'Did you bring
the salt ? ' 'No,' says Whitfield, 'never mind, we can
manage them without.' Six to eight apiece we thought
we could manage easily, and then we had bags to bring
home enough for all hands on the ship, and drills and
blow-pipes for the shells. So off we tobogganed down a
long snow-slope, regardless of our burberry trousers, and

soon we were in the thick of them—swearing, shouting, screeching, pecking at our legs on every side ; and how tight the hens sat on their nests. I stood and watched Whitfield and Cross as they shoved bird after bird off the nest, and yet I never saw either of them take an egg. Then I began to do the same myself—bird after bird I shoved off the nest and yet I never found an egg ; but I said to myself that *some* of these birds must have laid, and it's only a matter of hunting long enough, so I hunted longer—then I saw that Cross and Whitfield had joined up. What they said I heard later but needn't repeat it here, but when they saw that I had had the same luck we all roared with laughter, and Whitfield said Adélies' eggs weren't a patch on ordinary fowls' eggs ; and we sat under the lee of a rock and ate some cheese and biscuit and wished we had some water to moisten it down with, and watched the Adélies as they made love to one another and stole each other's nesting stones, and stood bolt upright with their heads in the air chortling to themselves as they slowly waggled their flippers, for they knew they had sold us a pup—as fair a pup as was ever sold to anyone in the Antarctic, and we knew that in a day or two the ground would be literally strewn with eggs and we could have filled a cart. Anyhow we couldn't wait while they laid their eggs, though we knew they couldn't hold on to them much longer, so we commandeered three apparently un-occupied male birds and carried them back to camp. Stewed, they were delicious ; but fried in butter, in blessed mouthfuls, they were heavenly ; though on the way home, carrying them—10 to 12 lbs. apiece—for 5 miles in soft fur boots over rough rocks against a wind of force 5 to 6 in our faces—well, we wished them at the bottom of the sea.

They reached camp late that night and with difficulty, grateful that the weather held sufficiently for them to pick up their line of guide-marks. But the next day and for two days following the blizzard fell on them with redoubled violence, and they lay wet and cold in their bags : ' the Adélie Penguins

were frozen like rock, so we applied the geological
hammer and cooked the crumbs—they were simply
excellent.' (The Adélie Penguin is generally considered most unpalatable.)

On November 2 the wind dropped, and though
the sky was still threatening they roped up and
started for home, having first paid a final visit
to the Emperors to count the remaining adults,
and the chicks alive and dead. Here Wilson made
a study for one of the best of his sketches of this
strange scene. Before they reached the ship Whitfield was in trouble with a badly swollen leg,
and Wilson's own feet were raw and bleeding every
day from the chafing of ski-straps through fur boots
and rough treatment over rocks. Their oil was
nearly finished, and Whitfield especially dreaded
the breaking of another blizzard—' so I decided
to push things a bit.' They got back in four
days ; and though the much-desired trophies—
eggs and young of the Emperor—had indeed been
secured, it had been a desperate journey, and
Wilson wrote home :

Bird-nesting at − 62° F. is a somewhat novel experience.
Those journeys to Cape Crozier were pretty average uncomfortable even for the Antarctic. It has been worth
doing—I feel that ; but I am not sure I could stand it
all over again.

Yet in 1911 he was to repeat the journey deliberately in mid-winter under infinitely worse conditions, including a forty-eight hours' exposure without shelter to a blizzard which, as he well knew
from this previous experience, might last for ten
days at Cape Crozier.

He had wished to investigate the tide-crack on

the southern side of Mount Erebus on this return from Cape Crozier ; and so now, after ten days' rest, he was anxious to be off again. With Hodgson and one of the seamen, he set out on November 16th for a ' picnic trip,' and returned on the 22nd, ' in time for the usual Sunday's breakfast of seal's liver,' with a very complete and valuable report of the glaciation of that limit of the Barrier, providing the correct solution to many problems connected with it which had puzzled Scott. As usual, he took risks, but used his judgment. An incidental discovery of minor interest was that of a line of eight fumaroles round the previous crater-ring of Erebus, having chimneys at least a hundred feet high. He took many photographs, changing the plates in his bag—

a disagreeable job, which takes longer than one's lungs take to use every scrap of oxygen in the bag, till at last one crawls out gasping, with a sweating sickly pallor. However, I got them changed.

Still he was not satisfied, and after five days on board was off again with Armitage and another seaman to the western side of the strait for a fortnight's exploration of the geology and ice-formation at the foot of Mount Discovery.[1] This journey was no picnic. There were frequent falls and sprains, and much capsizing of the sledges over rough surfaces and in gusty squalls of drift—on one occasion ' pulling through a surface of crusted thaw for 5 hours we gained a mile.' Footwear as well as sledges were badly punished.

---

[1] For a full account, see A. B. Armitage, *Two Years in the Antarctic*, chap. xvi.

I marched for some days through snow and ice and thaw-pools in my socks, the soles of my boots worn out by the rough ice. Luckily we had high temperatures throughout, never below + 17° F., and often above freezing-point on shore.

But the discomforts of the journey were more than compensated for by a valuable collection of rocks as well as of sketches, and a completion of topographical survey.

Wilson was fully prepared to set forth again, as he had planned, almost at once to pay a final call on the Adélie Penguins at Cape Crozier ; but finding that Scott had not yet returned from his great Western Journey with Evans and Lashly (probably the hardest he ever made save the last), and finding all hands busy, according to orders previously issued, at the arduous but hopeless attempt to free the ship by sawing through some ten miles of ice half-way from the sea, he immediately relinquished his own plans to join the toilers.

And never [he wrote] was a healthier crowd of ruffians than the thirty unwashed, unshaven, sleepless, swearing, grumbling, laughing, joking reprobates that lived in that smoky Saw-Camp.

When Scott returned a week later and realized the futility of this effort, sawing operations were abandoned in favour of the hope that nature would yet accomplish this task. He proposed to Wilson a ' saunter ' of a few days with a tent to Cape Royds, whereby, as unforeseen events proved, Wilson's expectation of seeing the Adélies again was not disappointed.

CHAPTER X

The ' Discovery ' Expedition (continued)

RELIEF AND RETURN

Thou, O God, hast taught me from my youth up until now : therefore will I tell of thy wondrous works.—For thou, Lord, hast made me glad through thy works : and I will rejoice in giving praise for the operations of thy hands.—O Lord, how glorious are thy works : thy thoughts are very deep.

' Three verses of the Psalms that always express what I feel.'—*E. A. W.*

FROM Hut Point, where the ship lay, to Cape Royds is a distance of some 25 miles across the sea-ice, but from ' Saw-Camp ' this distance was already lessened by ten ; so that Scott and Wilson, leaving camp on the afternoon of January 3, reached their destination early on the following day.

A notable find on this excursion was that of an enormous and totally unsuspected Adélie Penguin Rookery at Cape Royds ; ' it is exasperating to think of the feasts of eggs we have missed.' After a wash with soap and towels in a small rill of thaw-water in warm sunlight, followed by a dish of fried penguins' liver with seal kidneys, Scott opined that ' life in the Antarctic Regions can be very pleasant.' And the next morning he wrote :

135

We got up in the most leisurely fashion, and after a wash and our breakfast we lazily started to discuss our plans for the day. Our tent door was open and framed the clear sea beyond, and I was gazing dreamily out upon this patch of blue when suddenly a ship entered my field of view. It was so unexpected that I almost rubbed my eyes before I dared to report it.

The Captain and I [wrote Wilson] were writing in the tent ; it was a beautiful warm sunny morning, and we sat there on our sleeping-bags with the tent door open. He suddenly looked out and said, ' Why, there's the *Morning* ! ' I looked at him in surprise, because not five minutes before I had swept the horizon with a telescope and seen nothing ; but sure enough there, not three miles from us, coming round a cape which had hidden her, lay what we then thought was the *Morning* —certainly a whaler, and a black one. It turned out to be the *Terra Nova*.

A moment after, of course [continued Scott], all became bustle, and we began to search round for our boots and other articles necessary for the march. Whilst we were thus employed Wilson looked up and said, ' Why, there's another,' and sure enough there were now two vessels framed in our doorway. . . . We propounded all sorts of wild theories of which it need only be said that not one was within measurable distance of the truth.

We were dumbfounded [continued Wilson], and a host of surmises arose. Was it another Expedition—the *Gauss* ? or was it after all not the *Morning*, but two enterprising whalers or sealers who had no relief for us and no mails ? . . . It was a thrilling moment approaching the ships : no one was expected and everyone was below ; we were mistaken by each ship as stragglers from the other ; till at last four Dundee whaling men from the *Terra Nova* spotted us as strangers and came out to meet us. They spoke such perfect Dundee that we could hardly understand a word they said ; then we gathered that the Government had stepped in and was responsible for the *Terra Nova*.

Scott's orders from the Admiralty were disconcerting. He was instructed to abandon the *Discovery* if she could not be freed in time to proceed North with the relief ships.

Wilson, having spent ' most of a night in trying to take in a year's news ' [1] was back at Cape Royds studying the life there, and taking hourly observations on the tide ; and there on the 7th Scott rejoined him to get two days' quiet and consider the situation. He could not bear the thought of abandoning the *Discovery*, but 20 miles of relentless ice 7 feet thick, with a margin of only six weeks for it to break, still lay between her and the freedom of the seas. Experiments with explosives proved hardly more effective than the abortive sawing operations, and the *Terra Nova's* gallant attempts to butt it even less.

Old friends and new, in twos and threes, came to visit Wilson in his lonely camp : Ferrar and an officer of the *Morning* had the luck to be with him on the day that he bagged the first Sea Elephant yet seen in the Antarctic. A scientific description of this monster, and of its capture, may be read in his article in *Zoology* above-mentioned : his Journal records :

He was about as ugly a beast to walk close up to as

---

[1] Among the letters that pleased him most, next to his special home-letters, was a message of good wishes subscribed with 158 signatures, from St. George's Hospital men, at their annual dinner presided over by Sir Clifford Allbutt. A letter from Shackleton also contained the welcome news that the *Illustrated London News* would be pleased to accept work from him. This offer was made on the strength of his paintings in the *South Polar Times* which Shackleton had shown to the Editor.

I had ever seen outside a cage, but I wanted to get him. It took six of us to haul the beast up the beach, and then I skinned and flensed him, and arranged the skeleton for the skuas to clean. They were so bold and unsuspicious of what blood-thirsty brutes we were that they would take blubber out of our hands. They proved a trouble, for I had put the beast's tongue on one side, and his eyes, which were remarkably large, I buried in the sand. The skuas not only unburied these titbits but carried them off to sea and ate them. They also carried my jacket several yards, and I saw one fly off with a long seal-skin knife-sheath in his bill—about 18 inches long. I buried the skin in a big sand-heap, but the brutes got it out and made several bare patches in it. Total length was about 12 feet and his girth was enormous—just on 10 feet at the shoulders. There was from 2 to 3 inches of blubber on him, but nothing in his inside.

These few weeks of delay were in the nature of a God-send to Wilson, for his life in camp gave him opportunities for a close observation at the right season of the year of birds, seals and whales : all the material in fact he needed to complete those notes on Antarctic Zoology which formed one of the most valuable contributions to the Expedition's record.

But for Scott they were weeks of anxiety in which a capricious fortune rang the changes on hope and despair with nerve-racking persistency. His chronicle of this period is so vivid that the reader is carried away to the relentless ice-sheet that still separated the *Discovery* from her sister-ships. Human efforts to decrease it were long since realized to be fruitless : the question was—would Nature's be? When would the hurricane break over the McMurdo Strait as it had broken over the ice of Ross Sea two months previously and dispersed it in a night ?—But in the end it was neither wind nor storm nor blizzard that did the work.

On the night of February 14 ' when the wind had fallen to a calm, and not a sound disturbed the stillness about us,' to a hail of ' The ships are coming, sir ! ' Scott dashed out of the wardroom and up Arrival Heights to see the relief ships battling towards him through the fast-breaking floes. ' In the midst of this peaceful silence was an awful unseen agency rending that great ice-sheet as though it had been naught but the thinnest paper.' Such is the effect of a swell.

Yet fortune had still a card in hand with which she hoped to take the trick. Hardly was the ship freed, and before even she had weighed anchor or got up steam, when a sudden gale, rising with terrific force, smote her stern hard against the ice. When steam was made and the anchor tripped, the current pouring in past the Point added to the violence of the wind drove her helplessly ashore against Hut Point. There she remained for eight hours, pounding against the shoal, ' squeezed like a match-box, and with masts shivering ' ; a prey to the merciless fury of wind and sea. When at length she slid off the ledge, it was found to be with no more irreparable damage than the loss of a false keel and a twisted rudder. ' It is an eloquent witness,' wrote Scott, ' to the solid structure of our ship.'

I can remember Wilson on this occasion [wrote a comrade] working hard with the rest of us in the endeavour to get the ship afloat, with the cheeriest smile on his face and cheery words on his lips inspiring hope and courage in all. He was always cheerful and this cheeriness of character shone most in times of distress and difficulty.

As the remembered landmarks of the Victoria
Range came one by one again in view under stormy
threatening skies, Wilson wrote :

We are fast losing sight of Erebus, but Mt. Melbourne
is not yet clear of clouds. I shall not soon forget the
last view we had of our Strait as we last saw Mt. Discovery in the midnight sunset. It was a blaze of colour
astern of us—a glowing orange fire ; and standing out
black on our starboard quarter was the *Terra Nova* under
sail, and farther astern on our port quarter the *Morning*.

Quite the last thought in his mind was that he
would ever see these scenes again. He felt that
two years in the Polar Regions were enough for a
lifetime ; he had suffered very acutely from rheumatic pains during most of the second ; and he
had other fields of work of a different kind to look
forward to.

The Auckland Islands had been arranged as a
rendezvous for the ' fleet ' and here the *Discovery*
anchored on the night of March 14.

This sudden emergence from the grim and lifeless South, and the storm-girt sea, to land teeming
with life and verdure, ' clothed with bright green
and russet scrub to the water's edge,' was almost
magical : ' my joy was nearly complete when I
heard the well-known cry of a hawk, and looking
up saw a beautiful little falcon fly across. . . .
What a paradise ! ' Twenty-two pages of his
closely written Journal are packed with an account
of the natural history of these islands, from sea
lions to insects.

Out of the thirty birds shot I got paintings of over
twenty, and skins or formation specimens of nearly as
many. So the attempt to make a complete collection

in such a short while was worth it after all—only my letter-writing has suffered. It is at the expense of letter-writing that I have added 40 birds' skins to the collection since leaving winter-quarters.

The *Discovery* and her sister-ships were timed to make Lyttelton Harbour on Easter Day, but favoured at long last with fair weather they arrived off the Heads two days before their schedule—' and it was,' said Wilson, ' a Good Friday indeed.'

Mrs. Wilson, who had come to New Zealand a year previously when there was yet hope that the *Discovery* might have returned with her first relief, was now staying with her sister at a friend's house in Sumner, near Christchurch. The tale can best be taken up at this point by her, from a letter written to Westal.

I had woken early and was dozing again, when I heard a rush upstairs and breathless shouting—' All three ships are coming in ! They will be in in an hour !' You can imagine how quickly we huddled on clothes, and tore off on the road over the Port Hills to Lyttelton. We did that walk of four miles in record time ; but when we reached the top there was no sign of any of the ships. By a piece of great luck we found the Harbour Master, Capt. Clarke, who said he would take me out with him before any of the Harbour Board got down. . . . The Pilot's daughters were there ; they had gone early with the Pilot boat. I asked them whether they had any news of Ted, and imagine my joy when they said they had seen him on the bridge with Captain Scott ! . . . Presently the Mayor, Mr. Wigram, came up and said that he had been deputed to see that I was the first to be put on board the *Discovery*. When Ted at last appeared beaming, and I was helped on board, then indeed all was well.

' This sort of meeting,' said Wilson, ' beats a wedding hollow.'

The first month ashore was spent in visiting old friends, and in much necessary work upon skins at the Christchurch Museum ; after which they took ship to Wellington, and then began their 'real honeymoon.' It was a tour from end to end of North Island, through the volcanic region, across country which to-day can be travelled in civilized comfort, but which thirty years ago entailed many discomforts and much fatigue even to the experienced traveller. Wilson's travel-diary of this month's crowded tour contains material enough to form a small book. He was impressed with the enormous possibilities of the country as a field of exploration hitherto almost untried for the scientist and naturalist, as well as by its wonderful medicinal value ; but he was also sadly oppressed by a sense of the rapidly vanishing life of the wild, and wrote to his father :

New Zealand hasn't yet woken up to the fact that it is a ready-made world's Sanatorium—with the most astounding variety of springs at all temperatures and of all chemical combinations, all handy and workable. I had no notion of the wealth of this country from a therapeutic point of view.

. . . In a century, or less, all or most of this unique fauna and flora will be extinct—they are dying out before one's eyes. I could spend a few years here with advantage on a really classical piece of work.

After a short stay in Wellington as the guests of Bishop Wallis they returned to Christchurch to attend, on June 1, the ball given by the officers of the *Discovery* and the *Morning* to the people of the city : Mrs. Wilson and Captain Scott receiving the guests for the one ship, and Mrs. Evans and Captain Colbeck those for the other ; and it was voted an unqualified success. Wilson's letter home concerning it has little to tell of the function, though much of its principal hostess—' I could only stand in the crowd and admire her, and wonder how the deuce such a girl came to give herself to me.'

The last few days ashore were spent with their good friends the Kinseys, sorting and packing their trophies of rocks, bones, skulls, and ferns, and after a farewell dinner to the officers at which each had to speak, Wilson's being pronounced the speech of the evening because it ' set the table in a roar,' he and his wife were homeward bound by different ways, she by liner, and he once more aboard the *Discovery*.

The course was set for Cape Horn, but strong south-easterly gales drove the ship so far to the northward that it was decided to pass through the Magellan Straits, whose ' steep and broken shores were snow-covered almost to the water's edge ; the gnarled and stunted tree-trunks reminding me very strongly of Japanese paintings ; still more so the sight of a flock of flamingoes, pink against the glacier.'

With thoughts of home-coming uppermost in his mind, and with them grateful recollections of all that he felt he owed to the one man of whom he confessed, ' there's no man living I admire so much as him,' he wrote a long letter to his father.

My goodness, Dad, I am proud of you as a father ! I hope it's not impudent of me to say so. . . . I think few men have stepped into life with a better all-round education than you have given me. I don't mean so much my years at Clifton, Cheltenham, and Cambridge, though I realize their value ; nor even the Hospital, and you know how I value that ; but what I marvel most at now is that you saw the reasons for giving me those walking tours in Wales before I left school, do you remember ? and all that bird-nesting regardless of my school-work, Sundays and even meals ; and making me draw plants and birds and what not ; and then my visits abroad—and rather than spoil the whole show for six penn'orth of paint you were good enough to give me everything, and not a thing you have given me in the way of education but has helped to fit me for this sort of business, and I have only recently begun to see how fully I owe it all to your broad view of things. . . .

The last lap home was stormier than ever, and the sheep they took aboard were drowned in the hold.

The roar of a storm like this is indescribable, and the ship all the while is simply flying through the water, now on her beam ends, now coming up to windward with a roar, now plunging into a hollow depth of darkness to drown the fo'c'sle in a green sea, now lifting with a twist throws one off one's feet in a half-circle—and help the man that tries to move without hanging on to something, bang goes the freeing port, and splash comes the sea over the rail, and across it flies in a flashing cloud of driven spray that whips your face like a sprung twig and clicks against the sails and rigging as it passes, while the solid green comes thud upon the deck to join the constant swish and bang of the deck-wash shipped over the rail with each heavy roll to leeward. The crashes of thunder are completely drowned in the shriek of the storm in the rigging, but a dazzling flash of lightning every minute takes ten times the time that marked its image on the brain to fade it out of sight. Shist ! with a hiss comes the sea right over the fo'c'sle, while the masts swing quivering through an angle of eighty degrees or more, and then with a lifting wailing roar and shivering stays and a mast that bends and wags from truck to stepping, the whole great composite sheet of canvas rises to windward against the freshening blast and fills and bellies stiff till the braces are as taut as rods of steel. There is nothing made by man more wonderful than a sailing ship—and to realize this fully one must spend some hours at night under more sail than appears quite safe in a S.W.ly gale in the roaring forties with squalls of force 10 and 11 by Beaufort's scale. . . . She may look obstinate, she may be trying, but wait till you see her tried to the utmost and when she has either to bend or break she is like a perfect human being and will bend double first—then you can realize how instinct with life and therefore lovable is the work of man if only he has done his best.

The skin of the Sea Elephant, lashed to skid-beams, survived these tempests and its existence was forgotten by most till in the Tropics when, as Scott remarked, ' shift it from place to place as you would, it made its presence felt everywhere.'

Their last port of call was at the Azores. Here they fell in with the Prince of Monaco's yacht, and being invited on board were courteously entertained by that great deep-sea fisherman whose *Musée Géographique* is now one of the wonders of the scientific world.

On September 10, 1904, they landed at Southsea. Thus ended the Voyage of the *Discovery*.

CHAPTER XI

Grouse Disease : British Mammals and Birds

It is a most serious thing to be alive in this world ; to
die is not sport for man. Man's life never was a sport for
him ; it was a stern reality altogether, a serious matter to
be alive.

CARLYLE.

THE months that followed the return were
months of unceasing activity for Wilson.
What with the inevitable whirlwind of
invitations to dinners and social functions, work at
the Museum, making copies of his Antarctic pictures, illustrating Scott's book in colour and Armitage's in pen and ink, making lantern-slides for
Royds, lecturing to various scientific societies and
at public schools, and writing up his own scientific
reports for publication by the Natural History
Department of the British Museum—he had little
time to give to his family and friends. 'I want,'
he told his father, ' my monograph on the Emperor
Penguin to be a classic.' Though tenacious of his
own opinions he was always ready to take the advice
of one whose judgment he could trust ; and a year
later, having completed and submitted to his father's
criticism the manuscript of the volume embodying
his Reports on Antarctic Zoology, he wrote again,
' There was not a correction you made that I did
not adopt, and you greatly improved the chapters.'

The first noteworthy event was the exhibition of
his pictures in the Bruton Galleries in London, which
opened on November 7, simultaneously with Scott's
lecture at the Albert Hall, and for the first time
fame, from which he shrank, came to him.   During
the three weeks in which they were on view the
galleries were crowded.   But the commercial aspect
of the affair was as distasteful to him as it proved
unprofitable.   The originals of his pictures he considered to be the temporary property of the R.G.S.,
and therefore undertook to make copies of any
that were chosen for purchase.   He wished at first
to part with these for a modest figure, but on the
manager of the Gallery's assurance that they would
realize ten times as much, and request to be allowed
to undertake their sale at a high commission,
Wilson, innocent of the practical consequences of
the transaction, agreed.   In the result, though
orders for no less than eighty copies were placed,
and faithfully executed over a period of six
months, the artist realized a miserable return for his
labours.

London being now the centre of his work, he
and his wife rented inexpensive rooms in Bushey,
with a studio within a stone's throw, only a couple
of miles from his old lodgings at Stanmore.   Three
minutes' walk ' down our lane ' led them into a
mazy copse with marshy hollows full of all the
simple natural treasures that they loved.   He was
working in the studio on a picture of the Antarctic
coast for presentation to the King, when the sting
of a bee on a vein of his temple caused a sudden
swelling of his face and whole body.   The poison
had reached the heart and lungs, and the conse-

quences might have been serious unless Dr. Shackleton (a cousin of the explorer who as it chanced was in practice at Bushey) had been at hand to administer a timely injection.

Of the many lectures he was called upon to deliver, illustrated with his own slides, that to the Royal Institution was the most important. It was timed for a certain length, but he sat down amid shouts of ' Go on ! ' from the learned members, the Chairman, Sir William Crookes, remarking that he had but one fault to find with the lecture : it was far too short. At first he read his lectures, but as his confidence grew he delivered them in a simple direct conversational way, lit up with humour, which delighted his audiences. He was happy, he said, if only he could make them laugh. When lecturing on scurvy and its treatment his chief points were that fresh seal-meat is preferable to lime-juice ; that lumbago and muscular rheumatic pains were common, but that there was no arthritic attack ; nor was there anæmia, but the hæmoglobin was actually increased ; the taste for alcohol of all kinds decreased as the cold grew more intense. It required far more courage for him to face an audience than to cross a crevasse, and he could never accustom himself to the nightmare of after-dinner speeches in which he had to reply to a eulogy. At the first of these ordeals, at St. George's, he was speechless and was only rescued from dire confusion by the tactful intervention of his friend Fraser. Scott, too, with his native modesty, was at first equally nervous as a public speaker. Before addressing the Zoological Society on one occasion Wilson wrote to his father :

I have to say a word or two to-morrow for Protection
of Birds and mean to suggest that the Penguins want
more the intervention of the Prevention of Cruelty Society.
The hunting of King Penguins into red-hot cauldrons for
their oil will shock their graces, I think, but it is done
at the Macquarie Islands.

Later this iniquity was again exposed by his
friend Cherry-Garrard, and as a result its sup-
pression was eventually secured by Act of Parlia-
ment.

It was characteristic of Wilson that he should
give the proceeds of his most popular lecture, which
was delivered at the Queen's Hall when he was
racked with rheumatism, to the Caius College
Mission. Of his addresses to Public Schools those
which gave him greatest pleasure were at Cheltenham ; at Rugby, under the kindly auspices of
his old Headmaster, Dr. James ; and at Charterhouse, where his reception was thus described by
one of the masters :

Although he gave a vivid account of the party's experiences illuminated with a certain dry humour which
provoked torrents of cheers and laughter, he appeared
according to his own account to have done nothing himself. It was not till the Chairman rose to thank him
for his lecture (and some people said it was the best
they had ever known at Charterhouse) that the audience
began to realize the kind of man that this quiet humorous
stranger, with his lean capable figure and kindly twisted
smile, really was. Then they rose and cheered him to
the echo as if their enthusiasm would never cease.

On December 18, after presenting one of his
water-colour sketches to King Edward, he with his
comrades received the Antarctic Medal at His
Majesty's hands at Buckingham Palace.

So far from courting the attention of notabilities

he sought every means possible to avoid them, and was never really happy except when at work or in the seclusion of his little home. But among those of kindred tastes whom he was glad to meet may be named the artists Herkomer and Swan ; Pycraft the bird osteologist ; the Duchess of Bedford, who discussed with him the plans for her Cottage Hospital, and gave him the freedom of her Park; Sir Ray Lankester, who advised him to make himself *the* authority on seals ; and the brothers John and Hallam Murray, who encouraged him to write and illustrate for publication

and gave me to understand that they would be pleased if I came to them for an offer first. Hallam who paints came with me to the Exhibition. I have rarely met such a charming man or one so courteous and full of help and sympathy. He told me of several faults that run through all my painting—easily corrected, I am glad to say, now that my attention has been drawn to them.

In March 1905 he had the great pleasure of meeting Sir Joseph Hooker, then in his eighty-eighth year, after visiting whom he wrote home :

Our visit to the Hookers the other day was a real treat ; his mind is marvellously fresh about Ross's voyage and he showed us a portfolio of his pencil-drawings taken down there at the time. We came away with a beautiful souvenir of our visit from Lady Hooker—an oval piece of Wedgwood in which Sir Joseph's head in white appears on a dull green background—a copy of the gold medal presented to him by the Linnæan Society. . . .

Sir Joseph, having with difficulty paid a visit to the Exhibition, wrote in a letter to the Director at Kew :

I made an effort to see the Antarctic Sketches with my legs bandaged up to the knees (but not painful).

They are marvellous in number, interest, and execution. No naval expedition ever did the like. The heads and bodies of the birds by Dr. Wilson are the perfection of ornithological drawing and colouring. They are absolutely alive.[1]

Indeed, the aliveness of all his creature-studies was their distinctive quality, and proved to be their chief attraction at the Gallery.

He made the mammals and birds his own [writes Professor Stanley Gardiner]. They are not mere dull lists, but reports of enduring value, showing everywhere throughout the personal joyousness of their author. What could be more expressive than his drawings of the young chicks of the Emperor Penguin, or more maternal than that of the mother-seal with her week-old baby?

He was seldom out of touch with Scott. The publication of Scott's *Voyage of the Discovery* it was that brought to them both another friendship which can almost be said to have outlasted death. Mr. Reginald Smith, K.C., Head of the House of Smith, Elder & Co., was at that time also Editor of the *Cornhill*. The tale of their first meeting can best be told in the words of an unsigned article in the *Cornhill* of March 1913, entitled ' Two Heroes of the Antarctic.'

As the *Cornhill* is being made ready for press comes the news, so long looked for, so little expected, that tells of the fate of two best friends of this house—the leader of the Antarctic expedition and his close comrade and almost brother. Neither Robert Falcon Scott nor Edward Adrian Wilson ever wrote in these pages ; but both as writers and as men they were so intimately connected with the Editor and others in Waterloo Place that the magazine to-day must needs set down a few all-in-

---

[1] See also *Life of Sir J. D. Hooker* (Leonard Huxley), II, 457.

adequate words of affectionate remembrance and inexpressible admiration.

It is eight years since Captain Scott walked into this office at six o'clock one autumn evening and said, 'I am back from the Antarctic, and I want you to publish my book.' His perfect comradeship with Dr. Wilson, the closest companion of his first expedition as of the last, was delightful to behold as they sat together in this room and discussed various points in the forthcoming book, especially as regards the drawings, all of which were from Wilson's hand, for he was an accomplished artist as well as a skilful naturalist and counsellor to the expedition, as Scott was its moving spirit. One scene among these stands out unforgettably among many less defined memories. The question of the frontispiece to the first volume came up. It was proposed to give a photograph of the Southern sledge party led by Scott himself. Scott regarded it thoughtfully ; then suddenly looking up said, at first tentatively, then with growing emphasis : ' What do you think, Bill ? I don't think we ought to be there. The Southern party wasn't more than any other sledging party. No, we won't have it.' And it was thrown out to take a more modest place in the text. As substitute a sketch of the good ship *Discovery* was suggested. Time was short ; one remembers the cheery question, ' How long do you think you would take to do it, Bill ? ' and the quiet answer, in matter-of-fact tone, ' I can get it done in thirty-six hours if I sit up all night to it.'

Another recollection is of the first ' round table ' conference to consider the format of the book—a question in this case something like discussing plans for a new house with an architect. Both took infinite pains to get a clear notion of the details it was necessary to discuss and their bearing upon the work of writer and artist. At the end Scott turned to Wilson. ' How do you feel ? I hardly know where I am.' ' No more do I ! ' ' Then let's go and have a cup of tea.'

The subsequent publication of *The Grouse in Health and Disease* brought them into closer touch even more personally than officially. It was of

Reginald Smith that Wilson wrote later—'the friend whose friendship has made all but the very highest principles in life impossible—the memory of whom, on the Barrier, will be a help to achieve, and an incentive to return.' [1]   And it was of Wilson that Reginald Smith wrote—' To have known him is a life-long possession as to have lost him is a life-long regret.'

A new, and as it seemed a very congenial, sphere of work was unexpectedly opened to him after his address to the British Ornithologists' Union in March '05.   He was introduced to Lord Lovat, then Chairman of the Board of Agriculture's Commission on the Investigation of Grouse Disease. A field-naturalist was required for the work who was also a bacteriologist and a doctor.   Six months in the year were sufficient for observation on the moors and for laboratory research ; the remaining months of winter would give him freedom to sketch and write.   Lord Lovat invited Wilson to join him at Carlisle next day, where a group of experienced keepers were to be cross-questioned on the subject.   Wilson agreed, and the next day accepted the post of ' Field Observer.'

Almost at the same time an old Cambridge friend who had graduated equal with him in the Tripos of '94, and had been an unsuccessful competitor for his appointment on the *Discovery*, asked him to illustrate his new edition of Bell's *British Mammals*.   This was Major Barrett Hamilton, of Kilmanock, Co. Wexford, one of the keenest admirers of his Antarctic water-colours, who wrote

---

[1] *The House of Smith, Elder* (Leonard Huxley), p. 217.

subsequently of his mammal paintings, ' The only cause for regret is that the processes of reproduction have toned down Wilson's colour, always his strong point.'

And a little later Mr. Eagle Clarke asked him for a series of coloured illustrations for Yarrell's standard work on *British Birds*. He very gladly undertook to do both in the intervals of his work for the Grouse Disease Commission. With regard to the former, of which the premature deaths of both writer and artist prevented the completion, more must be said below. The request for the latter, when the illustrations were half-way towards completion, was unfortunately withdrawn.

He was now very busy with his sketches and skins at Bushey. In the early summer of '05 he and his wife removed from their lodgings at ' Windermere ' to the occupation of a small house, ' Tynecote,' near by, where they rejoiced in doing their own housekeeping, and from here he wrote to an aunt :

How we wish you would come and have a look at our cosy home. We are down at six every morning. O. does all the cooking and house-cleaning, and I do the kitchen-grate and light the fire and clean the flue. I don't smoke and I don't drink, and I have to swear horribly to prevent myself from becoming a little angel and flying away. So you must forgive O. if she shocks you when we next meet, because she *will* pick up such horrible expressions. Sometimes she says ' Oh bother,' and sometimes she says ' Well, never mind,' but it's awful to hear her when she breaks things washing up— luckily not our own things—she seems very careful about all our own things.

In August '05 he went for a well-earned respite to the south-west of Ireland, taking with him, how-

Blarney Castle, Ireland.

BLARNEY CASTLE

ever, some of his unfinished work. His parents
had taken a house for the month in a wild corner
of Kerry, where the whole family joined them. It
was the last of many such family picnic holidays.
Wilson and his wife enjoyed many a morning
watching the seals playing in the breakers or bask-
ing on the rocks ; rejoicing in the Irish tales of
E. Œ. Somerville and Martin Ross ; and in sketching birds, some of them already rare in England,
such as the Raven, the Grey Crow, Choughs,
Sheldrakes, Redshanks and many waders, Curlew
in immense flocks, and now and then a Buzzard
or a Kite wheeling in the sky. Here, too, many of
his finest landscapes were painted. His style had
lost none of its delicacy, its care for detail, or its
feeling for atmosphere since his Norway days
seven years before, but it had gained in breadth :
and his colour-sketches of Ireland have all the
charm and glamour of the ' Celtic twilight.'

He ended his stay there with a visit to Barrett
Hamilton at Waterford to discuss illustrations, and
to study the architecture of the abbeys and castles
in the south-east.

His illustrations of *British Mammals* were proceeding apace, and among the first to be dealt
with were bats. A raid was made on a cave, and
the captives found a temporary home in his studio
to be studied and sketched.

[To his father—Feb. 16, '06]—On Wednesday I went
bat-hunting. Met my friend Cocks [1] at Henley Station
and was driven to lunch with a Mr. Heatley Noble at a

---

[1] On a previous visit to Mr. Cocks he had in three days
made no less than seventy sketches of pine martins, wild
cats, badgers, and otters, which were kept on the premises.

very fine house in the middle of beautiful woods. In
his grounds is an underground passage about a quarter-
mile long, excavated 200 years ago right through a chalk
hill. We all had tapers and went along this and found
about 50 Bats, of four different species—Whiskered Bat,
Daubentons, Natterers and the Long-Eared. This is the
cave in which Millais found the rare Bechstein's Bat.
We have not repeated his find but as two of these were
new to me we were lucky. One simply picked them
off the chalk walls or hoicked them out of crannies. I
brought 20 home to O.! Noble is a great authority
on Birds and a very interesting man—said to be one of
the four best shots in England—but by no means only a
sportsman ; and he has asked me to go there for a night
any time I want another bat-hunt.

The bat-hunt had an amusing sequel. While
sketching one of the specimens in his studio at
'Tynecote' he was adjusting some fur with the point
of his pencil when a flea crawled on to the point.
Mrs. Wilson was engaged in whipping up a soufflée
in the kitchen when she heard her husband call for
help. On reaching the studio she was amused by
his request to hold the pencil and not to allow the
flea to hop away, while he ran to fetch a tube of
spirits. The flea was no common flea, but a rare
and precious species of its tribe, which he knew at
once would be a welcome addition to Mr. Charles
Rothschild's collection.

The year 1906 had opened with 'dead grouse
pouring in by every post' to 'Tynecote,' Bushey,
in every stage of mortality—and Wilson remarked
that he had 'got grouse disease.' The Field
Observer's task was from the outset no sinecure.
It proved to entail even more work in the laboratory
than in the field, for every dead grouse picked up
on a moor in the British Isles was at once trans-

mitted to him for examination. From the first he decided to make a Museum skin of every bird if possible. The crop contents had to be analysed, and the most accurate notes taken as to the sex, plumage, weight, and the condition of the intestines. Fortunately he found in his wife a competent and willing helper, for the work grew in importance till from being a half-yearly it became a full-yearly employment and it became apparent that, with his other illustrations, he had undertaken more than he could deal with alone.

April found him at Colinton, in Midlothian, hard at his laboratory work with his wife. Only at rare intervals was he able to enjoy the wild free life of the moors where, with a sturdy ghillie striding alongside, he strove to indoctrinate his companion with his views against the wholesale destruction of vermin and on the *value* of some of them, whether feathered or furred—especially hawks. Ghillies, a somewhat opinionative race, had to be conciliated, argued with and convinced, but they soon found that the stranger who could outpace them on the moor knew a thing or two about the habits of game. It was indeed, as Lord Lovat said, ' the *personal* qualities of Dr. Wilson' that secured him the willing assistance not only of his colleagues on the staff but also of the keepers.

The investigation was of a kind which from one point of view it may seem surprising to find Wilson engaged upon. For, though himself a good shot he had personally little interest in any sport in which living things are killed, hurt or hunted for recreation. It promised, however, to give him a much-desired combination of pursuits, independent research with the freedom of the wild ; but actually by far the greater part of his work was necessarily indoors. Two investigators had been in the field before him, Dr. Cobbold and Professor Klein, but it transpired that neither had hit upon the right solution.

The Inquiry was a very wide one, and had to be approached from diverse directions. For some time experts and ghillies had convinced themselves that in certain years the Grouse had suffered from a form of epidemic disease which had killed off great numbers, the birds dying quickly and in good condition. Klein was supposed to have confirmed this opinion by his discovery in the lungs of the dead birds of a bacillus of the Coli type. Grave doubt was soon thrown on this conclusion, especially when close investigation of the birds as shot on the moor showed that the bacillus was due to *post-mortem* changes. Three years were also destined to pass without the occurrence of a single instance of what had hitherto gone by the name of ' Klein's disease.' Search meanwhile took other directions and it was not long before the true cause was traced by the Field Observer to the existence of colonies of a minute Threadworm (Trichostrongylus pergracilis) which infested the cœca of weakly birds and by destroying the inner surface which absorbed their food brought about the death of the individual. This threadworm crawls up the fronds of the heather, infests the dewdrops or moisture condensed from mists at the ends of the young shoots on which the Grouse feed, and infects them with the lingering or pining form of the true ' Grouse Disease.' Many an early morning Wilson spent on the moors, collecting the precious drops, so beautiful and apparently innocuous, for examination through a powerful lens. The further search for the origin or 'host' of the Strongylus brought other observers into the field, including Dr. Shipley, afterwards Master of Christ's College, Cambridge; and Dr. Leiper, Helminthologist to the London School of Tropical Medicine. To them Dr. Wilson described the life-history of this pernicious nematode which he had studied under the microscope through all its stages.

On one occasion, having carefully dissected a couple of grouse sent through the post and having reported upon them to the sender that they were entirely free from disease, he received a reply that they had been intended for consumption, not for dissection!

In the summer of 1906 he moved to Fort Augustus, in order to be still nearer to his work. The landscape paintings that he made in Scotland, chiefly of this neighbourhood, are few in number compared with his usual output, for as his Grouse work expanded it made more and more demands upon his time: but they should be mentioned because here for the first time he tried a new method. His custom had been to paint on damped thin paper as being the most suitable for colour-blendings so delicate in their gradations that it appears as though hands had not touched them; he now tried his colour-effects on dry rough paper, but the results did not satisfy him, and he soon abandoned the new method for the old.

Here he made friends with the monks of St. Benedict's Monastery and with them went 'bat-hunting in the Belfry,' while they paid many a visit to his lodgings, to find him, as did other distinguished visitors, ' surrounded by a halo of grouse feathers and unravelled entrails.' But his own life was a constant round of visits to moor-owners in all parts of the country, interspersed with many visits from friends and relations to whom he and his wife were glad to offer their simple rooms as a ' convalescent home.' In a letter to his mother he says :

> Servants seem to be everyone's chief anxiety, and we are spared much by having none. . . . One of our worst troubles is being over-entertained ! It would suit many people very well, but it cuts into my work a lot.

He made himself responsible for the care of a sister in her serious illness, and his letters home contain frequent requests to help his home-folks personally or pecuniarily whenever help was needed.

The laborious nature of his work during these years, 1905–10, was known to no one but the companion who shared it. He was working harder than he had ever worked in his life. Much of his time was spent in travel from one end of Britain to the other for meetings, visits to Beaufort Castle, interviews with his colleagues on the Committee, journeys to moor-owners and even more to their keepers—all distracting to his actual work in hand which never seemed to get done. Even in the train more often than not he was correcting proofs or making up the arrears of correspondence. If ever a man knew how to ' fill the unforgiving minute with sixty seconds' worth of distance run ' it was he. Since he could never find time to

refresh his mind with reading, his wife read to him
while he skinned or sketched. Of any novel of
Dickens he confessed that he dared not open it,
for he could not put it down. And of a sewing-
machine—' I think it would knock anyone out of
a fit of the blues because it has got such a very
busy buzz ! ' The constant strain under which he
was living, and perhaps too the unpleasantly odor-
ous nature of his Grouse work, brought with it a
craving again for a narcotic, and after many an
ineffectual struggle at Fort Augustus he succumbed
again to the solace of a pipe, only to abandon it
entirely in 1908. During his journeys from place
to place he usually carried with him all the papers
necessary for reference at his destination : it was
therefore a terrible shock to him when, at Glasgow
in May 1907, his suit-case containing the results
of two years' steady work—all his dissection statis-
tics and others of equal importance—was stolen.
Over-wrought though he was with too much work,
he was of a calibre that ' could see the work he
gave his life to broken, and stoop and build it up
with worn-out tools.' Always methodical and
systematic in all he did, he had kept his rough
notes, and from them he set himself at once to
make good the loss, but very much additional
work was needed before it could be even partially
repaired.

The Committee meeting of 1907 opened with the
emphatic announcement of Dr. Shipley that the
first and most important decision to make was
that ' Wilson must have a holiday, as he has had
none for two years.'

On June 20 he wrote to his father :

The Grouse Commission has happily gone to sleep as it does during the month of June as a rule—chiefly because the Committee are in Camp—and because the birds have stopped dying, bless them ! . . . I am taking advantage of this lull in Grouse work to paint some more British mammals.

In September came indeed a much-needed respite. The Wilsons and Captain Scott were invited to the shooting-bungalow of their friends the Reginald Smiths at Cortachy, Kirriemuir; but even there, in the few days that he could afford, Grouse and correspondence followed him. There, however, in the companionship of his friends he enjoyed the complete freedom that no other visit could give him to the same degree, ' utilizing the idle lunch hour of a shooting-party to jot down the aspect of the moor on the nearest piece of sandwich paper, to be worked up later at home and given to his delighted host.'

An occasion is remembered at a shoot when Captain Scott allowed a roe-deer to pass near his gun unharmed ' because it was such a pretty little thing ' ; and another when he and Wilson leapt a fence together in pursuit of a Landrail.

Scott was now full of plans for a second expedition to the Antarctic, though as yet none but these friends knew of them : and when in the following year the Smiths lent their bungalow to the Wilsons for the summer, a young relative of the former, Apsley Cherry-Garrard, came to see them there. Two years later, hearing that Scott and Wilson were going South again he volunteered his services in a letter to Wilson, and was accepted as assistant zoologist—with consequences that neither

of them at the time foresaw. For many months
now Wilson's correspondence, which sometimes
took him an entire day to get through, was increased
by an exchange of many letters with Scott on the
subject of motor-tractors for use in the Antarctic,
and on securing a pension for an injured seaman of
the *Discovery*.

His services to the Grouse Disease Inquiry received formal appreciation in Lord Lovat's Introduction to the Commission's Report published in
the autumn of 1911.[1] But it may well be supplemented by some brief extracts from a long article
contributed to the *Cornhill Magazine* in April 1913
by Sir Arthur E. Shipley, his closest collaborator
on the Commission.

A combination of the artist and the man of science is
rare, but it is not so rare as one is apt to think, and
when it does occur it is often found in men of noble
character and of high purpose. Such a man was Edward
Adrian Wilson.

In the autumn of 1905 he had been appointed, at a
most modest salary, field observer, physiologist and anato-
mist to the recently established Grouse Disease Inquiry,
and from that date until five years later, when he sailed
in the *Terra Nova*, I saw him very frequently. I do not
think the Inquiry could have had a better man, or even
one so good. His singleness of purpose and his directness of address, coupled with the undoubted accuracy of
his knowledge, commanded at first the respect, and very
soon the sympathy both of the moor-owner and of his
keepers. Wilson was an indefatigable worker, and, besides visiting almost every important moor in Scotland,
and many in England, he dissected just under 2,000
grouse, and recorded under a dozen different headings
the physical and pathological conditions of the bird with

---

[1] *The Grouse in Health and Disease* (Messrs. Smith, Elder),
vol. I, p. xviii.

a minuteness that would put the most enthusiastic panel-doctor to shame. He thought nothing of sitting up all night on the moor to obtain a better knowledge of the sleeping and waking habits of the grouse and her chicks. I am reminded that he slept one May night on a Forfar-shire moor in order to obtain one or two drops of dew for the microscope. It was bitterly cold, but there was no dew. Many and many a time I have rushed up North to spend a few days with Wilson in his laboratory, hastily improvised in some Highland inn, or in a station hotel (we were not at all popular in station hotels), or in the gun-room of some moor-owner's castle. I think Wilson worked as hard as ever man did. Those were good days ; I would they were back again.

Of the two quarto volumes which form the ' Report ' of the Inquiry, Wilson wrote quite one-third, and the beautiful coloured plates were all drawn by him. He left, on his second Antarctic voyage, about a year before the ' Report' appeared : some of his unfinished work he took with him, and posted back to us from the several stopping-places ; others he left to us to prepare for press. . . . In his last letter to me (dated October 29, 1911) written two days before the Polar party started on their ' southern trek,' he says : ' I shall be fright-fully keen to see if the mail brings me a copy of the Grouse Report ! ' The mail did bring the copy, but he never saw it. The plates in the ' Report' hardly do justice to Wilson's skill as an artist. Although for the most part they are unusually successful examples of the three-colour process, the reproductions naturally fall far behind the originals. Wilson's sense of colour had been developed by a patient and for some time a daily study of Turner in the National Gallery. He always had a sense of form, and he had a real gift of putting on paper what his clear, calm eyes saw. He could in a subtle way indicate life or its absence ; motion or rest ; in his brilliant sketches of the Antarctic you could see the weather. His scientific work was on the same high level. ' Prove all things, and hold fast to that which is good,' was his habit. He made no revolutionary dis-coveries, he opened out no new realms of knowledge, but within the limits he set himself, his work was of a high standard, and, like everything about him, thoroughly sound.

Amongst his many fine qualities, his quiet simplicity and directness and his absolute loyalty and honesty of purpose stand out. He was not blunt or abrupt in any way, but it simply never occurred to him to finesse or—well, to use the methods familiar to politicians. His disposition was unusually serene, steadfast, and happy. I have never known him angry, and hardly ever put out. He never fussed. If something went wrong, and he could not put it right again, he simply did the next best thing, often without a comment. Though the most modest of men, he knew—but he never exaggerated—his own powers, nor did he underestimate them. With his frail body and his artist's hands he travelled and he worked throughout those long Antarctic voyages, but it was the brain and the will-power, which he knew and he alone knew, that carried him along. He was singularly unselfish, and although he enjoyed solving problems in Natural History or in Pathology, he never thought of his own reputation. He never sought recognition ; in fact, I doubt if it ever occurred to him that his work merited recognition in any form. In the best sense of the word he was an optimist, and never worried or troubled about the future. I cannot remember that he ever talked about religion ; yet if it be religion to dedicate one's life to ' whatsoever things are true, whatsoever things are honest, whatsoever things are just, whatsoever things are pure, whatsoever things are lovely, whatsoever things are of good report '—if this be religion, I have never known a more religious man.

Both morally and physically he was fearless ; and here again I do not think it ever occurred to him that anyone could be otherwise. Like his religion his high courage was part of himself, inherent in him. To him death was but a step, a change to something further, something better, and the death of a relative or friend hardly ruffled his trustful serenity. Of his own death I cannot write. Browning foresaw it.[1]

His illustrations of mammals had brought him

---

[1] ' Prospice.'

into contact with Messrs. Oliver & Boyd, of Edinburgh, who, he wrote to his father, are

publishers of the real old stock, you would love to see
them—they remind me of the Dickens type. . . . They
tell me that the work I am doing will put me in the
first rank, [and on their having shown one of his drawings of a Stoat to Eagle Clarke and Grimshaw], they
were told that Millais couldn't do anything as good : this
is of course humbug but they took it in and congratulated
me most heartily, so I have something to live up to now.

One result of this connection was an order for
a frontispiece to a new edition of *The Birds of the
Border*, by Abel Chapman. He also made an
illustration for the ' Ice Age ' in Knipe's *Nebula to
Man*. And it was not long before he had the
pleasure of doing his Scotch friends a good turn
by persuading the authorities of the Royal Society
to place the half-tone work of the volume he was
engaged in editing into their hands. This was the
Album of Photographs and Sketches (Nat. Ant. Exp.
1901–4). The task had brought him into close
touch with Sir Archibald Geikie, then Secretary
to the Society, who in his prefatory note to the
volume paid Wilson a high tribute, and wrote to
him that its completion gave him but one cause
for regret, namely ' a close to our pleasant co-
operation, if I may call it so.'

But as he never saw the visible results of his
work on the Grouse Disease, neither was he destined to see the results of his work on *British Mammals*,
of which the first number appeared in October
1910, though his illustrations therein continued to
appear for many years after his death. The four-
teenth number (April 1913) was prefaced by an

appreciation from the hand of his friend Major
Barrett Hamilton. This has a special interest, for
before the next issue Barrett Hamilton himself had
died, and the fifteenth number (March 1914) contains an appreciation of him by their mutual
friend, Oldfield Thomas.

Barrett Hamilton wrote :

. . . One could not associate with him without feeling
that one had gained something. While his natural breadth
of mind must sometimes have revolted against the minute
detail inseparable from mammalogy, he yet lavished
the most careful attention on the numerous technical
diagrams, to master the meaning of which meant much
study on what was to him a novel subject. A dreamer
of great dreams, it was sometimes necessary to call him
to earth for a demonstration on murine osteology, but
no man ever took criticism in better part. As a rule
he forestalled it by a genial counter-attack : ' You are
so polite this morning, that I know you are going to
tear my drawings to pieces,' was his typical opening to a
discussion. . . .

Wilson has gone ! His long, lean figure will no longer
stalk down the galleries of the British Museum of Natural
History to a conference on Mammal illustrations, but
we, his fellow-workers, will treasure his memory, proud
that for a brief space he journeyed with us, lightening
our labours with the encouragement of the truest good-
fellowship.

Side by side with his rapidly growing collection
of pictures of *British Mammals* grew his pictures
of *British Birds*. On these he expended all the
love and care that his heart held for them, for birds
were his very life. His letters evince the privilege
he felt in being asked to illustrate the standard
work on them and the sense of responsibility with
which he approached the task. But the apprecia-
tions of his publisher and of the Editor were so

encouraging, and their criticisms so few and slight, that he went to work at them with high hopes.

Eagle Clarke is genuinely pleased with the Birds and quite spontaneously told me that he was very glad the whole was to be done by me alone. . . .   I am delighted to find that there is no shadow of a doubt about his appreciation. He says that they are so much my own that he cannot find a suggestion of any other bird-artist's work in any of them, and that pleases me perhaps more than anything in these days of plagiarism. . . . The Dipper, he says, is the best Dipper anyone has ever drawn ! And so on.

It may therefore be imagined with what dismay he opened a letter on December 10, 1909, which informed him that they were ' not satisfactory,' and the agreement was terminated, the reasons never being understood by him. The project itself was subsequently abandoned by the Editor, and the work was never published. But some few of Wilson's studies of British Birds in the Highlands were after his death reproduced in Major Hesketh Prichard's *Sport in Wildest Britain* (1921), with a foreword by the author who was himself dying when he wrote it. In it he stated that ' he wished the book to be regarded rather as a tribute to Dr. Wilson's genius than in any other light.' This is the sole recognition ever given, and that posthumously, to an infinitesimal part of what was probably his greatest work in art.

His output of work, at the age of thirty-eight, is such that would satisfy most men as the achievement of a long lifetime, but by far the greater bulk of it is buried in obscurity ; his Natural History Book alone—which he called his ' stock in trade ' for future compilation, representing as it

BULL-FINCHES.

does a mass of material in original notes and
sketches in pencil and colour all culled from personal observation—is a life-work in itself. Started
in his schooldays and each fresh discovery added
bit by bit with patient care, it had grown to pro-
digious dimensions. Had he lived to complete it
there is no doubt that its importance would have
eclipsed all his other work.

His unremitting labour during these four years
had been accomplished at the price of continual
fatigue, frequent rheumatic aches, occasional cramp
and attacks of migraine. But physical pain served
only to spur him into further activity.

The following extracts from letters to his wife
cover the period of their short but frequent separa-
tions during the last two of these busy years. They
are selected as representative of the thoughts which
were uppermost in his mind, and the pensiveness
of their expression bespeaks a tired man.

Here we have no abiding-place—and I feel it more
as I grow older and the days for service and for doing
and for making often seem so few ahead and so few
behind too. It is amazing and most puzzling when one
tries to think what is the object of our short life on earth
—a mere visit—and how desperately this must represent
our effect on the little part of the world with which we
come into contact. I get such a feeling of the absolute
necessity to be at something always, and at every hour,
day and night, before the end may come or I have done
a decent portion of what I was expected to do ; each
minute is of value, though we so often waste hours and
hours, not because we want rest, nor because as sometimes it is a duty, but out of sheer want of application. . . .

The more one does the more one gets to do, and I
don't ever really want to have less to do than I have
these last few years—I want to be able to feel and to
know that *you* feel, when my end comes, that I couldn't

have done more—and then I shall die quite happy, and
I shall know that you will always be proud. . . . Anything I do which leaves nothing to *show* gives me a
feeling of lost time, but before God I know it isn't.   He
judges the effort and the motive, not the result.

You will be glad to hear that I have really finished
off the Royal Soc. Vol. completely except for two maps,
and copying out the Index which I shall leave for you.
I sat at it yesterday from breakfast till 2 o'clock this
morning—but I knew I could sleep all this afternoon
in the train.

My old beliefs are all every atom as strong as ever.
It isn't that any of my convictions or any of my longings
have altered or died out ; it is that they are out of sight
only, as the foundations of a house are out of sight, but
they are there for as long as the building lasts, and they
are quite sound.   I am reminded of the Fort Augustus
Chapel of the Monastery.   Once foundations are laid
they should be built on, and the more they are built
on the more they disappear from view.   If ever you see
signs of the foundations giving way, then tell me it is
time to stop building—but until then and as long as God
puts the bricks and mortar before us so constantly, and
each day more than we can get finished with, so long
must we go on building and building.   Every now and
then one must glance over the whole show, even look
into it carefully, to see that the foundations are not
giving way . . . to see that there aren't any cracks or
signs of settling.

I feel so horribly unideal and so different to what I
could and might and ought to be. . . .   I am getting
more and more soft and dependent upon comforts, and
this I hate.   I want to endure hardness and instead of
that I enjoy hotel dinners and prefer hot water to cold
and so on—all bad signs and something must be done
to stop it.

I feel that every picture I draw will live and effect
something after our death. . . .   I always feel so certain
that I shall be given time to write and publish some of
the things that are in my head, and also to paint some
others, not in a hurry as I have to now, but my best
possible.   This conviction makes me absolutely fearless

as to another journey South, for whatever happened I
know I should come back to you, and as to you—I
cannot bring myself to think that you would fail, or to
be afraid on your account. . . . I should not feel it
was right now to desert Scott if he goes. . . .

I suppose that anyone who has any feeling at all for
trouble in other people finds more and more of it every
year as he grows older. Sometimes it seems overwhelm-
ing—as though one could see no way of getting clear
of it except by running away. . . . Summer is over
and autumn will still be through, but let us thank God
because this is not our rest, and the sooner it's over the
sooner to sleep. . . . We are perhaps half-way, who
knows, we may one or both of us be much farther towards our rest than we can guess. I feel myself that I
have a long way yet and much to do. It makes me
inexpressibly sad when I think of it these autumn days,
with their early-closing dark cold wet grey evenings,
cheerless to a degree, most suggestive of what my life
would be in its latter half if I had to finish it without
you. God give us courage to persevere and die in
harness, remembering this is not our rest. As our lives
quiet down God will grant us to be gentler, less ready to
take offence, less likely to give it, more ready to remember Him as a friend at hand, a guide, a counsellor,
and a great companion—as you indeed are and have
been all along to me, and oh it's sad I feel without you.

For real happiness our marriage would be hard to
beat, and our married life hard to improve upon.

You from the first have always been different—yes,
from the very first . . . and I am the man you have
blessed above all.

. . . It looks almost as though in real love anything
short of death is insufficient ; and yet, though death
for one's best and truest love is the highest thing of all,
it is to be avoided by every means so long as any minor
hardship can be endured for the joy, the very blessed
joy, of proving one's love.

May God guide and keep you in the happiest path of
life, peace of mind and a firm determination to be silent
and say nothing when things go wrong, and to look
always for something that is lovely and of good report,

worthy of your notice and your words. Better to say nothing than to condemn, and to laugh with than to criticize, and so *much* happier. Ignore things and people that insist on going wrong, and assist the right in the least of all things by your approval and by your notice.— Isn't this better? Whatsoever things are of *good* report are worthy of your praise. Whatsoever things are of evil report are not even worthy of your notice, let alone your words.

DINGLE BAY.

CHAPTER XII

Some Antarctic Correspondence

Like a cog-wheel with a catch—our law of life should be one tooth higher in the wheel every day.—E. A. W.

DURING the winters it was Wilson's custom to come south from Scotland in order to deal with the accumulation of his work, and for this purpose he made Westal as far as possible his headquarters, where a disused conservatory in the garden was requisitioned as a depot for dead grouse. But the Natural History Museum in London had its claims on his time, and his business in connection both with Grouse and British Mammals took him far afield, so that he was seldom in one place for any length of time. It was while he happened to be in Westal in February 1907 that he was surprised by the news which gave rise to the following correspondence. Of only one of his own letters did he write a draft, but the tenor of the rest can easily be gathered from Shackleton's replies.

Shackleton had successfully enlisted financial support for a second and independent expedition to the Antarctic; his plans were formulated and approved on February 8 and made public a day or two later. Applications from volunteers poured in from every quarter, but before considering any he wrote to Wilson, and the following letters evince the urgency with which he sought to secure the partnership of his old friend.

LETTER FROM LIEUT. SHACKLETON TO DR. WILSON

MY DEAR BILLY,—   Edinburgh, *Feb. 12, '07.*

You will have seen in the Press that I am going South again. It was only settled on Friday night and I did not think there was much of a chance before. . . . Will you come as second in command—you know me well enough to know that we can work together. I want the job done and you are the best man in the world for it, and if I am not fit enough to do the Southern journey there could be no one better than you. Your advice and help from the beginning would be invaluable. I know you don't think motors any use, but the main thing will be Siberian ponies. . . .

Come, Billy. Don't say No till we have had a talk. Don't say No at all. Wire me to Edinburgh that you are considering it and write there.

Yours ever,
SHACKLES.

That Wilson declined, though reluctantly, on the ground of his work is apparent from the following telegrams both dispatched on the same day.

TELEGRAMS FROM LIEUT. SHACKLETON TO DR. WILSON

Edinburgh, *Feb. 14, 1907.*

Please send letter to Lovat at once. He must let you go. It is the country before the grouse. Everyone I know wants you to go. I cannot speak too strongly. The expedition will be a thousand times better with you.—SHACKLES.

Would it be any use if I asked my friend the Marquis of Graham—who is one of our strongest backers to the expedition and he knows all about you and the importance of your coming—to write Lovat. I can get any number of men to write also if you like.—SHACKLETON.

LETTER FROM DR. WILSON TO LORD LOVAT

MY LORD,— Westal, *Feb. 15, 1907.*

I think that you may perhaps receive letters asking that I may be liberated from my Grouse work to go on another expedition to the Antarctic. I write therefore to say that I have refused the offer, and that I am quite prepared to stand by the Grouse. For many reasons of course I should like to have gone, but I feel that it would be absurd and unfair to throw up the Grouse Inquiry work just when I have begun to get a grip of it. I referred Lieut. Shackleton, who is organizing the Expedition, to Leslie as he was in Edinburgh, that he might assure himself that I was still wanted on the Grouse Inquiry. Shackleton is of course a great friend of mine as we were together in the *Discovery*, and in refusing to go with him I told him that it was a great disappointment. Under the circumstances I should be equally sorry now not to see the Grouse Inquiry through to the end.

Believe me, my Lord,
Yours very truly,
EDWARD A. WILSON.

TELEGRAM FROM LIEUT. SHACKLETON TO DR. WILSON

Edinburgh, *Feb. 15, '07.*

Letters and wire received. This is almost as bitter a disappointment as when I left *Discovery*. I understand your position. Have seen Secretary and realize how much they depend on you, but am making you a proposition which you might arrange. Writing.—SHACKLES.

LETTER FROM LIEUT. SHACKLETON TO A. S. LESLIE, ESQ.

Edinburgh, *Feb. 18, '07.*

DEAR SIR,—

I beg to thank you for your kindness in granting me an interview last week. I must say that, when I left you, I had but little hope, after hearing what you had to say, that I would be able to have as my companion again Dr. Wilson. No one knows better than I how valuable his services are in any direction in which he is interested, and I quite well see your point.

Following my interview and your advice I have not

written to anybody. Indeed, on returning to my house, I received letters from Dr. Wilson which left me no hope, as he pointed out to me that he was in honour bound to the Commission, and felt that he could not even ask to be relieved of his appointment. Knowing as I do his great interest in such a matter as the Expedition, I understand well that it must have cost him something to refuse my offer, but that he did so only shows his character in a stronger light. The loss is the Expedition's, and to me personally that of a good friend and adviser.

With renewed thanks for your courtesy, and trusting that the labours of the Committee will be crowned with success.   Believe me,
                    Yours very truly,
                    ERNEST H. SHACKLETON.

LETTER FROM LIEUT. SHACKLETON TO DR. WILSON
                    Edinburgh, *Feb. 15,* '07.
MY DEAR BILLY,—

I wired you to-night, but wires and letters are all too feeble to express what I feel, though you have finally decided and though I fully realize your honourable attitude which is your nature and has made you what you are. I am hoping against hope, perchance in ignorance, that there may still be a loophole, though I fear there is not much chance. I went to see the Secretary with a lively hope of success, I came away in fear—a fear that was confirmed when I was met by my wife with your wire and opened your letters. The Secretary said that if I had asked for any other man they could spare him —*you* were unique. . . . I said I would do anything if I could get you and that, Billy, is the idea I want to put forward.—If you had this season with another man, and also with a secretary to do your notes, etc., could you come out by mail? I feel it is a forlorn hope after your letters, and I know that you will not think of it unless you feel it is right, so I leave it to you. Heaven knows how I want you—but I admire you more than ever for your attitude. A man rarely writes out his heart but I would to you. If I reach the Pole I will still have a regret that you were not with me. . . . Beardmore

writing to me to-day hoped you would come.   Everyone
wants you.   I don't want to make it harder, Billy, my
friend, but I am sad at heart.

Your wife is splendid to be glad for you to do this
work if you could have done it.   Write me in answer.

Yours ever,
SHACKLES.

LETTER FROM LIEUT. SHACKLETON TO DR. WILSON

London, *Feb. 20*, '07.

MY DEAR OLD MAN,—

Thank you very much for your last letter.   In time
the disappointment on my side may grow less, but now
it is very keen, and out there will be keener.   I know,
though you are very rushed, you will give me the benefit
of your advice and experience, and I wonder would you
be able to find time if I could come and see you for one
day soon ? . . .   There is a far-away chance of you
having perhaps an opportunity of seeing the old land
once more.   I mean by this that the ship will not be
coming back to us till Feb. 1909 : by then you will
have finished the Grouse, and I would gladly arrange
for you and your wife to come out to N.Z. and you
come down in the ship and see the old place, and continue in the exploration of Wilkes' Land . . . and you
are the only person I have ever mentioned it to . . .
only a talk with you would do us both good. . . .

The news of Shackleton's intended enterprise
only reached Scott through the public Press on
H.M.S. *Albemarle* with the Atlantic Fleet on February 21, when he wrote at once to Wilson, requesting his judgment on the situation in view of his
own plans, of which Wilson equally with Shackleton was at that time unaware.   Apart from showing the esteem in which both men held their old
comrade, there would be no point in referring to
an old controversy were it not that the correspondence which followed clearly shows it to have
been based, as Wilson correctly surmised, on a

misunderstanding for which neither was responsible. The authorities which should have kept
each in touch with the other's plans had failed
to do so. But there was a further complication.
Scott felt that he had a claim on his old winter-
quarters in the McMurdo Sound as a base for
future exploration, and that an infringement of
his rights in that quarter was in the nature of a
trespass. For there is an etiquette between explorers as there is an etiquette between professional
men, and the mediation of Wilson was again called
upon to make this point clear to Shackleton. For
this purpose Shackleton made a special journey to
Westal early in March, and with Wilson's guidance
there and then formulated an agreement in detail
engaging not to use McMurdo Sound as his base,
nor to operate west of meridian 170° unless compelled by unforeseen circumstances. The controversy, and the compromise which thus ended it,
does credit to the moderation and generosity of
both, but much more to the mediation of the man
on whom both leant—a man utterly impartial because devoid of personal ambition, and only anxious
to do justice to the reputation of each of them :
Scott writing to him, 'I wanted your opinion
because it is one that I consider conclusive in
a question of honour'; and Shackleton, 'I am
sorry you are having all this worry, but it is the
penalty of being considered capable in judgment.'
Shackleton continued to exchange letters with
Wilson right up to his departure in connection
with questions as to the best medical outfit and
other subjects concerning his expedition, and left
England in August with his old friend's best wishes

for his enterprise. The world knows with what success it was attended. Force of circumstances compelled him to winter in McMurdo Sound [1] which he made the base for his operations and for his great Southern Journey, when he discovered the gateway to the Polar Plateau through the Glacier which he named after Mr. Beardmore, and pitched his last camp in latitude 88° 23'— only 97 geographical miles from the Pole. On his return two years later Scott immediately cabled ' Unqualified congratulations on magnificent success,' and received in reply, ' Deeply appreciate your cable.'

During these months of interim Scott again from time to time sought Wilson's advice on his own project, and correspondence between the two was frequent. His preparations for another venture were still tentative and it was not until after the return of Shackleton that they matured, nor was it indeed till then that Wilson, who had been glad to further his plans in any way possible, seriously considered accompanying him himself. But meanwhile Scott wrote to Wilson under various dates :

If I should go South again you know there is no one in the world I would sooner have with me than you, though I should perfectly understand the ties which might make it impossible. I hesitate to suggest such a thing till there is something to offer. Meanwhile you know my opinion of your judgment, and you will believe that I have no wish to cut across Shackleton except in so far as the *Discovery* corner is concerned. . . .

The letter you last wrote was just like you and what we called your ' blooming modesty,' and therefore it was the more delightful. As to wanting you when and

[1] *Life of Sir Ernest Shackleton*, by H. R. Mill, pp. 118–21.

if I go South there is no question you would be wanted
more than anyone else in the world. I only wonder
that you should care to come with me, and can scarcely
hope yet that you will be free if the time comes. If
you are, why it's worth it—it really is worth it.—I'm
going to try and get South again if circumstances permit
you to come too. That's all that need be said for the
present. . . .

At the time of his visit to Cortachy in 1907
Scott was already contemplating marriage : as he
whimsically confessed, it was the double example
of its felicity there that ' drove him into matri-
mony '—but it was not till the autumn of the following year that Wilson received the following
letter (undated) :

H.M.S. Bulwark.

My Dear Old Bill,—

What a ruffian I am not to have thanked you a thousand times for your splendid loyal letter, and for the
congratulations. What with the really arduous work in
this ship and the exacting demands of my engagement I
really haven't had a moment to do anything but answer,
or attempt to answer current notes. These are stupidly
expressed excuses—I really haven't a sound one—you're
a brick and I'm a ruffian.

My dear Bill, wish me well, will you? You must
and your wife also, because you're a glaring example of
how happiness may be achieved without a large share of
worldly gear. . . . Good-bye, old chap—excuse such a
wretched and belated answer to the nicest letter I have
ever had.

Yours ever,

R. Scott.

Nov. 14, '08, H.M.S. Bulwark.

Dear old Bill,—

You are just you—there never was anybody so absolutely straight and honest. In a world of grinding axes
it's pure refreshment to me to see you or hear from you.
Imprimis, will you drop my title—I understand per-

fectly, but I liked one letter written 'dear old chap'
immensely. Next, *do* make use of our funny semi-
occupied house in London. My wife has written, I know
—but what I want you to understand is the *real pleasure*
you'd give us both by staying there. . . .[1]

And in a postscript to a letter written a year
later—in reference to his arrangement that Mrs.
Wilson's first-class return passage to New Zealand
should be defrayed :

My message to Mrs. Wilson is that the people who
cannot distinguish between their rights and their privileges
are always delightful.

In July 1909, Scott having obtained from Shackleton the assurance that another effort in the Antarctic would be disconcerting no plan of his, proceeded vigorously with the preparations that he
had been provisionally negotiating for several
months ; and on September 16 sent Wilson a
telegram requesting him to organize and lead the
Scientific Staff of the Expedition to leave England
in June of the following year. It was a fateful
decision for Wilson to make, though from the first
his acceptance was almost a foregone conclusion.
The Grouse Disease Inquiry was well on the way
to its conclusion ; the results of his artificial in-
fection of grouse had proved, on July 12, to be
entirely satisfactory ; his collection of illustrations
for *British Mammals* now needed comparatively few
to complete it ; but he had still a long way to
go towards even half of his illustrations for *British
Birds*. On the editor's written assurance, however, that half only of these illustrations would
be required from him before the expedition started,

---

[1] See also *Captain Scott*, by Stephen Gwynn, p. 143.

as publication was not anticipated for four or five years, he felt, on the score of his work and with several months yet in hand to give to it, free to accept Scott's offer. Besides, he had left a job unfinished there that no one else could do.

On September 16 he wrote to his father :

Scott is a man worth working for as a man.—No one can say that it will only have been a Pole-hunt, though that of course is a *sine qua non*. We *must* get to the Pole ; but we shall get more too, and there will be no loopholes for error in means and methods if care in preparation can avoid them. I can promise you it is a work worth anyone's time and care and I feel it is really a great opportunity.

We want the Scientific work to make the bagging of the Pole merely an item in the results.

As regards his wife's contribution to the decision, it is best expressed in Sir A. E. Shipley's words (from the article quoted above) : ' With that heroism, and above all with that patience of waiting, which is so often the gift of great women, she acquiesced and aided in every way her husband's adventure on both his Antarctic voyages.'

From the day of his appointment to lead the Scientific Staff, to the day the *Terra Nova* sailed, he was literally working against time every day. ' My work is endless ; it seems as if I could not possibly get through it all, and yet bit by bit it gets done.' Apart from his labours to finish his work on Grouse Disease and *British Mammals* and *Birds*, he was now immersed in much of the business of the Expedition, and was consulted in almost every department of it besides his own : inspecting every scientific instrument ; calculating food values and their quantities for men and animals ;

consulting Peary and Borup on the subject of
depot-laying in the Arctic, and Mawson about
spheres of operations in the South. On December
19 he wrote from London to his father :

As an antidote to the pressure of business, I have quite
deliberately undertaken to sit absolutely still for four
hours on end for 3 or 4 days running. Soord, originally
a pupil of Herkomer, is painting my portrait for O.

The incident is mentioned, partly because the
portrait found a place in the Royal Academy Exhibition of 1910, and partly on account of his
strangely prophetic words in a letter to the artist :

I, too, learned a lot in our conversations. You have
done more good than to paint a picture which will be a
great comfort to my ' grass widow.' . . . My character
is weathered or ought to be as you have painted it, and
I pray God it may be increasingly to the end. It isn't
enough so yet, but it will be some day, and the more the
better, for ' here we have no abiding place and this is
not our rest ' are two lines from our book of instructions
which keep me moving on always. If you are hewn
down it will be for some better purpose than you could
fulfil by standing, and I shall envy you. Funny if I
go all the way to the South Pole to drop into a crevasse.
That will give you something to think about. What
good ? and why so far to so small a purpose ? Still
funnier if I am allowed back again, don't you think ?

He spent his last Christmas with his wife in
England, at Westal, when (says his father) he was
the gayest and liveliest of the party.

By the end of January his Staff was nearly complete. Its selection was a grave matter which had
given him much anxiety, and one of his greatest
regrets in regard to it was his necessary rejection,
on the ground of youth, of Julian Huxley, who
had applied for the post of biologist.

But the harder he worked the more work there seemed to do, and he kept falling asleep over his work. To prevent this he stood up to write or sketch, and it is significant that his sole Lenten resolve was ' never to go to bed before midnight.' The excessive pressure of his work led some of his old friends to imagine that he was neglecting them, and a letter from Dr. Fraser calling him to book for this drew from him the following reply :

I never forget you, nor do I ever forget your kindness to my wife when I was away. And I am going to hope that you will keep an eye on her health in my absence next trip to the South Pole—we start probably in August. But apart from all this, can it be the right and proper result of a happy marriage that one should become so wholly independent of all one's old friends and associates that one never makes time to write them a line to find out if they are alive or dead ? I don't know ; but it seems to have been the result in my case.

If I meet a friend or hear from one, I like, as much as anyone living, to feel that he is the same as when I last saw him. I like to take up the friendship where it was put down, and then no matter how long a blank intervenes I am contented with my wife : she is *all* my friends put together and all my relations. I often wonder why she has not been taken from me as good things so often are when they become the breath of one's very existence. . . .

I must come and see my Godson before I go South and am myself seen no more. Now, many people send their godchildren ridiculous rattles and gollywog dolls. I don't, because I know that Hugh Munroe will have everything he can possibly pull to pieces in that way. But I want now and again to deposit with you things that he will be glad to have when he grows up ; and it strikes me that a copy of the *South Polar Times* may serve as a connecting link between him and his Godfather some day, when it is possible he may be pleased to find

that he was godfathered by one of the people who was
fired in the South by the same enthusiasm that fired Dr.
Cook in the North !—let us hope with better regard of
the conventionalities and Truth.

A letter to his parents, dated May 18, indicates
the spirit with which he accepted the last adventure.

I am sure there is more for me to do when I come
back than I've done yet, and all the past has seemed to
be like an education for something more useful than as
an end in itself ; even the disappointments and the
apparent checks are all in their proper place and have
been first-rate schooling ; and even as long ago as the
Battersea days I felt that willing intention was everything
in this life, and not achievement. . . .
Well, it only means that free-will in the eyes of God
means the willingness to do one's best at whatever comes
in our way, however difficult it may seem ; but though
He does not like us to look back after putting our hands
to the plough, He often takes the plough away as soon
as He knows we mean to carry through. . . .

He found time before he sailed to visit his
brother-in-law Bernard Rendall's school at Cop-
thorne in Sussex, to thank the boys for their help
in providing a sledge for the Expedition and for
having contributed to the scientific instrument
fund. A window in the Chapel there has since
been erected to his memory. It is a small lancet,
bordered with the Rose of England and the Cross
of St. George suspended from the apex. In the
centre of the device is one of his sketches of Erebus
in stained glass and his motto ' Res non Verba,'
and at the base is the figure of Wilson kneeling
in prayer. Part of the inscription beneath the
window reads—

His body lies far away in the Antarctic,
but his name shall live for ever.

CHAPTER XIII

Whaling Expedition

There go the ships, and there is that Leviathan . . .
                                                —*Psalms.*

THE *Terra Nova* sailed from the East India Docks, where for some days Wilson had been aboard her at intervals packing gear, for Greenhithe on June 1, *en route* for Cardiff. Dr. Shipley had contrived a visit to her while in dock, after which he wrote to Wilson the following humorous farewell :

> Christ's College,
> Cambridge,
> *27 May, 1910.*

MY DEAR WILSON,—

I got down to the *Terra Nova* yesterday, and I am glad I have seen her. I shall be able to picture your life on board her much better than had I not gone.

I had, however, one tiresome experience. Someone had arranged, just outside the cabin door, a species of ' drop ' such as, I imagine, exists on a gallows. I had cautiously and rather shyly made my way down a steep ladder leading to the cabin, in search of some of the Officers, who at that hour were lunching.

For the fraction of a second they must have beheld, framed in the doorway, a stout, middle-aged gentleman, taking off a decent top-hat, and then suddenly, in the twinkling of an eye, one half of him disappeared and the other half lay, more or less at right angles to the former, prone on the ground. I had fortunately only put my right leg on the ' drop,' so that my right foot

186

alone was angling about in the dark and unexplored abyss for some sort of foothold. The rest of me was in some queer rectangular sort of way lying on the floor.

It must have been excessively funny to see. I think your people are perfectly splendid—they didn't even smile. They came and hauled me up and made me sit down, and comforted me with beer and bread. Fortunately, Bruce was there, whom I know, and he was able to explain to them who I was. I feel quite certain that after the way those men treated the half-disappearing stranger, that they are the right fellows to tackle any unexpected problem which may present itself.

I do not think I have done more damage to myself than bruising a lot of muscles, but it has made me dreadfully lame, and I am like the late Mrs. Finch—'gradually stiffening.'

I want you to regard me as a kind of 'Agent' for you in every way whilst you are away. Anything I can do I will. There'll be things you remember at Madeira you want, and some of them I can see to and send out by Scott.

Lovat desires a Meeting. With this infernal Tripos I am not sure I *can* come, but probably *shall* if only to see you again.

Yours ever,
A. E. SHIPLEY.

For three successive summers, while in Scotland, Wilson had promised himself a Whaling Expedition from the Shetlands. Now, however, he was determined to snatch a few days, come what might in the way of night vigils to make up for it later on, to fit it in somehow before the *Terra Nova* sailed. He had promised to read a paper before the Zoological Society on June 14, but gave it, with permission, to Ogilvie Grant to read instead. After three days' sketching of Grouse skins, another of writing and drawing the remainder of his *Mammals*, furiously packing up to the last minute, he boarded a night express from Cheltenham on May 31 : did business with his publishers in Edinburgh the next morning, and with Mr. Leslie the same day, and reached Aberdeen the same night.

For the first time for many months his Diary, a mere record of daily events, expands into several pages of graphic description, from which a few are taken, and they are fresh with a tang of the brine. He has much to tell of the herring-fishery, the types of steam-trawlers, drifters, and tugs, that ply their industry in these areas, the amount of harbour-dues exacted on their registered tonnage being determined by space, and not weight, of cargo : of the frustration of attempts to evade the regulations : of the method of fishing employed by each type of craft : the lighthouse watchers of Fair Isle : and, lastly, of a Dutchman he made friends with on the *St. Sunniva*, who described the hunting of a school of whales in the Faroes, and with whom he talked ' herrings and theosophy.'

Arrived at Kirkwall in the Orkneys on the night of June 1, ' just in time to get a view over the Cathedral, which I had seen three years before,' he was much impressed by a monument in the nave—

which I liked before and determined to sketch this time : a full-length figure of ' John Rae, M.D., LL.D., F.R.S., F.R.G.S., Arctic Explorer. Intrepid Discoverer of the fate of Sir John Franklin's last Expedition. Born 1813. Died 1893. Expeditions 1846–7 ; 1848–9 ; 1851–2 ; 1854–4. Erected by public subscription in 1895.' That is the whole inscription—and the man is a life-size figure lying asleep wrapped in a buffalo sleeping bag, with moccasins on and a gun and a book open by his side.

TERN.

The whole thing looked rather natural and nice, and although the 6*d.* guide-book claims credit from McLintock for John Rae, there is no suggestion of it in the monument itself. He was a member of the Hudson Bay Company and so was probably in a position to help a good deal ; and sleeps soundly in this little out-of-the-way beautiful Cathedral at Kirkwall—honoured by his own people and caring nothing about the rest. This is what the monument suggested to me in the darkening nave of Kirkwall Cathedral at about 10 p.m. that evening just before the verger turned me out.

The next day he met a future comrade, E. W. Nelson, biologist to the Expedition, ' who has known the Shetlands all his life and will one day own half of them ' ; talked with the lighthouse-keepers of Fair Isle ; and learnt of the breeding habits of the sea-birds on the cliffs, and the lore of the Shetland sheep. The next day he was driven over 36 miles of moorland to interview Mr. Lange, the Norwegian manager of the whaling station at Olna-firth, as to the prospects of finding a suitable whaling gunner to take to the Antarctic. On June 4 he boarded the steam whaler *Haldane* of the Queen Alexandra Whaling Company—

and the first day was an experience I shall not soon forget. The motion of that whaler all day was the worst I have ever experienced. I lay down in my bunk in the afternoon during intervals when I hung my head over a save-all, wishing devoutly or otherwise that it would drop off and stay there. The blessed boat lay first on one side then on the other, then moved like a screw and with a jerk came round to try a reverse—and generally made me feel sick unto death. But joy came at Baltasound, where I crawled up on deck to breathe air instead of concentrated Chief Engineer and whale oil which alone filled the space below.
[To his wife]—Close to my bunk over the propeller was the door of the Chief Engineer's cabin—a perfectly hugely

fat pendulous mass, who always came down the gangway backwards and squeezed into his cabin door sideways, at once shutting himself in tight and going to sleep in his bunk in his overalls. I can assure you the heavy reek of whale oil which came out with him every time he awoke and squeezed out, with the admixture of shag smoke, was not a ' smell ' nor a ' pervading atmosphere ' —it was a heavy *presence* far and far more stiff than the large bag of jelly-like material which, with two blue, sad, dreamy-looking eyes and a tiny fish's mouth, composed the Chief Engineer. . . .

I wasn't sure I could go on . . . but I was glad I kept it to myself. . . . The sea is a most wonderful reviver, and the North Sea is exceptionally lively in that respect. I slept all night, my bunk being right aft, and when I awoke and got up I knew I was over my sickness. There was still any amount of motion. The Whalers are awful for motion, they say ; they go too fast for their size and are totally unaccommodating. They run so low in and through the waves that the deck is always awash from amidships aft—often sweeping to one's knees, so I was glad I had my sea-boots. The meals are in a small deck-house which is the galley and dining-saloon in one —*just* room for four men to squeeze in and eat close-packed. . . . Fish-pudding—the only thing I couldn't stick. I tried it, as it was kept overnight for me as a treat for breakfast ; but if you can imagine starting the day, having been sick the whole day previously, with ice-cold blancmange strongly flavoured with some faint white fish which had sufficiently altered in keeping to have produced bubbles all through like Gruyère cheese —cold, soft, white, fishy, and with complete absence of subsistence of any kind—no, I couldn't do it . . . black pipes of shag smoking indiscriminately before and after during the meals, and all the fat greasing steam of the galley crowding into that hot little box of which the door and the only port-hole were tight shut. And I tell you I thought I should never survive it on Friday —but on Sunday I positively revelled in it all, and could have enjoyed it twice as bad.

[From his Journal]—Henriksen and I went on shore together and up to the Post Office and then to the one Hotel, which was kept by an old whaling skipper. On the way we had the good fortune to find two whaling boats hauled up on the beach, one of which had all the equipment for Bottlenose Whale-fishing. Henriksen showed me exactly in this boat how all the men and lines and harpoons and guns were to be arranged, and I picked up many points which I couldn't have learned otherwise. . . .

I turned in early, and the whaler started out again in a N.E.^{ly} direction at about 2 a.m. on Sunday morning, as the wind had dropped and the weather promised to be better. When I turned out in the morning we had got over the 50 miles limit from the coast, and had sighted whales, and the chase began. It was a most awfully interesting and exciting show.

[To his wife]—I know nothing more suggestive of the bold, rather brutal, self-confident and a little boastful daring of the Viking spirit than the assurance of this first-rate and exceptionally successful and intelligent whaling captain. Sober, strong, alive in every look and movement, genial, and completely careless of cold, wet, difficulty, danger, or of risk, this man was now with a Captain's Certificate—a self-made expert from a start as cabin-boy ; despising drink and drunkards as fools, he allowed no spirits on the ship ; contemptuous of greed, alive to business, keen for wealth but only for its bigger opportunities, this young Viking of 33 years old has already lost four ships, has tramped the oceans from end to end as a whaling skipper, and has seen and killed every whale of the two hemispheres except the now rare Right Whale of the Greenland Ice and the unknown whales of the Antarctic. Five years whaling with Japanese in the Pacific, Corean seas and California ; Bottlenose whaling in Iceland and Spitzbergen—Spermfinner, Humpback, Blue Whale, Atlantic Right Whale, Devil fish, Killer, and a host of others have fallen to his gun, and I saw him take three shots at three large Seivhal in the North Sea that Sunday and kill every one unfailingly. The slow, lazy, deliberate security of these whales, their comfortable systematic rise with obese and breathless blow of immense size and volume, is what strikes me most on a close acquaintance with these huge bovine sea monsters. Their confidence and the blunder that eventually brings them up to blow within range of this infernal gun, and the quick mind which forsees their movements and continually heads them off—two solid hours we followed the first whale before we shot him. ' I tink I know vhat dat vhal will tink—dat chap—he tink, ven I go down, I go dis way— ja—den I tink, ja, dis way ; den I tink again, dat vhal he go dis vay, but den he go dis vay, 'gain I tink— so I go not dis vay, but dat vay—so—dat feller he come and blow, an' I shoot—ja. Often I tink I know vat dat vhal tink in my het.'

[From his Journal]—Henriksen was on the firing platform in the bows with the heavy gun loaded ; the harpoon and forerunner and line and everything all in place—and then appeared the whales. There were two of them swimming together and blowing every now and again a cloud of spray. We constantly saw their broad heads appear and the blow-holes open and close—they were a dull brown colour and had a dorsal fin. They showed but little of the body above water, a characteristic of the species they represented, which was Balaenoptera borealis, the Northern Rorqual, or, as the Norwegians call it, the Seivhal. No one can tell whether the whale will go straight on or turn right or left below the water—no one but the whaler—and he will often catch the whale's next blow by moving exactly in the (apparently) wrong direction, which he somehow felt was coming, so he gets his shot. And the shot—an immense explosion like the bursting of a gun—a cloud of black smoke, a huge hurtling half-ton of iron harpoon, a ridiculous wriggling rope rising suddenly upwards into coils and a smother of cotton waste ; and as the air clears, a column of white smoke like a smoke-stack rises from the huge harpoon hole in the whale's back for a few seconds, a number of convulsive blows, a gush of blood reddening the sea water, a flipper swung out, another blow, and the whole of the vast brown beast's head comes vertically out of the water to look round ; another blow, and another, and another, and an attempt to swim away on the surface without sinking, and the blows the while more and more occasionally superficial, but blowing up solid water instead of spray—and eventually he sinks.

Out runs the line with its turns round the massive

winch—out and out it runs till the whale finds bottom
or ceases to sink. Then a seaman runs up the foremast,
hitches the line into blocks by which the huge strain is
broken on strong springs in the body of the hold, and
then heave up on the steam winch until the whale
appears under the bows. If it is not quite dead a cry
soon warns the man at the engine, who slacks out a bit,
and with a 20-feet hand lance the whale is then pierced
by hand through the heart or lungs to prevent damage
to the ship by any action of the immense tail flukes in
the dying flurry. These flukes are appalling in their
immensity and strength, 12 feet from tip to tip, and to
be used with the whole bulky strength of the whole
whale's back and body—should the beast but know and
wish to sink the ship. But it is generally too far gone.
The tail is now caught in a line, and so a minute later
in a chain cable and shackled—the flukes cut off—and
then a hollow iron pipe with a lance head driven into
the body of the whale, and air pumped in by a pipe of
rubber tubing till the whale floats high out of water.
Remove the pipe, plug the hole with waste, and the big
beast floats belly up along the length of the ship's side,
secured to the ship by the chain cable only round its
tail ; and so reload the gun with a new charge of powder
—400 grams—a new detonator, a new harpoon, with a
new explosive cast-iron head, the whole huge piece of
metal to be fired weighing just as much as two men can
lift and carry.

The hollow cast-iron point of 10 or 15 lbs. was full of
powder, and this was exploded and shattered by a time
fuse fired by the shock of firing by means of a detonator
at the junction with the harpoon shafts close to the barbs.
The barbs are thus released at the same moment and
the whale is killed. Meanwhile we had sighted other
whales blowing, and now we made for them towing our
first alongside. This time I stood on the bridge well
back and saw the harpoon fly out with its forerunner in
coils, strike the whale through the upper ribs, to be lost
in a hole which then showed only the rope coming out
—and at once a column of smoke issued from the hole
showing that the shell had burst and done its work : a
few blows, high at first and infrequent but rapidly in-

creasing in frequency and decreasing in force—while the
poor beast slowly flapped its fins on the surface and
lazily, as it appeared, wallowed there, unable to swim
away or to sink, until at last the blows died down and
then the dead whale sank.

A page is here devoted to a description of the
colour, shape and height of the blows of the following : Blue Whale, Finner, Northern Rorqual,
Humpback, Lesser Rorqual, Atlantic Right Whale,
Greenland Right Whale.

The third whale which we killed was also a Northern
Rorqual and it was killed dead almost instanteously.
After this we spent an hour or two chasing another
couple and several times came almost within range, yet
Henriksen would not fire. The patience of this man
was quite extraordinary, and it accounts for the fact
that a miss is almost unknown. Unless the whale is
within range and in a position to be hit in such a way
as to be probably killed, the gun is not fired.

[To his wife]—It is a great and thrilling sport, no more
cruel in proportion than is the shooting of a stag and far
more merciful, since the very magnitude of the weapon and
the terrific shock produces frequently an instantaneous
death. The dead or dying whale just turns over and
wallows a minute or two in its unconscious agony, the
spine as often as not is shattered and all sensation lost
below. If sport can be not cruel then whaling can be
not cruel. I don't know.

The sea remaining too rough to attempt to tow
a fourth whale with safety, they made for port
some 70 miles away, at 3–4 knots, reaching Olna-
firth on the morning of Monday, June 6, the whole
of which day he spent in ' collecting details of the
business.'

On the return voyage from the Orkneys to
Aberdeen he was favoured on June 8 with a very
rare spectacle.

About 4 o'clock this afternoon I had been packing my bags below on the *St. Giles*, and then casually strolled on deck and looked over the bows, and saw four or five small whales right ahead, coming up and going down a long way off; but sure enough we bore down on them, and then they saw the ship and came straight to her, and turned and came along with us under the bows for about a quarter of an hour—and I recognized them as white-nosed Dolphins—there wasn't even a ripple in the clear water to distort them : it was wonderful : and am I not lucky, or isn't God good in giving one unexpected treats like that just for fun? You remember on my last trip I saw the ca'aing whales disporting as I have illustrated them in the Mammal book—I do think it's so wonderful being shown these things. Why did I come up at that moment?—taken by the scruff of the neck by an invisible angel and told off to see what very few people in the world have seen—this particular dolphin alive in the sea, and at the same time with knowledge of dolphins sufficient to recognize it.

He returned by the same route without delay, transacted more business at Aberdeen and Edinburgh, caught a night express again, and reached Cheltenham on the morning of the 10th.

We have had work to get all done [he wrote], but thanks to O. who has worked like a solid brick as she is, it has been done. I couldn't have done it without her. She has had no holiday, as I had in the Shetlands. On the contrary she has had very heavy packing to do in London in very great heat, without me to help her. She then got ready and packed up all my clothes for the whole voyage as well as for the ports of call and the Antarctic. I left all to her and she managed it all wonderfully. Then when I came home I had to work late every night, and she would not be sent to bed until I was near to coming also. We were both tired out and dreadfully short of sleep, but I remember these last days with her as days of the most perfect companionship I have ever known.

Up at 6 o'clock on the 13th, they caught the early express to London, he writing hard the whole journey at his promised paper on plumage changes for the Zoological Society; 'squared off *British Mammals*' with Barrett Hamilton; arranged for the transport of the Expedition's whaling gear to Cardiff; purchased his own scientific instruments; made his farewells to friends; and wrote at his Grouse papers on the journey home, which he reached at 2 a.m. Still at Grouse work the whole of the next day, they caught a late train for Cardiff.

It was about 4 p.m. the next day when we parted— full of good hope for our next meeting at the Cape. Nelson lent me his glasses for a last look; and then O. and I looked forward instead of back. I plumped hard at once into shifting cases until too dark, and then to bed.

A month later Mrs. Wilson received the following letter :

MRS. DR. E. A. WILSON,—

I will in fjo words send to you, end your Husbond Dr. Wilson, my hartliest many tanks for the nise present of a teleskope you senth to my. I am verry glad to have a membry after the Whaling trip Dr. Wilson doi wit my. I hope he vil kome back from the Sout Pol soun the first man to have ben ther. I have just sendth a lether to him to N.Z. hoping he will receiv it. I have ben verry lokki this cisun, caugt 33 Whales end one Richt Whale. I wil send soun enother lether to the Dr. and tel him my best. Pleas send him from my, my bedst and hartliest tanks for all.

Yours faithfully,
ERIC HENRIKSEN,
Master of Wales, Haldane, Sjetland.

CHAPTER XIV

The Last Expedition

THE VOYAGE OUT

I would not take life but on terms of death,
That sting in the wine of being, salt of its feast.
O death, thou hast a beckon to the brave—
Thou last sea of the navigator, last
Plunge of the diver, and last hunter's leap !
                              STEPHEN PHILLIPS (*Ulysses*).

THE literature on the subject of Scott's
Last Expedition is considerable. His own
Journal as it stands unrevised in the first
volume, with the various minor reports that form
the subject of the second, is the highest monument to that heroic endeavour, and a permanent
source of moral stimulus and inspiration to the
race ; Lieutenant Evans's *South with Scott*, Mr.
Ponting's *The Great White South*, Professor Griffith
Taylor's *With Scott—The Silver Lining*, Mr. Priestley's
Antarctic Adventure, Dr. Levick's *Antarctic Penguins*,
are each in their way valuable contributions ;
while finally Mr. Cherry-Garrard's *The Worst
Journey in the World*, the completest record of the
Expedition from start to finish, is a classic of
Antarctic literature.

The scientific objects of the Expedition have
been briefly outlined in Sir Clements Markham's
Introduction to *Scott's Journal*, where he pointed

out that never before (and it might with equal
truth be added—or since) had a fuller complement
of trained scientists composed the staff of a Polar Expedition. Indeed one may wonder if ever before had
a collection of men of such calibre, mental, moral
and physical, been gathered together into one place.

The first Expedition had been launched as a great
national enterprise with the aid of a large national
subsidy, backed by the generosity of a few indi-
viduals, so that expenditure for its needs was un-
stinted. But the way had thus been opened for
other explorers, foreign as well as British, who had
followed or were contemplating similar enterprises,
and the possibilities of the Antarctic had come in
a sense to be exploited, so that by the time Scott's
last Expedition was ready the first flush of public
enthusiasm had already somewhat waned. His
last Expedition therefore was launched on a much
more modest scale than his first had been, with
considerably less financial support, so that its
provision and equipment called for the strictest
economy. ' The *Discovery*,' wrote Wilson, ' was a
palace compared to the *Terra Nova*.' But the
members of the Staff, though they fared more
frugally and worked more strenuously on the
voyage out, did so even more happily, in spite of
acting as navvies and stevedores.

Wilson's responsible position gave him at once a
prominence he would have been glad to avoid, but
his obvious capacity to fill it ensured for him the
confidence of every soul on board : a confidence
conferred at once and by all, not gained point by
point as on the *Discovery*, and one that grew deeper
and deeper with the experience of all who gave it.

Even his own unstudied Journal is an unconscious
testimony to the affection in which they held him.

June 16. Slept soundly—no sea-sickness. Got to filthy
work right off, shifting cases and hunting for my gear
which had got buried in every part of the ship. Cherry-
Garrard was invaluable, as he had kept an eye on the
whereabouts of everything that had been sent to the
Docks. Several of the ' After-Guard,' i.e. the Wardroom
mess of officers and scientific staff, were very sea-sick,
but nearly all stuck to their work. . . .
  Sea-sick people are not always careful about making
gear safe against motion, and one is unwittingly tired
out by the fatigue of unwonted exercise in trying to
keep balanced from morning till night and from night
till morning. . . .
  Generally I am in bed by 10 p.m., and am called
regularly before midnight to a huge mug of thick cocoa,
just to help me to go to sleep again. Nelson or Gran
always make this. They all declare that nothing wakes
me now like a spoon being stirred in a mug ; and I
must confess it has a better chance than any alarum
clock, and is much more fattening ![1]

Amongst his mails at Madeira was a long letter
from Ogilvie Grant, who had read his paper before
the Zoological Society, ' and agreed with it all
except on one point where I unwittingly upheld
Millais against Grant. But as a matter of fact I
believe Millais is right ! '[2]

[At Madeira]— . . . Titus Oates, Atkinson, and Lillie
insisted on carrying my gear ashore to a café, where I
worked at Grouse from early morning till 2.30 a.m.,

---

[1] In the Antarctic midwinter, be it added, a cup of cocoa
was not considered by him of the right consistency unless a
spoon could stand up in it !
[2] Wilson's point was that the change in plumage of ptarmigan in winter is not due to protective colouring, but to
loss of energy, and so of heat.

and was up at 6 next morning, having slept 7 hours in
48, and I fear that some of my 25 letters may read like
it too, for I was latterly quite unable to keep awake for
more than a line or two at a time. . . . I slept with
Cherry-Garrard on the ice-house, where 5 hours' sleep
is more good than 8 below : and from now onwards
life became sheer enjoyment, with plenty of air, food,
and exercise in a routine. I feel myself putting on flesh
every day and am as fit as can be. . . . After breakfast there is a call for volunteers for the coal-trimming—
transferring coal from the main hold to the 2 bunkers
—from 9 to 12, and 1 to 4, and we take it in 3-hourly
spells. In ten minutes we are streaming with sweat and
as black as Kaffirs. The air in the hold is always tested
first to be sure it is breathable. . . .

In the intervals of coal-trimming he was working at sledge-rations for the forthcoming depot
journey with Campbell and Evans in the wardroom. On one of these occasions when there was
an alarm of fire in the hold, Wilson was the first
on the spot to extinguish it.

Stoking in the Tropics was even more arduous.

. . . While shovelling in coal one gets stung by ' stoke-
hold flies '—they are drops of hot oil from the engines
above and catch one in the back of the neck as one stoops
to shovel. . . . If between whiles one finds a minute
to lean up against or sit back upon a stationary part
of the engines it either scalds or burns one. I think
that three hours of this at 4 a.m. on a cup of cocoa only,
is the hardest work I have ever put myself to. Perhaps
the most trying part of it is the continuous noise—a
clanging and clatter of iron and a roar from the furnace
and the engines all round and above one.

July 11. Several of the cabins have now got names :
one is the Rogue's Retreat, another the Abode of Love,
and yet a third is the Wine-bin. We have also quite a
number of nicknames. Pennell is ' Penelope,' Rennick is
' Parny,' ' Birdie ' Bowers, ' Max ' and ' Climax ' are the
inseparable Atkinson and Titus Oates ; Levick is ' Toffer-

ino,' otherwise known as the 'Old Sport'; and Nelson
is 'Marie Ducat' or 'Antonio the Immaculate'—he
wears always a clean collar at dinner-time; Simpson is
'Sunny Jim'; Cherry-Garrard is, of course, 'Cherry' or
'The Cheery One'; and Wright is the 'Julius Verne';
while Lillie is commonly spoken of as 'Hercules.' As
I am the oldest of the party at present on board, I am
generally known as 'Uncle Bill.'

July 16. [His wedding day.] I was up at 4.30 this
morning as usual before any sign of sunrise, and then
the sun rose and I tried to sketch it, but this must be a
special one for you if only I can make it worthy of you.

July 24. My birthday was celebrated last night between 12 and 1, when Evans, Rennick and Birdie Bowers
came and danced and sang on the main hatch dog
kennel—and turned everybody out of bed to come and
wish me many happy returns of the day as I slept in my
bag on the top of the ice-house. This was done to make
up for having forgotten to celebrate the event at dinner.
I was glad that no one minded being turned out for such
a purpose, but I saved some of them by going round myself; happily, everyone is overflowing with good nature.

On the 26th they made South Trinidad.
Accounts of this second exploration of the island
have been given so graphically in the diaries of
Bowers and of Cherry-Garrard in the *Worst Journey*,
that it requires no further expansion from Wilson's
Journal. He has a special note on the identity of
the Trinidad Petrel—

which has two phases, a black and a light one. This
bird has been given no less than three specific names,
but I am sure they all interbreed and are really the
same species. Besides being called Æstrelata trinitati, it
is also called Æ. arminjoniana and Æ. Wilsoni after me;
but we found every phase together—nesting along the
cliff-ledges, dark and pale, young and old. . . . They
made a most delightful noise between the drumming of a
snipe and the bubbling note of a cuckoo, arranged rather
like the spring song of the common sandpiper.

In the perilous attempts to embark on the boats in a tremendous swell he lost his watch and aneroid, his Goertz field-glasses and heavy nailed boots, but happily not the chronometer (given him by the Duchess of Bedford)—

yet the whole show was very excellent sport and quite worth the cost. I regretted most of all that the large collection of birds we shot there having been dragged through salt water made only very second-rate skins. This was especially regrettable on account of the doubt concerning the specific positions of the petrels. . . . Cherry-Garrard was so keen to save them too that he continued skinning all night till breakfast.

From now till arrival at the Cape he gave up his early morning sunrise sketches to write up the arrears of his Grouse reports at an improvised desk (a wash-stand and a suit-case) in a corner of a lumber-cabin—

purposely standing, as I invariably fall asleep at once if I sit down. Work under these conditions is awkward. The cabin is minute and full of gear—no table or room to spread papers—very little light and less air—and a heavy roll which spills one's balanced papers on to a wet and greasy floor. It will be a miracle if what I am now writing is acceptable to the Committee, for I feel as though I had left the Grouse work behind me years ago. Still it has to be finished and sent home from the Cape. Then adieu, with every pleasure.

Aug. 11. This evening we had a tremendous scrap. Campbell, C.-G. and I held the Nursery which has two doors against the rest of the Wardroom. It lasted an hour or two, and half of us were nearly naked towards the finish, having had our clothes torn off our backs— all in excellent fun and splendid exercise.

I doubt if a class of Ladies' College girls could be more unselfish in looking after each other's interests than we are on the ship, even if they were all preparing for confirmation. The way in which every one fights for

the worst jobs is really amusing. The pump is really
hard work four times a day, and the competition for it
is ridiculous. . . .

Evans is the most boisterously good-tempered individual imaginable. I never knew anyone so per-
sistently high-spirited, and we are all infected with his
noisy good-nature. But almost every one of the Wardroom mess has some exceptional qualities, mental, moral,
or physical, or all three. . . . Bowers, whom you will
remember by sight, a short red-headed thick-set little
man with a very large nose, is a perfect marvel of
efficiency—but in addition to this he has the most unselfish character I have ever seen in a man anywhere.
Of the naval men the oldest is Campbell (3 years younger
than myself)—he is a delightful man, pleasant and
sensible, and rather quieter than most of the others. I
should have liked to have him (to be with our party),
or Pennell who will return with the ship. I wish with
all my heart that Pennell was not booked for the ships'
cruise, for he would make an excellent companion for
the hut. He is at work as a rule from 4 a.m. until past
10 p.m. and yet I have never known him sleep in the
afternoons. He gets through a perfectly extraordinary
amount of work every day—always cheerful and genial
and busy, but never too busy to talk birds and to be
interested in other work than his own. He is wonderful
in the way he picks up new things and in the accuracy
with which he tackles them. Rennick will prove a
splendid man for the whole show—he can't say a word
without putting it in the driest, funniest way : a born
humorist, and his humour is of the kindliest. Nelson is
even better than I thought, and a favourite with everyone. So is Atkinson, very quiet still, but most reliable—
as good as anyone we could have got. Oates is extraordinarily silent and laconic, but works all day at painting,
hauling—any heavy work, and the dogs.

On August 15 they made Simonstown Harbour,
where Mrs. Wilson and Mrs. Evans met the ship.
Here Wilson successfully completed and dispatched
all his Grouse work, a great load off his mind at

last. Four days later they were joined by Captain and Mrs. Scott (who had been with the Governor at Pretoria). He surprised them by a change of plan. This was that he should take on the ship to New Zealand, and that Wilson should proceed with the ladies by liner to Melbourne to select a third geologist and also to undertake a diplomatic mission to Sydney in connection with a grant from the Federal Government towards the Expedition. This latter was not at all in Wilson's line, and he regretted losing the fun of the voyage on the *Terra Nova*, but the chance of his wife's company made up for all. He left the observations of birds to the quick eyes of Pennell, comparing them later with his own observations 7° North.

His Journal while in Cape Colony is taken up chiefly with botanical notes of great interest : and most notably his account of a visit to the whaling station in Saldanha Bay, where he obtained much valuable information supplementary to his knowledge gained in the North. His mission to the Australian Government was performed with conspicuous success, though its end was achieved without diplomacy or ' finesse,' but simple and direct statements of fact to the authorities concerned. With considerable relief he handed ' the business reins ' over to Scott again on October 13, and for the voyage to New Zealand they again, also to his great relief, changed places.

A month in Lyttelton was passed in a continual whirl of social functions, further State interviews, and much business with the Expedition's personnel : and husband and wife saw too little of each other,

and less still of their many good friends in New
Zealand, before they joined the ship at Port
Chalmers on November 28.

Yet we have really had a very great deal of real happiness together up to the very last, and the people we
have most of all to thank are the Bowens, who allowed
us to live at Middleton the whole of our long stay exactly
as though it was our home, even when we left for
Wellington and stayed with Bishop Wallis and his wife
there.   And the Kinseys—they are dear good friends both
to the Expedition and even more to us. . . .   Lady
Bowen was actually up to see us off at 7, which was a
sad thing to remember too, for I don't think the dear
old lady was a bit happy over it, and I was made to
promise to come straight there first upon our arrival
back, a promise I was only too pleased to make.   And
after the Bowens, to the Wigrams on our return—they
are all too good and kind to us, every one.

Before sailing he found time for a last letter to
his friend Dr. Fraser :

Christchurch, N.Z., *Nov. 27, '10.*
MY DEAR OLD BOY JOHN,—
In two days from now we shall be away for the South.
This short line is to assure you that my thoughts often
fly back to you as my most faithful friend John, the
same old John of old days at the Corner, notwithstanding
the way I have treated you and the few times I have
written to you or fulfilled my promises to come and see
you.   My dear old boy, I shall often remember you,
and your kind wife and the Godson—whose welfare I
have and always shall have much at heart.   I hope he
will grow up as honest as his Father—and then he isn't
far wrong.   Everything to do with the Expedition is first
rate, and I have never been thrown with a nicer lot
of men, and some are perfect treasures.   We have indeed been most fortunate.   My wife too is fit and well
and is so much stronger for the trial than she was
nine years ago.   Keep an eye open for her, John ; she
will be back in England somewhere about Feb. or March

1911, and she will like to get a line of welcome from an old and reliable friend like yourself. My love to you all.

An impression of the effect of his personality at this stage is given by the young geologist who had joined the Staff in New Zealand (Mr. Frank Debenham, now Professor of Geography and Director of the Scott Polar Research Institute at Cambridge), in the *Caian* in 1913.

Imagine a small queer-shaped ship alongside a quay which is thronged with people. The clean white crow's nest on the mainmast and the new gilt ' *TERRA NOVA R.Y.S.*' give her purpose and title. . . .
At the stern are gathered most of the officers, dressed for the last time for many months in gold-laced uniforms, awaiting the arrival of the Bishop for the parting service. Someone among them suddenly says ' There's Bill,' and immediately a chorus of ' Come on, Uncle,' ' You're late, Bill,' and ' Shake your long legs, Director,' draws attention to a tall, grave-looking man coming through the crowd. The chorus and the answering smile revealed more than many words could do the perfect understanding that already existed between the Chief of the Scientific Staff and his subordinates, an understanding that did more than anything else to promote and sustain the harmony which will always remain one of the chief features of Captain Scott's Last Expedition.

Among those who watched the ship from the quay was the Editor of a New Zealand newspaper, who had made the acquaintance of all the officers. When news of the Expedition's achievement reached New Zealand eighteen months later he wrote, ' All were great, but I am sure that the greatest figure of all was my gentle friend, Wilson.'

Next day [Wilson wrote] we were boisterously and very cheerily seen off, and O. was with us on board to the last, and there on the bridge I saw her disappear out of sight waving happily a good-bye that will be with me till I see her again in this world or the next. I think it will be in this world and some time in 1912.

Thus, with a high heart and good hope, he sailed South.

From this point onward Scott's Last Expedition becomes the story of a succession of adverse circumstances in which—' It looks as though fortune is determined to put every difficulty in our path.' The Expedition came near to being utterly wrecked almost immediately it was launched. Setting sail from Port Chalmers on November 29, the *Terra Nova* ran on the second day out into one of the worst storms a ship could live through. The *Discovery* had been laden to an extent at which no company would insure her, but the *Terra Nova* was far more heavily laden still. The risk of overloading the ship (especially with coal) was a legitimate risk that had to be taken, and nothing but the human spirit strung to the highest pitch of courage and endurance kept her afloat. Only when the hurricane had been weathered Scott allowed himself the comment, ' It was touch and go.'

To quote Wilson's detailed account of it is not possible here, but it has three descriptive touches which unconsciously reflect the man.

Dec. 1. I must say I enjoyed it all from beginning to end, and as one bunk became untenable after another owing to the wet, and the comments became more and more to the point as people searched out dry spots here and there to finish the night in oilskins and great-coat on the cabin or ward-room floors, I thought things were becoming interesting. . . . Then dawn came and with it things began to go wrong again all at once.

. . . Some of the staff were like dead men with sea-sickness. I have no sea-sickness on these ships myself under any conditions, so I enjoyed it all. And as I have the run of the bridge and can ask as many questions as I choose I knew all that was going on.

There came the choking of the pumps and the forlorn attempt to bail out the ship with buckets.

Dec. 2. It was a weird night's work with the howling gale and the darkness and the immense sea running over the ship every few minutes, and no engines and no sail, and we all in the engine-room black as ink, singing chanties as we passed slopping buckets full of bilge, each man above slopping a little over the heads of all of us below him; wet through to the skin, so much so that some of the party worked altogether naked like Chinese coolies ; and the rush of the wave backwards and forwards at the bottom grew hourly less in the dim light of a couple of engine-room oil-lamps whose light just made the darkness visible—the ship all the time rolling like a sodden lifeless log, her lee gunwale under water every time.

And when the outlook appeared as grim as it could be, a surprising observation shows the man of action for a moment lost in the visionary.

. . . Just about the time when things looked their very worst—the sky was like ink and water was every-where and everyone was as wet inside their oilskins as the skins were wet without—there came out a most per-fect and brilliant rainbow for about half a minute or less and then suddenly and completely went out. If ever there was a moment when such a message was a comfort it was just then : it seemed to remove every shadow of doubt not only as to the present but as to the final issue of the whole expedition. And from that moment matters mended, and everything came all right.

But what his Journal leaves untold, namely his own personal bearing and example in this peril, is finely suggested in the words of one who watched and worked with him. Professor Debenham continues the story :

The same small ship in a howling gale, hove to under all but bare poles, heavy in the water and wellnigh foundering. On the decks a wet confusion of half-drowned dogs, loose cases and labouring men ; the lee bulwarks awash and a bleak desolation of wind-whipped sea all round. Grave faces in the ward-room, talk of provisioning the boats, heavy work in the engine-room bailing with buckets—and readiest, if possible, for the hard work, calmest in counsel, and hopefulest in outlook, is the same tall, grave-looking man with the kindly smile. And one realized as one toiled beside him that there was a man who knew no fear, in whom there was some mysterious force that triumphed, some faith that upheld. A faith that could read in the momentary rainbow at the height of the storm that only he had eyes to see, the hope or rather the assurance that all was to be well.

And afterwards on the ship as she steadily ' chunked ' across those stormy seas one was more and more aware of the same tall figure constantly at work, yet never too busy to lend a hand aloft with the sails or below trimming coal. A favourite place was on the stern grating, where one might see him seated for hours, with binoculars slung round his neck, now searching the waves to identify the long smooth back and small jet of steam that are the only visible signs of ' Whale,' now catching in a few inspired strokes of his pencil that peculiar curve of the albatross's wing as he rockets across the stern. Bad weather sees him at work in the captain's cabin with pen and brush, amplifying his hasty field sketches. That is his own work—but what of the work he did for others ? Perhaps the charm of it was that it was rarely apparent, and each member of the staff knew only for himself for how much of his inspiration and for how much of his data he had to thank Dr. Wilson's keen eyes and ready help. The phrase ' Ask Uncle Bill ' was like to become a wardroom byword.

In the days that followed the gale, discussions as to a possible landing at Cape Crozier were frequent between Scott and Wilson, and Wilson made his sketch of it from memory, which is here reproduced, at the same time setting forth its advantages as a winter-quarters : close to the Barrier surface ; in an enormous rookery of Adélie Penguins, and only three miles from the Emperors ; sheltered from heavy winds, and entirely so from the southerly blizzards, though only by a bare half-mile ; Hut Point and Cape Royds easily accessible ; on the shore of Ross Sea, with the advantage of noting movements of the sea-ice in winter, never watched before ; seals all along the coast ; new points to be examined—parasitic volcanic cones, raised beaches, old moraines, erratic boulders, old remnants of glaciers, new glaciers from Terror and névé slopes ; finally, the movement of the Barrier itself so gaugeable at its junction with the Cape where it raises a tortuous mass of pressure ridges, and yet leaves a clear hard roadway along the border of the Island to the South. From all points of view its advantages as a winter-quarters seemed obvious.

On December 9 they entered the pack.

At 7 a.m. we ran into loose streams of broken pack-ice at last, little thinking at the time that what we had been looking for so eagerly we should be jolly glad to see the last of in 3 weeks' time . . . the soft seething noise of moving ice and an occasional bump and grating along the ship's side gave one a feeling of old times.

For Scott the prolonged struggle through the pack called for as much fortitude as the fight through the storm. Perhaps nothing he ever wrote is more revealing of the man than these pages of his *Journal*, so eloquent of the vicissitudes

SKETCH-MAP OF CAPE CROZIER
(looking south)

of life's pilgrimage that one wonders if the writer were conscious of the parallel. ' It is certainly a case,' he wrote, ' of fighting our way South.'

But these long days gave to Wilson the opportunity of studying the infinite wonder of the life of the pack—from whales to minute crustaceans— and they were record days not only for marine observation, but also for sketching the pure and pale glories of the ice. To his less busy companions it was a holiday in fairyland.

Now and again one hears a Penguin cry out in the stillness near at hand or far away, and then perhaps he appears in his dress tail coat and white waistcoat suddenly upon an ice-floe from the water, and catching sight of the ship runs curiously towards her, crying out in his amazement as he comes, from time to time, but only intensifying the wonderful stillness and beauty of the whole fairy-like scene as the golden glaring sun in the South just touches the horizon and begins again to rise gradually without ever having set at all. We have now broad daylight night and day, but the beauty of the day with its lovely blues and greens amongst the bergs and ice-floes is eclipsed altogether by the marvellous beauty of the midnight, when white ice becomes deepest purple and golden rose and the sky is lemon green without a cloud. No scene in the whole world was ever more beautiful than a clear midnight in the pack.

On New Year's Eve they sighted land.

A magnificent view of the Admiralty Range with the wonderful peak of Mount Sabine on our starboard beam at midnight, 120 miles away. I went up last thing into the Crow's Nest and then turned in, to be awakened by a general midnight hurrah party and the steam syren with which the New Year was welcomed.

Jan. 2. Mt. Erebus came in sight and the double-topped knoll which overlooks the Emperor Penguins' Rookery Bay. We ought to be at Cape Crozier to-morrow, and everyone is keen to see the place where we expect to winter during the coming year, but there is a horrible swell rolling in from the N.E. which may make a landing there impossible, and we have expended so much coal that we cannot afford to wait. . . .

Here we brought the ship close in and then we lowered a boat in which were Capt. Scott, Campbell, myself, Cherry-Garrard, Titus Oates and Taylor. We were to examine the possibilities of landing, but the swell was so heavy in its break amongst the floating blocks of ice along the actual beach and ice-foot that a landing was out of the question. We should have broken up the boat and have all been in the water together. But I assure you it was tantalizing to me, for there, about 6 feet above us, on a small dirty piece of the old bay ice about 10 feet square, one living Emperor Penguin chick was standing disconsolately stranded, and close by it stood one faithful old Emperor Penguin parent asleep. This young Emperor was still in the down, a most interesting fact in the bird's life-history, at which we had rightly guessed, but which no one had actually observed before. It was however in a stage never yet seen or collected, for the wings were already quite clean of down and feathered as in the adult ; also a line down the breast and part of the head was shed of down. This bird would have been a treasure to me, but we couldn't risk life for it, so it had to remain there with its faithful parent asleep. It was a curious fact that with as much clean ice to live on as they could have wished for, these destitute derelicts of a flourishing colony now gone North on floating bay-ice should have preferred to remain standing on the only piece of bay-ice left—a piece about 10 feet square and now pressed up 6 feet above water-level ; evidently wondering why it was so long in starting North with the general exodus which must have taken place just a month ago. The whole incident was most interesting and full of suggestion as to the slow working of the brains of these queer people. Another point was most weird to see, namely, that on the *under* surface of this very dirty piece of sea-ice which was about 2 feet thick, and which hung over the water as a sort of cave, we could see the legs and lower halves of dead

Emperor chicks hanging through, and in one place even a dead adult. I hope to make a picture of the whole quaint incident, for it was a corner cram full of Imperial history in the light of what we already knew, and it would otherwise have been about as unintelligible as any group of animate and inanimate nature could possibly have been. As it is, it throws more light on the life-history of this strangely primitive bird.

We rowed round the bay trying at every likely spot for a landing, but without success : the swell was too heavy for us. We rowed all along under the overhanging cliffs of Cape Crozier close in to examine the beautiful arrangement of the unusually fine columnar basalt which formed the face all along the lower half of the cliffs. We were joking in the boat as we rowed under these cliffs and saying it would be a short-lived amusement to see the overhanging cliff part company and fall over us. So we were glad to find we were rowing back to the ship and already were two or three hundred yards from the place and in open water, when there was a noise like crackling thunder and a huge plunge into the sea, and a smother of rock dust like the smoke of an explosion, and we realized that the very thing had happened that we had just been talking of. . . . We could see the post which we put up ten years ago, and on it the two cylinders ; the lower one of which I attached myself when I was there in 1903. There was no pack-ice here, but there were several stranded bergs ; but alas, no shelter of any sort or kind from the swell which rolled straight in from the North-East and made our proposed landing here impossible, and the place as a winter quarters, admirable in every other respect and beyond every other place interesting, out of the question. . . .

Jan. 4. . . . These days are with one for all time— they are never to be forgotten—and they are to be found nowhere else in the world but at the poles. The peace of God which passes all understanding reigns here in these days. One only wishes one could bring a glimpse of it away with one with all its unimaginable beauty. . . .

[To his wife]—I simply love the Crow's Nest—my private chapel. I have spent the happiest times you can possibly imagine there . . . alone with God and with you . . . and

nothing above but the sky and snow-squalls, and nothing
below but the sea and miles of ice. I have an excellent reason
for being up there, for I am making pencil sketches, and no
one wonders why I am there so often, and the pull of the rope
always warns me when anyone is coming . . . I feel as
much at home there as in a church. It is not very warm in
a bitter wind, but as private as can be, and therefore a very
easy place to find you . . . and I just love it for my prayers
and daily reading with you.

He was in the Crow's Nest on Jan. 4 when he
was joined there by Captain Scott and Lieutenant
Evans for consultation as to an alternative site for
winter-quarters. Cape Royds and Cape Barne
were both isolated from the south by open water.
A decision was therefore made in favour of a cape
of moraine and rock called the 'Skuary' in
Discovery days, and now renamed Cape Evans.

SNOWY PETRELS.

CHAPTER XV

The Last Expedition (continued)

THE DEPOT JOURNEY

The eternal silence of the great white desert. Cloudy columns of snow-drift advancing from the south, pale yellow wraiths, heralding the coming storm, blotting out one by one the sharp-cut lines of the land.

The blizzard, Nature's protest—the crevasse, Nature's pitfall—that grim trap for the unwary—no hunter could conceal his snare so perfectly—the light rippled snow bridge gives no hint or sign of the hidden danger, its position unguessable till man or beast is floundering, clawing and struggling for foothold on the brink.

A dog must be either eating, asleep, or *interested*. His eagerness to snatch at interest, to chain his attention to something, is almost pathetic. The monotony of marching kills him.

This is the fearfullest difficulty for the dog-driver on a snow-plain without leading marks or objects in sight. The dog is almost human in its demand for living interest, yet fatally less than human in its inability to foresee.

CAPTAIN SCOTT (Impressions on the March : Depot Journey).

WITHIN a week the stores were landed, the hut was up though not yet occupied, the ponies sheltered, and Scott called Wilson into his tent

and showed me a long letter he had written home, in which was absolutely nothing but the fullest appreciation of everybody's work. He also told me all his plans for the future . . . and for our depot journey on which we shall be starting in about ten days' time. He wants me

215

to be a dog-driver with himself, Meares and Teddie
Evans. And this is what I would have chosen had I
had a free choice of all. . . . Moreover, if any traction
except ourselves can reach the top of Beardmore Glacier
it will be the dogs—and the dog-drivers are therefore
the people who will have best chance of doing the top
piece of the ice cap at 10,000 feet to the Pole.[1] May I
be there ! About this time next year, may I be there
or thereabouts. With so many young bloods in the hey-
day of youth and strength beyond my own I feel there
will be a most difficult task in making choice towards
the end and a most keen competition—*and* a universal
lack of selfishness and self seeking, with a complete
absence of any jealous feeling in any single one of the
comparatively large number who at present stand a
chance of being on the last piece next summer.

It is impossible [wrote Scott privately] to speak too
highly of one and all, but of course the most valued
and valuable of all is Wilson. He is a positive wonder
and has by sheer force of character achieved a position
of authority over the others whilst retaining their warmest
affection.

Yet never [writes Professor Debenham] was a Chief
of a Scientific Staff so unceremoniously treated by his
men. One remarks here the strange inversion of terms
in the language of comradeship ; as officer he was
universally ' Uncle Bill ' to all ; as merely one of a
band of light-hearted explorers, chaffing and chaffed, he
was addressed as ' The Director,' with many uncom-
plimentary adjectives. One recalls many such scenes as
the following. One night in the pack-ice, when all the
officers were about to turn in, someone suggested a raid

---

[1] As late as October 15 he writes further :
' No one yet knows who will be on the Summit Party : it
is to depend on condition and fitness when we get there.'
It is told of Scott, while still in New Zealand, that being
pressed on the point, he playfully said, ' Well, I should like
to have Bill to hold my hand when we get to the Pole,'
but the Diary shows how the actual choice was made on
the march. (*Scott's Last Expedition*, vol. i, p. 615 (Appendix).)

on the Director's cabin. Immediately scantily clothed figures emerged from each door and the storming of the stern cabin began, but owing to the narrowness of the gangway most of the assailants had to become spectators. After many minutes of grunting and heaving in the tiny cabin there appeared the dishevelled figure, hardly clothed, of our revered Director, dragging the prostrate forms of a Captain of Dragoons and a Helminthologist [1] along the floor and depositing them in the dirtiest part near the stove.

The wonder was not that he was able and willing to take a prominent part in such scenes and even to provoke them, but that in spite of it he never for an instant lost the respect and the reverence due to his office. Many superior officers would long to join thus in the games of their men, few would dare to try, and fewer still carry it off as he did.

The object of the Depot Journey was to dump a large store of provisions at a point 130 geographical miles on the road South from Hut Point, as a reserve for the party returning from the Pole the following year.

The main Hut at Cape Evans was separated from the old Discovery Hut below Observation Hill by two deep bays, which when frozen over represented a day's march. Midway between the two a snout of ice descending from the ramps of Erebus, named Glacier Tongue, jutted out some 6 miles into the sea. At this season of the year the sea-ice in the bay between Cape Evans and the Tongue had already broken up, while that to the south still held. Scott knew that it could be but a matter of days or even of hours, until this ice also broke away. He accordingly made use of the open water to transport twenty-six dogs with sledges, and eight tons of stores, by ship to the

---

[1] Oates and Atkinson.

Tongue, and disembarked them on the still-fast
sea-ice. Meanwhile the eight ponies piloted by
Wilson and Meares were led afoot by a narrow
track close inshore over the steep slopes of the
Tongue, where they joined the dog-teams ; and
the whole party made across the sea-ice to camp
near Castle Rock. The next day, January 25, the
party comprising nine officers and four men sledged
back to the ship for the remainder of their stores.
Here they took leave for the last time of the Ship's
Party (Pennell, Rennick, and Lillie and crew) ;
and of the Eastern—subsequently Northern Party
(Campbell, Levick, Priestley and three men)—they
little knew of the tribulations that were in store for
the latter. But for Wilson the loss of Pennell's
companionship was the worst—' such an exceedingly nice chap, and by far the most capable man
on the whole Expedition.'¹   Scott now definitely
handed over the charge of the dog-teams to Meares
and Wilson, and the latter's Journal has some
enlivening adventures to tell which their per-
formances in the traces provided.

Jan. 26.　. . . It was interesting to watch a couple
of Rorqual whales which kept feeding close round the
ship all the while she lay alongside the Glacier Tongue.
They showed themselves well—constantly coming up to
blow and diving under the fast ice. While I was dog-
driving they would occasionally blow and show a dorsal
fin in an open crack in the middle of what was apparently fast sea-ice and then nothing would hold the dogs ;
they were simply mad to get at it, and they would tear
off in the direction of the blow, where I knew there
was a great lane of open water. I had awful trouble

¹ Commander Pennell went down with his ship the *Queen
Mary* in the Battle of Jutland.

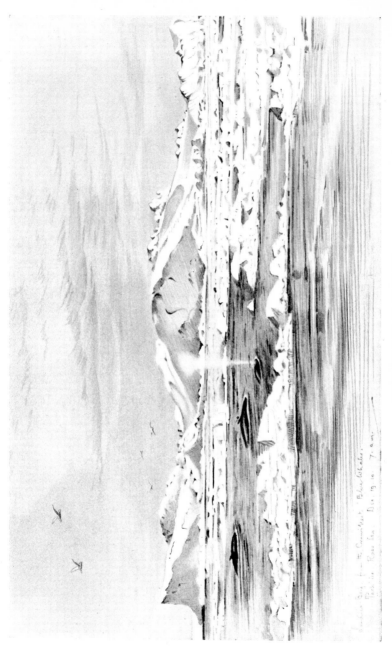

BLUE WHALES IN FLOE-ICE

to stop them from going in with me and the sledge and loads. Seals too and stray penguins are a constant source of trouble when one is on sea-ice. It is so hard that the iron-shod stick with which one puts on the brake will not bite and one simply rushes along in a shower of ice chips.

Jan. 30. The seals have been giving us a lot of trouble, that is, Meares and me, with our dogs. The whole teams go absolutely crazy when they get wind or sight of them, and there are literally hundreds of them along some of the cracks. Occasionally when one believes oneself to be quite away from trouble, an old seal will pop his head up at a blow-hole a few yards ahead, and they are all on top of him before one can say ' knife.' One has to rush in amongst them with the whip, and then every dog jumps over the harness of the dog next him, and the harnesses become a muddle that takes much patience to unravel, not to mention care lest the whole team should get away with the sledge and leave one behind to follow on foot. I never got left, the whole of this depot journey, but I was often very near it, and several times had only time to seize a strap or a part of the sledge and be dragged along at full length until the team got sick of galloping and one could struggle to one's feet again. One gets very watchful and wide awake when one has to manage a team of eleven dogs and a sledge load, but it was a most interesting experience ; and I had a delightful leader Stareek by name— the Russian for ' Old man '—and he was a most wise old man. One has to use Russian terms with all our dogs. *Ki, ki,* means Go to the right—*Chui,* means Go to the left—*Eshte,* means Lie down—and the remainder are mostly swear words which mean everything else that one has to say to a dog-team. Dog-driving like this, in the orthodox manner, is a very different thing to the beastly dog-driving we perpetrated in the *Discovery* days. I got to love all my team and they all got to know me well, and my old leader even now (I am writing this six months after I have had anything to do with any of them [1]) never fails to come and speak to me when-ever he sees me, and he knows me and my voice ever

---

[1] i.e. writing up his Journal from his sledging notes.

so far off. He is really quite a ridiculous ' old man,'
and quite the nicest quietest cleverest old dog gentleman
I have ever come across. He looks in face as though
he knew all the wickedness of all the world and all its
cares, and as though he was bored to death by both of
them. I must get Ponting to photograph him with me :
he's a dear old thing.

On the first stage of the journey they had got
their stores across the sea-ice in the nick of time,
for it actually all broke up the following day. The
next point to be made due east was ' Safety Camp ' ;
so called because it lay well up on the permanent
ice of the Great Barrier. Here Wilson was obliged
to attend Atkinson who was lame with a badly
septic heel, in the intervals going back and forth
with the dogs to the Barrier edge for the stores
which had been dumped there ; and if ever the
maxim that ' human activity mainly consists in
moving matter from place to place ' was exemplified,
it was so on this journey. The ponies having made
very heavy going in the first stages across the soft
snow surface of the Barrier, it was decided that
Wilson and Meares should return to Cape Evans,
a distance of 20 miles, in the afternoon for snow-
shoes. The attempt was vain, as they found the
sea-ice already gone out.

Jan. 31. We covered about 15 miles and reached the
Glacier Tongue almost without a stop. We had a little
trouble here and there with seals, but we went at a very
good pace, and on nearing Glacier Tongue came to a
crack which had opened too wide for the sledge to go
safely over. I got off and ran along it to find a nar-
rower place, when the dogs suddenly took it into their
heads to cross it and Meares and the sledge, of course,
followed happily without going in : but for myself there
was no alternative but to jump and as it was too wide

and with rotten edges I naturally went through with
my legs and one of my finnesko got filled up with water,
but I scrambled out and was not cold, as it all froze
up and kept the wind out. We ran up a snowdrift over
the tide crack and on to the top of the Glacier Tongue
and across it, in a biting wind and drift ; and then we
saw that the sea-ice had gone out and we were cut off
from Cape Evans. So we turned and ran across the
Glacier and then down the same drift, and over the
same tide crack which gave us a terrific bump, and
looking back I saw we had run over a crevasse which
had let half the length of the sledge down in its run, only
the dogs were going downhill so fast that it had to come
up again. Then we ran over the wide crack again ;
this time both on the sledge trusting in Providence that
we shouldn't go in the water, so we didn't.

On arrival at 'Safety Camp' Wilson at once
resumed transporting stores from the Barrier edge
single-handed ; and was obliged to direct Atkinson,
whose heel was still troublesome, to return to Hut
Point.

The pony teams now went in advance of the
swifter dog-teams, and night marching took the
place of day marching owing to the extreme softness
of the snow by day. The advance was made east-
south-east, avoiding the crevassed region near White
Island, to ' Corner Camp ' ; so called because from
this point the trail turns due south. It had been
Scott's intention to lay the Depot in the 80th
parallel ; but at ' Corner Camp ' the party was
held up by a three-days' blizzard, and the ponies
were fast losing condition. Consequently he could
only reach latitude 79° 30'. This untimely blizzard
therefore was a contributory cause of the final
disaster, for if One Ton Depot had been 30 miles
nearer on their return from the Pole the party

might have been saved. On February 11 Wilson notes, ' There was a sunset light on the Western Mountains for the first time, warning us that the season is closing in.' [1]

From the ' Bluff Depot ' on the 13th Lieutenant Evans was sent back with two of the men and three weak ponies ; and the depleted party—Scott, Oates, Bowers, Cherry-Garrard and Gran—pushed on with the remainder, Meares and Wilson with the dog-teams.

Feb. 14. . . . Coming into camp to-day one of the horses known as ' Weary Willie,' led by Gran, foundered just as Meares with his team of dogs was passing. The whole team turned into wolves like a wink and made for the horse as it lay in the snow, and were all on top of it in a moment notwithstanding all that Meares could do to check them ; they knew at once as they always do that the horse was done. Gran and Meares both broke their sticks on the dogs' heads and the horse kicked and bit at them, and they were at last driven off, but not before the poor beast of a horse had been pretty severely bitten. I was behind Meares when his team took charge, and my own dogs at once spotted what was going on and wanted to rush ; but I was prepared for them and stopped where I was till the whole show was done and the horse on his legs and in camp again.

Feb. 15. . . . The surface was good generally, but here and there were heavy drifts of soft sand-like powdery snow. There were also innumerable subsidences of the surface, the breaking of crusts over air-spaces under them, large areas dropping a quarter of an inch or so with a hushing sort of noise, or muffled report. My leader—Stareek—the nicest and wisest old dog in the whole of both teams, thought there was a rabbit under

---

[1] Compare their position on the same date the following year when they were among the crevasses of the upper reaches of the Beardmore Glacier, 500 miles from their base.

the crust every time one gave way close by him and he would jump sideways with both feet on the spot and his nose in the snow ; the action was like a flash and never checked the team ; it was most amusing. I have another funny little dog, Mukaka, small but very game and a good worker ; he is paired with a fat and lazy and very greedy black dog, Nugis by name. And in every march this sprightly little Mukaka will once or twice notice that Nugis isn't pulling and will jump over the trace, bite Nugis like a snap, and be back again in his own place before the fat dog knows what had happened.

Feb. 17. . . . We reached our final camp and made a large cairn and a depot of a ton of food for men, dogs and horses. It was very cold and windy ; everyone getting frost-nipped. The building up of this and the planting of a flag and 2 sledges and the sorting out of provisions took us all our time and we made no march. This is to be called ' One Ton Depot,' and it is in sight of the Bluff.

On the return journey the party was divided. Scott and Cherry-Garrard joined the dog-teams, and the ponies proceeded at their own pace with the rest of the party. The first day the dog-teams made 23 miles, the second 25, and the third 33. On the fourth day Scott made the mistake (and it was against the strongly expressed judgment of Wilson that he did so) of trying to shorten the distance by cutting the corner, and keeping in too close to White Island.

Feb. 21. The light was bad to-day, but there was no wind happily. We got too near in towards White Island and found ourselves running over irregular ice, soft snow-drift alternating with weathered blue ice surfaces, the sort of stuff that I knew would be crevassed. We however kept running as before, and as I ran I knew from the noise and the feel under foot that every now and then we were crossing rotten lidded crevasses. Once my

foot went through and I leapt on to the sledge and saw
my leading dog at the same moment scramble out of a
crack into which he had broken with his hind feet, but
the sledge was running fast and all the team and the
sledge with Cherry-Garrard and myself ran over all
right. This sort of surface continued for a mile or a
mile and a half, and I was running my team abreast of
Meares, but about 100 yards on his right, when I suddenly saw his whole team disappear one dog after another, as they ran down a crevasse in the Barrier surface.
Ten out of his thirteen dogs disappeared as I watched,
they looked exactly like rats running down a rat hole;
only I saw no hole: they simply went into the white
surface and disappeared. I saw Scott who was running
alongside quickly jump on the sledge and I saw Meares
jam the brake on, as I fixed my sledge and left Cherry
with my dogs and ran over to see what had really happened. I found that they had been running along a
lidded crevasse about 6 to 8 feet wide for quite a distance, and the loaded sledge was still standing on it,
while in front was a great blue chasm in which hung
the team of dogs in a festoon. The leader, Osman, a
very powerful fine dog, had remained on the surface,
and the two dogs next the sledge were also still on the
surface—the long trace hung in a long loop down the
crevasse between these two rear dogs and the leader
Osman, and from it hung the remainder of the team in
their harnesses, whining and yapping and trying to get a
foothold on each other and on the crumbly snow sides
of the crevasse. Two of the dogs had slipped out of
their harness and fallen 40 feet down to a snow ledge
where they immediately curled up and went to sleep!
The crevasse was 40 feet deep to this ledge and then blue
holes went deeper here and there. The miracle was
that the sledge hadn't followed the dogs with Meares
and Capt. Scott. We first got the sledge off the crevasse
lid, and then unpacked it in case it should be dragged
in with the tent and sleeping-bags while we were re-
trieving the dogs. We had an Alpine rope, and having
bridged the crevasse with the empty sledge we tied the
rope to Meares and lowered him till he could reach the
nearest two or three dogs, which he cut out of their

harness and hoisted out one by one. We meanwhile
were hanging on also to the sledge end of the trace and
saving Osman from being throttled, for the only reason
that he did not go down the crevasse with the rest was
that the trace had cut into the edge of the crevasse edge
and was using him as a sort of toggle, and as it had a
turn round his chest it was all but choking him. We
then got the Alpine rope attached nearer to the weight
of the remaining dogs on the trace and hauled until
one by one the dogs came within reach, and could be
cut loose and hoisted up and so by degrees we got all of
them up, though it took about an hour and a half.
There were still two more on the ledge at the bottom,
and after testing the length of the Alpine rope we let
Scott down at his request ; we all wanted to go instead
of him ; but he insisted, and so we recovered all the
dogs that went down. Several of them suffered a bit
from their adventure, having hung head down in their
harnesses for a long time by a tight band round the
hind quarters ; they showed signs of damage inside for
some days : and one dog never got over it and died
about a month later. We luckily had no wind all the
time we were working at this business ; it was cold for
the hands as it was, holding on for an hour or two and
hauling on thin taut rope. When we had all the dogs
up they were of course loose, many in cut harness ends ;
and the first thing they did when we were not watching
was to wander over one or two of them to my team
and start a fight, and in a second the whole 24 dogs were
in a furious fighting, biting, barking, ravening heap with
my team's trace and harness tied up in knots that took
me about an hour to unravel when they had finished,
which they did pretty quickly with the four of us—no,
three of us—hammering them promiscuously and dragging
off the loose ones. Capt. Scott was at the bottom of
the crevasse at the moment, and we had to leave him
there till we stopped the dog-fight. One of my dogs
was badly bitten all over—evidently had been the centre
of attraction ; it was the fat little black dog, the lazy
one, but he soon recovered and was none the worse
for his doing. We camped here and had lunch—and
then made another march on a bad surface but with-

out any more crevasse incidents, and then camped for the day.

On the 22nd when within 6 miles of Hut Point they overtook Evans and his two men with one surviving pony, and proceeded to the old Hut for expected letters from Atkinson which should bring news of the Ship's Party and Campbell's Party, but it was not till they arrived at 'Safety Camp' that these came to hand, together with the startling news that Amundsen had landed in the Bay of Whales. Campbell had therefore determined to push northward to Cape Adare and leave the eastern area to the Norwegian. Wilson appears to have been cheerfully sceptical of Amundsen's chances of reaching the Pole, but—

. . . he may be fortunate and his dogs may be a success, in which case he will probably reach the Pole this year, earlier than we can : for not only will he travel much faster with dogs and expert ski-runners than we shall with ponies, but he will be able also to start earlier than we can, as we don't want to expose the ponies to any October temperatures.

But Scott did not underrate his rival.

Every incident of the day [he wrote] pales before the startling contents of the mail-bag which Atkinson gave me : a letter from Campbell setting out his doings and the finding of Amundsen established in the Bay of Whales. One thing only fixes itself definitely in my mind. The proper, as well as the wiser course for us is to proceed exactly as though this had not happened. To go forward and do our best for the honour of our country without fear or panic. There is no doubt that Amundsen's plan is a very serious menace to ours. He has a shorter distance to the Pole by 60 miles : I never thought he could have got so many dogs safely to the ice. His plan of running them seems excellent. But above and

beyond all, he can start his journey early in the season—
an impossible condition with ponies.

After a week of refitting at 'Safety Camp,' the
pony-teams arrived, and the dog-teams were sent
back to Hut Point with all the gear. The next
chapter of accidents provided a ' piece of education
on an impressive scale.'

Feb. 28. . . . Meares and I are now to take our dog-
teams to Hut Point, with all our gear, and the horse
party will follow us. We had a somewhat lengthy discussion on the advisability of going there by the Gap—
or by the other way round Cape Armitage, which meant
round the large thaw-pool off Cape Armitage. I was
all for the Gap, for I didn't believe that the sea-ice
would still be safe the other way without making a very
big detour round the Cape Armitage thaw-pool, and
this point I urged : but I was overruled to the extent
of being told to go round Cape Armitage if possible, but
to feel quite independent, and so far as the dog-teams
were concerned to be guided by my own judgment. As
it turned out, this freedom of movement saved Meares
and myself from getting into great trouble with the
dog-teams.

Before we had run two miles on the sea-ice we noticed
that we were coming on to an area broken up by fine
thread-like cracks, evidently quite fresh, and as I ran
along by the sledge I paced them and found they
occurred regularly at every 30 paces which could only
mean that they were caused by a swell. This suggested
to me that the thaw-pool off Cape Armitage was even
bigger than I thought and that we were getting on to
ice which was breaking up to flow north into it. We
stopped to consider and found that the cracks in the ice
we were on were actually working up and down about
half an inch with the rise and fall of the swell. Knowing
that the ice might remain like this with each piece tight
against the next only until the tide turned, I knew we
must get off it at once in case the tide turned in the
next half-hour ! when each crack would open up into a

wide lead of open water and we should find ourselves
on an isolated floe. We at once turned and went back
as fast as possible to the unbroken sea-ice. Obviously
it was unsafe now to go round by Cape Armitage—and
we therefore made for the Gap.

From here they watched the pony-team (led as
they then thought by Scott and the rest of the party,
but actually by Bowers, Cherry-Garrard and Seaman
Crean) change direction and go south towards
White Island, evidently to avoid the tide-cracks.

. . . Then I thought they were all right, for I knew
they would get on to safe ice and camp for the night.
We therefore had supper, and were turning in at midnight, when I had a last look to see where they were
and found they had camped, as it appeared to me, on
safe Barrier ice : the only safe thing they could have
done. They were now about 6 miles away from us and
it was lucky that I had my Goertz glasses with me so
that we could follow their movements. Now, as everything looked all right we turned in and slept. At 5
a.m. I awoke and as I felt uneasy about the party went
out along the Gap to where I could see their camp ;
and was horrified to see that the whole of the sea-ice was
now on the move and that it had broken up for miles
further, right back past where they had camped, and
that the pony party was now adrift on a floe. They
were running the ponies and sledges over as quickly as
possible from floe to floe whenever they could, trying to
get near the safe Barrier ice again. The whole strait
was now open water to the North of Cape Armitage with
frost smoke rising everywhere from it, and full of pieces
of floating ice, all going up North towards Ross Sea.

They searched the Barrier for signs of a tent,
and seeing one at ' Safety Camp ' immediately made
off without waiting for breakfast, to join up with
the party and render what help they could. The
route by the Gap being now impracticable they

were obliged to make a wide detour to reach the
Camp at noon, where they found Scott ' in a dreadful state of anxiety,' and in time to see Seaman
Crean leaping from floe to floe towards the Barrier.
Eventually Bowers and Cherry-Garrard helped
themselves off the floes on to the Barrier ice unaided,
using their sledges as bridges and ladders. The
weather all the while had been very bitter, with a
low drift obscuring landmarks. Bowers then with
the help of Oates made a gallant attempt to rescue
the three surviving ponies that he would never have
abandoned at all save under a peremptory order
from Scott. Among all the exploits of the Last
Expedition this one, performed by that ' most
undefeatable little sportsman,' was as thrilling as
it was heroic. It has been told very modestly by
Bowers himself in a graphic letter home.[1]

The ice having broken up all over the Strait, and
even (an unexampled happening) 2 miles off the
end of Glacier Tongue, the party were cut off from
their base and marooned at Hut Point until the
sea should freeze again. The weather continued
thick and bitterly cold. The roof of the old hut
was lined with a solid sheet of ice. They made the
best of their comfortless plight with an improvised
stove and blubber for fuel. They even contemplated a return to Cape Evans over the heavily
crevassed slopes of Erebus at a height of 5,000 feet.
Wilson found a route, but it was abandoned as
impracticable. On March 14 they were joined by
the returning Western Party (Griffith Taylor,
Wright, Debenham and Seaman Evans), and with
them Wilson, never unoccupied, went geologizing.

---

[1] The Worst Journey in the World, vol. i, pp. 138–54.

Life in the Hut, in spite of its discomforts, was merry and convivial. On one memorable occasion Wilson nearly ruined his reputation as cook by experimenting with seal liver in a ' fry ' of penguin blubber. ' Three heroes,' says Scott, ' got through their pannikins, but the rest of us decided to be contented with cocoa and biscuit after tasting the first mouthful.' ' Fun over a fry I made in my new penguin lard,' says Wilson cheerfully. ' It was quite a success and tasted like very bad sardine oil.' But his ' chupatties ' were in much request, especially by Oates. Professor Debenham also recalls that—

Together with others of the party Oates pretended to have a grudge against the ' medical faculty ' in that certain medical comforts, namely brandy, taken for emergencies on sledge journeys, were never opened. Over the blubber stove one day at Hut Point Oates complained somewhat as follows : ' Saw them again this morning in the medical stores. *All full.* What *do* they give brandy for, anyway ? ' Various answers elicited the fact that epileptic fits required brandy, whereupon Oates went and cross-examined Atkinson on the phenomenon of fits. Later in the day Oates went out to where Wilson and others were shovelling snow and threw a very realistic fit at Wilson's feet. An accomplice said to Wilson : ' It looks as if Oates had got a fit.' ' Yes,' said Wilson, ' he's got a fit all right ; rub some snow down his neck, and he'll soon get over it.'

Meanwhile the weather showed no improvement.

March 17. Bad weather again : a heavy snowstorm from the N. went round later to a regular gale from the S. and by night a tremendous sea was running in on to the Hut Point icefoot and breaking over the Point. By midnight things looked very bad indeed for the dogs, and Meares and I turned out to let them loose from the picketing lines for they were getting frozen into solid jackets of sea water. It was a dreadful night and Meares and I were both coated from head to foot with frozen sea water before we had finished. The breakers were 20 to 30 feet high and the spindrift froze and rattled on the hut, and blew right across the Hut Point promontory. The Magnetic huts and even Vince's Cross about 40 feet up on the hill were an inch deep in frozen salt water by the morning. We got the dogs in under the lee of the hut where they were more sheltered, but they were in a pitiable condition of cold and wet.

On April 5 he records that new ice had formed to the depth of an inch, in some places 8 inches : on the 6th ' if the weather holds we are to try and get across in two days ' ; on the 7th ' several people walked on the sea-ice ' ; on the 8th ' Blizzard. All the ice gone out to within half a mile of Hut Point ' ; on the 9th ' all the ice gone out except a small corner South of Glacier Tongue.' Yet on the 11th the majority, under Scott, made a bid for it by an untried route, partly by land and partly by ice close inshore, leaving Wilson with Oates, Atkinson, Meares and Cherry-Garrard to bring the animals along when the ice should hold.

April 13. . . . Here, we have come to an end of our sugar to-day. We have also finished our flour, so we can't make chupatties. We have also finished our oat-meal—but we have lots of seal meat and biscuit and cocoa. Butter is running out, but we can't starve ! And we are a very happy party of bohemians. Our clothes are soaked in seal blubber and soot, and we are all bearded and very dirty.

When on the 18th Scott returned with a relief party and provisions he found them ' all well and in excellent spirits—didn't seem to want us much ! ' On the 21st he left Meares with six of the relief still in charge of the animals, and led the main party back to Cape Evans, which was with much difficulty reached the same night.

CHAPTER XVI

The Last Expedition (continued)

WINTER QUARTERS

The more I get to know of Dr. Wilson, the more I see that he was a man to love whom was indeed a liberal education, and to be loved by whom was to enter a little circle of the elect.

A. A. MILNE.

THE Depot Journey had been a gruelling experience in more ways than one, and the enforced imprisonment at Hut Point which succeeded it, with its reeking atmosphere of greasy soot, blood and blubber, must have been akin to the barbaric existence of primeval man. Perhaps the best indication of what the life was really like is the fact that the first man who met the returning party at Cape Evans failed to recognize them at once, believing them to be strangers of the Norwegian Expedition. In the comparative comfort of the Hut at Cape Evans a few days later Scott wrote :

I do not think that there can be any life quite so demonstrative of character as that which we had on these expeditions. One sees a remarkable reassortment of values. Under ordinary conditions it is so easy to carry a point with a little bounce ; self-assertion is a mask which covers many a weakness. As a rule we have neither the time nor the desire to look beneath it, and so

232

it is that commonly we accept people on their own valuation. Here the outward show is nothing, it is the inward purpose that counts. So the ' Gods ' dwindle and the humble supplant them. Pretence is useless.

And again, after a lecture by Wilson a few days later :

The lecture was delivered in the author's usual modest strain, but unconsciously it was expressive of himself and his whole-hearted thoroughness. He stands very high in the scale of human beings—how high I scarcely knew till the experience of the past few months.

There is no member of our party so universally esteemed ; only to-night I realize how patiently and consistently he has given time and attention to help the efforts of the other sketchers, and so it is all through ; he has had a hand in almost every lecture given, and has been consulted in almost every effort which has been made towards the solution of the practical or theoretical problems of our Polar world.

The achievement of a great result by patient work is the best possible object lesson for struggling humanity, for the results of genius, however admirable, can rarely be instructive. The chief of the Scientific Staff sets an example which is more potent than any other factor in maintaining that bond of good fellowship which is the marked and beneficent characteristic of our community.

This is high praise. So high indeed that it might seem to be extravagant were it not confirmed again and again both by Scott himself, and every member of the Expedition without exception. From these we can but select a few, but they are representative of all. Taking up the tribute of Debenham from the point at which we left it :

In the hut life at headquarters he was as quietly prominent as ever, never in the limelight if possible but always at hand. Living all in one room, so to speak, without any real privacy, one there got a better idea of

his semi-ascetic habits and his stern sense of duty. Up
with the cook, his first business was a bath of frozen
snow, a method of ablution in which none but Lieut.
Bowers joined him, followed often enough by a long
walk before breakfast to read one of the outlying ther-
mometers. In bad weather he would be at his desk all
day, sketching, revising notes or giving friendly advice
to all and sundry. He usually cut meal hours a little
short, but often after dinner he sat on while others
smoked, and though he rarely entered into the long and
frequent arguments one might often trace the original
statement to Dr. Wilson, and his quiet wit and balanced
criticism kept many such an argument from degenerating
into either banality or acerbity. The very reverse of
dictatorial, he yet made his points with a quiet firm-
ness that carried far more weight than any loud-voiced
assurance could have done.

In reasonable weather he was always out and was
second only to Bowers in his absolute disregard of cold
or discomfort. His was a common figure to meet on
one's walks round the icebergs in the bay, over the
domed hills of the little cape or on the bare slopes of
the glacier behind, for there was no part of the district
that he did not know and visit. The neat dress with
belt outside the wind-blouse, balaclava carefully folded
to form a cap, and a cross gartering of the tapes of the
putties, was the most easily recognized of all the queer
collection of garbs affected by the party, while the long
stride and the slight characteristic stoop, distinguished
him from others at a still greater distance. From these
walks—whether in exercising a pony or alone—he rarely
returned without a little store of observations and these
he quietly passed on to those into whose branches they
fell ; there was little that escaped the sharp eyes or the
recording pencil whether in ice forms, meteorology or
new varieties of rocks. . . . Between and amongst all
these hours of hard work there were moments of the
lightest gaiety when he entered into or led the fun that
in every possible form made that winter the cheeriest
time in the lives of many there. . . .

As doctor, and therefore responsible for the general
arrangement of our diet, he kept a particularly sharp

look-out for the possible symptoms of scurvy. . . . And
the titles frequently hurled at him of 'The Scorbutic
Director' or 'Livery Bill' remained, in spite of their
virulence, merely tributes to his never-varying good health
and his unfailing good temper.

And Cherry-Garrard has written:

However much of good I may write of Wilson, his
many friends in England, those who served with him
on the ship or in the hut, and most of all those who
had the good fortune to sledge with him (for it is sledging
which is far the greatest test) will all be dissatisfied, for
I know that I cannot do justice to his value. If you
knew him you could not like him : you simply had to
love him. Bill was of the salt of the earth. If I were
asked what quality it was before others that made him
so useful, and so lovable, I think I should answer that
it was because he never for one moment thought of
himself. . . . Scott and Wilson worked hand in hand
to further the scientific objects of the Expedition. . . .
Wilson's own share in the scientific results is more obvious
because he was the director of the work. But no published reports will give an adequate idea of the ability
he showed in co-ordinating the various interests of a
varied community, nor the tact he displayed in dealing
with the difficulties which arose. Above all his judgment
was excellent, and Scott as well as the rest of us relied
upon him to a very great extent. The value of judgment
in a land where a wrong decision may mean disaster
as well as loss of life is beyond all price. . . . Nature
is sometimes almost too big an enemy to fight : all this
wants judgment, and if possible experience. Wilson could
supply both, for his experience was as wide as that of
Scott, and I have constantly known Scott change his
mind after a talk with Bill.

And Wright:

We who knew him realized that though he kept himself as much in the background as possible, not a single
man on the Expedition from Captain Scott down to
myself ever undertook any serious step without first asking Dr. Bill's advice. Always ready to help—the best

influence and the finest character I for one will ever
meet in this life.

His own comments on some of his comrades,
written in his Journal and his letters home at intervals
since landing, may find an appropriate place here :

[To his wife]—If you ever go anywhere near the
Bowers', do go and see them—he would so like it and
he is such a real good sort, and says that no living person
could have a happier home to go to than his. I should
so like you to go and see them, he is such a brick.
He takes the edge off a lot of difficulty for everyone
by accepting everything that is said to him as a matter
of course in the most solemn manner imaginable, when
he always becomes irresistibly humorous, and there isn't
a thing that happens that he doesn't find a ridiculous
side to. He is a perfect treasure—and improves every
day I think.

So do Titus and Atkinson, and I have a great deal
of talk with both of them. Atkinson is splendid in the
way he has always played the game by me, for he does
nothing without telling me and asking if I approve—
knowing quite well that he knows a lot more about it
all (medicine) than I do. I like them both, I think, as
much as anyone in the mess, and Titus has lost all his
shyness. He is a ripper and a thoroughly good sort.

Ponting is very artistic and he has said some very
flattering things about my pictures, and indeed I have
also learned a good deal from talking with him about
Japanese art and from looking at his perfectly beautiful
collection of Japanese photos and lantern-slides. He is
an artist with genuine feeling to his finger-tips. I like
him more and more. He is most critical of his own
work but he has plenty of appreciation of good work
by other photographers, and what I like about him
especially is that he won't allow the shadow of untruth
in his work, and faking, which is so frequent now in photo-
graphy, he simply refuses to touch. His work is beautiful,
and one knows it is absolutely true and untouched.

Meanwhile his own collection of sketches was

PETRELS ON PACK-ICE

growing with enormous rapidity and by June 7
he had completed no less than fifty.

[To his wife, from Cape Evans]—You can't think how
the thought of you and your encouragement stirs me to get
sketches done. . . . I have got a whole sketch-book filled
with pencil ones—dozens—during the past month at Hut
Point and they have all to be worked out, before I go to
Cape Crozier in July, by acetylene and candle-light—so
they may have to be done over again [a pencil note later
—' no, they are all right by daylight ']. . . . If I can
bring home a dozen really large water-colours and some
scores of smaller ones I shall be content. Oh, but this
place is *full* of beautiful subjects for painting ; much
better than Hut Point. The trouble is that we shall
be here such a short time during daylight, and there is
such a dreadful lot of other work to do. . . .
   To-day I tried body colour painting on grey paper
and they have been successful beyond my hopes—and
so I am going on that way. It was Turner's way, so it
can't be very wrong. . . . I feel that I know more about
what is worth aiming at now than I did 10 years ago,
and I am doing many of my sketches much larger. The
chief trouble is shortage of time. . . . It is all done
with the thought of you in my heart and mind all the
time, and I love it all. I am now sure it is better work
than I have done before.

Yet in his passionate devotion to his art he was
never, it appeared, too preoccupied or absorbed
to be of use to others when needed, and he was
seldom free from these interruptions. An instance
of his remarkable disregard for himself is mentioned
by Griffith Taylor :

Atkinson found some parasitic grubs in some fish and
took them over to Dr. Bill. He was engaged upon some
wonderful sunset sketches, but abandoned this task and
nonchalantly proceeded to make water-colours of pink
parasitic grubs on a purple background of liver and gall.
He would always help anyone if it lay in his power. I

think what touched some of us as much as anything was his willingness to take the last and longest hour of anyone's night watch. ' I don't mind getting up at 7 a.m.,' he used to say, ' I'll get on with my painting. Just put a kettle on to boil, and wake me and then you can turn in. . . .'

I thought him the finest man in the whole Expedition, and the least self-seeking spirit I have ever met. He was the kindly buffer between naval ideas of discipline and those to which scientists were more accustomed and so managed that we all worked smoothly and thought the more of him. . . . I am sure he was the heart of that long-drawn agonizing march. His example will ever encourage one of his mates who is proud to have been associated with him.[1]

He would willingly and cheerfully leave the work in hand to draw ice-crystals for Wright, a rare fish for Nelson, or for walks with Scott and long discussions with him on glaciation, dietary, sledge-rations and hosts of other things ; exercising ponies, caring for the dogs, besides his unfailing daily pilgrimage with Bowers to the Ramp for observations.[2]

On one of these occasions, Scott's diary has this entry :

May 20.[3] Blowing hard from the south with some snow and very cold. Few of us went far ; Wilson and Bowers went to the top of the Ramp, and found the wind there force 6 to 7, temperature $-24°$; as a consequence they got frost-bitten. There was lively cheering when they reappeared in this condition, such is the sym-

---

[1] *With Scott—The Silver Lining*, p. 304 (supplemented by a letter).

[2] The flashlight photograph of Wilson sketching Bowers while reading the meteorological screen on the Ramp was taken by Ponting on June 7. (*Scott's Last Expedition*, I, 321.)

[3] Ponting's photograph of Wilson at work in the Hut on his sketch of a paraselene was taken on this day. (*Scott's Last Expedition*, I, 260.)

pathy which is here displayed for affliction ; but with
Wilson much of the amusement arises from his peculiarly
scanty headgear and the confessed jealousy of those of
us who cannot face the weather with so little face protection.

It was Wilson's pleasant conceit (wrote Cherry-Garrard)
to keep his balaclava rolled up, so that his face was
bare, on such occasions, being somewhat proud of the
fact that he had not, as yet, been frost-bitten. Imagine
our joy when he entered the hut one cold windy evening
with two white spots on his cheeks which he vainly tried
to hide behind his dogskin mitts.

The hardihood of these two Spartans was always
a matter for envy and banter from their companions, but not for emulation.

There is a stretching of limbs and an interchange
of morning greetings, garnished with sleepy humour.
Wilson and Bowers meet in a state of nature beside a
washing basin filled with snow and proceed to rub
glistening limbs with this chilling substance. A little
later with less hardihood some others may be seen making
the most of a meagre allowance of water (Scott).

And yet in civilization Wilson had been sus-
ceptible to cold, and had always much ado to
restore his circulation after his morning's cold bath.

The characteristic of his lectures was their
simplicity and clarity. He was called upon for
three, and he prepared them with the same care
and thoroughness that he gave to all his other
work. His own notes of them have been preserved,
but those taken at the time by Scott and others
are not without interest also. He opened the
lecture series with a paper on ' Antarctic Flying
Birds,' and in this explained his own theory of
pigmentation (that in which he had supported the
view of Millais). ' Does the absence of pigment,'

he asked, ' suggest absence of reserve energy ? Does it increase the insulating properties of the feathers ? Or does its white clothing cause less radiation and expenditure of the bird's internal heat ? ' In his second lecture he traced the descent of Penguins from the primitive lizard-bird, explaining their anatomy, and finding corroborative evidence in their prehistoric fossilized remains. The theme for his third lecture on ' Sketching ' became (said Scott) ' the extreme importance of accuracy, his mode of expression and explanation frankly Ruskinesque.'

As to his illustrations for the *South Polar Times*, of which Cherry-Garrard was editor, the standard of this production was even higher than that of its two *Discovery* predecessors ; Wilson's artistic contributions to it are maturer, and his lighter fancies excellently witty and humorous. There is, however, one contribution made by him of which more must be said. This was his first and only poem. It is entitled ' The Barrier Silence ' and is published at the beginning of Vol. II of *Scott's Last Expedition* with the editorial remark : ' It is characteristic of the man that he sent these verses in typewritten, lest the editor should recognize his hand and judge them on personal rather than on literary grounds.' Dr. Griffith Taylor has given a fuller explanation of this.

One day Bill came to me with a poem he had written. He asked me to type it so that Cherry should not recognize his writing. A few days later Cherry brought me all the MS. and complimented me on the ' Barrier Silence.' So I had to disclaim authorship. Then he wanted two lines cleared up and asked me to do it. I declined but said that evidently the Author expected

The silence was deep with a breath like sleep
    As our sledge runners slid on the snow,
But the fate-full fall of our fur-clad feet,
    Struck mute like a silent blow
On a questioning "hush", as the settling crust
    Shrank shivering over the floe,
And a voice that was thick ~~from~~ as a soul that ~~was~~ sick
    Came back from the Barrier.. ~~No~~!
~~And this was~~   ~~the thought~~
They ~~were~~ only ~~sounds~~ that the silence won brought
~~As it scorched & froze us through~~
    In the heat of the sun, & the glow
    And the glare from the glistening floe, .
As it scorched & ~~froze~~ us ~~throughs~~ through
    With the bite of the drifting snow.
That we were the men God meant should know
    The ~~heart~~ soul of the Barrier snow.

MANUSCRIPT OF "THE BARRIER SILENCE"

Bill (the artist) to see the poem and that I was sure
that whatever he and Bill agreed to would satisfy the
Author. Whereat I heard Bill chuckle! Later it was
returned to me emended, as subsequently printed.'

But what is not generally known is that many of
the phrases and rhymes of this poem were simmering
in Wilson's mind in the *Discovery* days, and had
been jotted down by him then and laid aside.
Now he re-cast them into verse form, with a typical
self-criticism, ' pathological I am afraid, perhaps
an early symptom of Polar anæmia.'

¹ The Silence was deep with a breath like sleep
    As our sledge runners slid on the snow,
And the fate-full fall of our fur-clad feet
    Struck mute like a silent blow
On a questioning ' hush,' as the settling crust
    Shrank shivering over the floe :
And the sledge in its track sent a whisper back
    Which was lost in a white fog-bow.

And this was the thought that the Silence wrought
    As it scorched and froze us through,
Though secrets hidden are all forbidden
    Till God means man to know,
We might be the men God meant should know
    The heart of the Barrier snow,
In the heat of the sun, and the glow
    And the glare from the glistening flow,
As it scorched and froze us through and through
    With the bite of the drifting snow.

[From letters to his wife]—It is a great joy to feel one
is not useless or out of place, and everyone is so exceedingly nice all round. Moreover I feel just as strong and
as active as the majority of our party and I believe I

---

¹ The reproduction opposite is of a fragment of the first
draft of the poem. The version here printed is taken from
the typescript before its final revision.

shall last out any or all of them. Oh, my love, I know I am wanted here, and they all *make* me feel they want me here : it is a great joy to feel appreciated. . . . They all more or less come to me to talk things over in matters of work or trouble or what not. Captain Scott has been very good—and I felt that if I was to be of any use it must be on account of what they found useful in me and not on account of what I thought I could help them in. They are all so exceedingly pleasant and friendly. . . . The Scientific work of this expedition is going to be on a very high level, thanks to the excellency of our workers.

Everything seems to have gone wrong with the Expedition's prospects so far.—We start fully handicapped, but all will come right and as God wills, and everyone is cheerful. . . . The ship will return while we are still on the Southern Journey, so I shall not have a chance to see your letters, or to answer a single question for a whole year more after receiving them.—It all seems cruel and cold but it is God's will to make good stuff of us both. Anyhow you will do your duty, my brave kind lady, and your ' kind sir ' will do his, and we will both trust in God. . . . You are the very breath of life to *me* . . . my most living prayer is that we may both fulfil the purpose for which God gave us life. . . .

I dreamt of you singing at a piano, impromptu, to a number of people. You were trying to pick up a tune, and every time you tried it ran into a sea-chanty that we sing down here, and that wasn't what you wanted. You looked lovely because you were sitting with your back to a large window through which was a perfect glory of buttercups in a lovely hayfield in bright sunshine. I love to think of you enjoying May sunshine and the flowers and birds, and oh, how beautiful it is all to remember.

The time is quickly coming when I start on my winter sledge journey to Cape Crozier with Birdie Bowers and Cherry-Garrard, the two I like best of all our party. It is going to be a regular snorter, I can see that : but I

have got the two best sledgers of the whole Expedition
to come with me. Scott has allowed me to have them,
and they are desperately keen to come. . . . 'Neither
count I my life dear unto myself, so that I might finish
my course with joy.' . . . My own love, I count not
my life dear to myself, but I count it dear to you as I
know well it is. . . . Life is a gift that we are to use in
His service, doing what is expected of us at all cost and
at all risks ; and this we are doing, thank God, and thank
you, my beloved, for having made it easy and possible
by your courage, and I just honour and worship you
for it as I love you for yourself. . . . I don't think
anyone has tried travelling in midwinter before, and yet
as there is no other possible way in the world to do this
particular piece of work, it is up to me to try it. . . .
Capt. Scott hopes I shall bring them back safe and sound
for the Southern Journey. He told me to-day again
that I had the pick of the sledging element and mustn't
get them crocked. . . . Our sledging-bags and clothes
may get so bad that we may have to return very much
earlier than we expect. Still, the thing is worth trying.
To-morrow we start, but you come with me in my heart.
You are all in all to me in this life and in the next.

CHAPTER XVII

The Last Expedition (continued)

THE WINTER JOURNEY

Thou whose far-reaching ray heralds the dawn of day,
At last begun,
Scatt'ring with glorious light darkness of winter night,
Dazzling in brilliance bright,
Hail mighty Sun !

Greatest of Heaven's lights, grandest of earthly sights,—
Cape, island, shore,
Limitless plains of snow, peak, boulder, berg and floe,
Lit with thy radiant glow,
Greet thee once more.
Lieut. Henry R. Bowers (*The South Polar Times*).

ON June 27, having sped the ' Cape Crozier Party ' a little distance on their way, Scott returned to the Hut and completed a MS. book of his diary with the words :

This winter travel is a new and bold venture, but the right men have gone to attempt it. All good luck go with them !

More than five weeks later he put on record the words that follow :

Wilson is disappointed at seeing so little of the Penguins, but to me and to everyone who has remained here the result of this effort is the appeal it makes to our imagination as one of the most gallant stories in

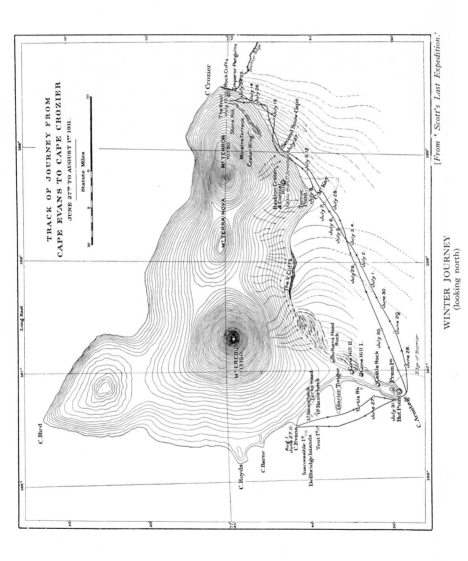

TRACK OF JOURNEY FROM
CAPE EVANS TO CAPE CROZIER
JUNE 27TH TO AUGUST 1ST 1911.

Statute Miles

WINTER JOURNEY
(looking north)

[From 'Scott's Last Expedition.'

[244]

Polar History. That men should wander forth in the depth of a Polar night to face the most dismal cold and the fiercest gales in darkness is something new ; that they should have persisted in this effort in spite of every adversity for five weeks is heroic. It makes a tale for our generation which I hope may not be lost in the telling.

He called it ' the hardest journey that has ever been made ' : and this is the well-considered judgment of a man not prone to exaggerate, whose knowledge and experience in such matters was and still is second to none. For whatever claims other feats of endurance of which we have record may have to compare with it, the verdict of those best qualified to judge still gives the palm to this journey. It was always open to them to return, without dishonour : the uniqueness of their achievement is in the fact that they deliberately elected to go on. There may have been other journeys which called for a fortitude as great because they were determined by the sheer necessity of self-preservation, as a record of human endurance *voluntarily* accepted and undergone the Winter Journey of 1911 stands, and will probably for long remain, without parallel. Two of the three men who survived it were to die eight months later on the journey from the Pole, but it is certain that the Polar Journey itself, five months in duration and terminating in death, had no conditions to offer more terrible than these five weeks miraculously ending in preservation.

Wilson's official Report of the Winter Journey— ' the weirdest bird-nesting expedition that has been or ever will be '—can be read at the beginning of Volume II of *Scott's Last Expedition* ; and perhaps no document could be more characteristic of the man than this, with its strict and faithful adherence

to facts, its accuracy of observation, its exactitude
of detail—above all, its complete self-effacement :
a terse and simple chronicle of facts, set down
without comment except in praise of his companions, yet 'sedulously stripped of the fuller
human colouring, simple and reticent to the last.'
But if anyone wishes to see what it cost him to
write it one may turn, with careful reverence, the
pages of the pocket notebook, filmed with his
frozen breath, across which his numbed fingers
painfully traced in scarcely legible lines the record
for each day.[1] It is difficult to conceive how a
man in such straits could write at all ; more
difficult still to read it with undimmed eyes.

In introducing the text of Wilson's official Report
to the public Sir Clements Markham outlined the
objects : firstly, to secure eggs at such a stage of
incubation as to furnish a series of early embryos,
for it seemed probable, as Wilson had said, that 'we
have in the Emperor Penguin the nearest approach
to a primitive form not only of a penguin, but of a
bird ' ; secondly, to obtain an exact knowledge of
the winter conditions on the Barrier at this extremity
of it—achieved, in fact, by Bowers' remarkable
meteorological record ; thirdly, to experiment with
sledging rations for future guidance.

The Report was amplified for publication with
annotations from Cherry-Garrard's diary ' which
tells of incidents and impressions in their more
personal bearing.'   But since then Mr. Cherry-
Garrard has, in his chapter ' The Winter Journey,'
abundantly realized the hope of Scott : ' it makes

---

[1] The notebook is in the South Polar Research Institute
at Cambridge.

a tale for our generation which I hope may not be lost in the telling.'

'The right men have gone to attempt it.' There was never any doubt in Scott's mind as to that. The prospect of such an enterprise being attempted at all had given him considerable anxiety ; he had more than once endeavoured to dissuade Wilson from it, and consented finally on Wilson's reassurance that he would bring his companions back unharmed. Wilson had made up his mind to it ever since the discovery of the Emperor rookery at Cape Crozier nine years before, ' but I'm not saying much about it—it might never come off' he had confided to C.-G. in London.

His monograph on the Emperor Penguin, published by the British Museum under the ' Zoology' section of the National Antarctic Expedition's Report 1901–4, had concluded with the following words :

The possibility that we have in the Emperor Penguin the nearest approach to a primitive form not only of a penguin, but of a bird, makes the future working out of its embryology a matter of the greatest possible importance. It was a great disappointment to us that although we discovered their breeding ground, and although we were able to bring home a number of deserted eggs and chicks, we were not able to procure a series of early embryos by which alone the points of particular interest can be worked out. To have done this in a proper manner from the spot at which the *Discovery* wintered in McMurdo Sound would have involved us in endless difficulties, for it would have entailed the risks of sledge travelling in midwinter with an almost total absence of light. It would at any time require that a party of three at least, with full camp equipment, should traverse about a hundred miles of the Barrier surface in the dark, and should, by moonlight, cross over with rope and axe the immense pressure-ridges which form a chaos of crevasses at Cape Crozier. These ridges moreover, which have taken a party as much as two hours of careful work to cross by daylight, must be crossed and re-crossed at every visit to the breeding site in the bay. There is no possibility even by daylight of conveying over them the sledge and camping kit, and in the darkness of mid-winter the impracticability is still more obvious. Cape Crozier is a focus for wind and storm, where every breath is converted, by the configuration of Mounts Erebus and Terror, into a regular drifting blizzard full of snow. It is here, as I have already stated, that on one journey or another we have had to lie patiently in sodden sleeping-bags for as many as five and seven days on end, waiting for the weather to change and make it possible for us to leave our tents at all. If, however, these dangers were overcome there would still be the difficulty of making the needful preparations from the eggs. The party would have to be on the scene at any rate early in July. Supposing that no eggs were found upon arrival, it would be well to spend the time in labelling the most likely birds, those for example that have taken up their stations close under the ice-cliffs. And if this were done it would be easier then to examine them daily by the moonlight, if it and the weather generally were suitable ; conditions, I must confess, not always easily obtained at Cape Crozier. But if by good luck things happened to go well, it would by this time be useful to have a shelter built of snow blocks on the sea-ice in which to work with the cooking lamp to pre-vent the freezing of the egg before the embryo was cut out, and in order that fluid solutions might be handy for the various stages of its preparation ; for it must be borne in mind that the temperature all the while may be anything between zero and $-50°$ F. The whole work no doubt would be full of difficulty, but it would not be quite impossible, and it is with a view to helping those to whom the opportunity may occur in the future, that this outline has been added of the difficulties that would surely beset their path.

With regard to his own competence to lead this

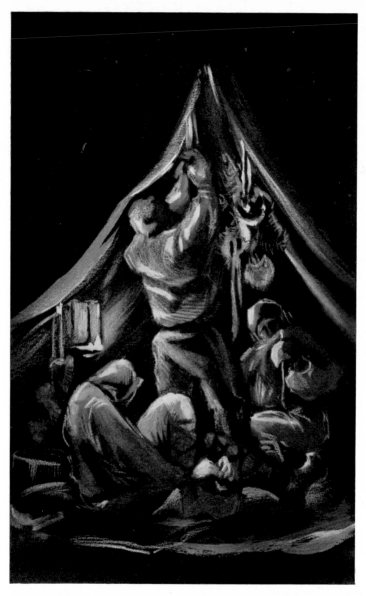

THREE IN A TENT

expedition, the bare imagination of which had never before been entertained by any explorer north or south, it is sufficient to say at once, and quite simply, that probably no one else could have done it. No one else possessed in the same degree in combination the necessary resolution, judgment and patience : in a word, practical idealism. It is almost equally unnecessary to comment on the selection of Bowers, ' the incomparable, the indomitable '—Scott's diary abounds in references to his reliance and resource. Transferred from service in one of the hottest quarters of the globe, the Persian Gulf, to the Antarctic, he seemed equally impervious to heat and cold. There is little doubt that the party as a whole owed its preservation as much to Bowers as to Wilson, though Bowers was not equipped with the experience required to lead it.

I believe he is the hardest traveller that ever undertook a Polar journey, as well as one of the most undaunted. His untiring energy and astonishing physique enable him to continue to work under conditions which are absolutely paralysing to others.—(Scott.)

Cherry-Garrard was also one of Scott's picked men, and already on his list for the Southern Journey. He had left Oxford with a reputation as an oarsman, having helped to win the Grand Challenge Cup at Henley in 1908. There is probably no better training than toil at the oar for toil in the traces of a sledge ; at any rate before the close of the Expedition he had more sledge-journeys to his credit than any member of it.

He is another of the open-air, self-effacing, quiet workers : his whole heart is in this life, with profound eagerness to help everyone. One has caught glimpses of him in tight places ; sound all through and pretty hard also.—(Scott.)

Between himself and Bowers, moreover, there existed a bond of personal friendship which needed but the experience of a common hardship to cement, and both had an unbounded affection for Wilson. On all points therefore the trio could not have been better selected.

The conditions they encountered on their outward journey of 67 miles across the ' Windless Bight ' to the pressure-ridges of the Great Barrier can be baldly stated here, but they cannot be imagined ; to be imagined they would have to be experienced.—Total darkness, in which the ever-present danger of crevasses could only be guessed at by the sound of ice-cracks or the feel of the footfall in the snow ; a darkness which for a time was lifted, but scarcely relieved, by fitful gleams of moonlight, or in which its glow was suffused in a white density of fog as bewildering as the darkness had been ; a surface over which for days together the sledge-runners could not glide—compelling the travellers to ' relay ' their two sledges and thus to cover three times the distance actually made good for the day's march ; days together when one mile per hour, or less, was reckoned a marvellously good march, and other days when 3, $2\frac{1}{2}$, 2, or $1\frac{1}{2}$ miles could only be accomplished with the utmost effort after eight hours' solid sledging ; hands blistered with frost-bite on the march, the fluid in them freezing, to be thawed out and pricked when in the tent over the primus—but not before straps had been untoggled, ropes lashed, lanyards tied, and strings like wire unloosed ; temperatures a reduction from which to −55° F. was felt as an enormous relief[1] ; perspiration which froze into ice-flakes on the skin and shook down from between it and their clothing as they moved ; breath freezing with a crackle as it left their lips in the open, coating the face with an ice-mask like a visor—a grateful protection from the wind ; but far worse, freezing into their closed-up sleeping-bags as they lay in them, breathing their own breath ; balaclavas encased with ice about the head and neck like steel helmets ; garments like armour-plate. . . . These were some of the conditions they experienced *before* they ' reached bed-rock.' ' They talk of chattering teeth : but when your body chatters you can call yourself cold.'

And yet they went on. Sometimes unaware of their position, most often feeling, not seeing, their probable direction, they struggled blindly, vaguely, hopefully on—Wilson apparently guided by the instinct of a homing-bird. Would any but suicidal maniacs bent on a peculiarly lingering death have done it ? Yes, there is one other species of the genus man, and one only, that would do it : he is the pure idealist—a species that is very rare.

In civilization men are taken at their own valuation because there are so many ways of concealment, and there is so little time, perhaps even so little understanding. Not so down South. These two men went through the Winter Journey and lived : later they went through the Polar Journey and died. They were gold, pure, shining, unalloyed. Words cannot express how good their companionship was.

Through all these days, and those which were to

---

[1] The lowest temperature recorded was −77·5° F., i.e. 109½ degrees of frost.

follow, the worst I suppose in their dark severity that men have ever come through alive, no single hasty or angry word passed their lips. When, later, we were sure, so far as we can be sure of anything, that we must die, they were cheerful, and so far as I can judge their songs and cheery words were quite unforced. Nor were they ever flurried, though always as quick as the conditions would allow in moments of emergency. It is hard that often such men must go first when others far less worthy remain. . . .

I am not going to pretend that this was anything but a ghastly journey, made bearable and even pleasant to look back upon by the qualities of my two companions who have gone. . . .

More than once in my short life I have been struck by the value of the man who is blind to what appears to be a common-sense certainty : he achieves the impossible. . . . We were quite intelligent people, and we must all have known that we were not going to see the Penguins and that it was folly to go forward. And yet with quiet perseverance, in perfect friendship, almost with gentleness those two men led on. I just did what I was told. . . .

And now Bill was feeling terribly responsible for both of us. He kept on saying that he was sorry, but he had never dreamed it was going to be as bad as this. He felt that having asked us to come he was in some way chargeable with our troubles. When leaders have this kind of feeling about their men they get much better results, if the men are good : if men are bad or even moderate they will try and take advantage of what they consider to be softness.[1] . . . Always patient, self-possessed, unruffled, he was the only man on earth, as I believe, who could have led this journey.[2]

Somehow the spirit and the will within them drove their tortured, toil-racked bodies to drag their laden sledges up between heaped-up pressure-ridges where the Barrier ice abuts on land, and here Wilson lengthened out his trace and pulled

---

[1] *The Worst Journey in the World*, I, 246–251.   [2] *ibid.*, 240.

ahead, sounding for crevasses—' nice for us but not
so nice for Bill. Crevasses in the dark *do* put your
nerves on edge.' And at last in a snowy dip
between the twin peaks of the Knoll, 800 feet above
the sea, they pitched their last camp nineteen days
out, in the bleakest, least hospitable corner of that
desolate coast ; began at once to build their
' house ' of boulders, to chip out slabs of snow
weathered to the consistency almost of marble,
cementing all the crevices with gravel and drifted
snow : and mostly by the light of a hurricane lamp !
For two days and part of two nights they built it,
with jokes about the transitional period from the
Glacial to the Paleolithic Age. Before they had
even roofed their shelter—it was blowing too hard—
they made an attempt in the faint twilight of midday to reach the Rookery by a way between the
rock-wall and the ice-cliff that Wilson remembered.
One obstacle after another they surmounted till
faced with the insuperable last of all, an impasse
of pressure-ridges abutting on the sea-ice, behind
which they heard the Emperors calling. Twilight
was failing, total darkness again at hand, their
tracks hard to see, they found and lost and found
them again, reached their igloo just in time,
snatched a few hours' rest in their ice-hard bags,
up at three and worked at their roof till breakfast,
and with the first glimpse of light went down to
the Rookery again. Somehow they scrambled
over, climbed up, slithered down, wriggled along,
tumbled in and out of that tortuous maze of
crevassed and ridgy ice-upheaval to the rocks
where they left their battered sledge ; roped up,
worried their way lower, and then—

came up against a wall of ice which a single glance told us we could never cross. One of the largest pressure-ridges had been thrown, end on, against the cliff. We seemed to be stopped, when Bill found a black hole, something like a fox's earth, disappearing into the bowels of the ice. We looked at it : ' Well, here goes ! ' he said, and put his head in, and disappeared, Bowers likewise. It was a longish way, but quite possible to wriggle along, and presently I found myself looking out of the other side with a deep gully below me, the rock-face on one hand and the ice on the other. ' Put your back against the ice and your feet against the rock and lever your-self along,' said Bill, who was already standing on firm ice at the far end in a snow pit. We cut some fifteen steps to get out of that hole. Excited by now, and thoroughly enjoying ourselves, we found the way ahead easier, until the penguins' call reached us again and we stood, three crystallized ragamuffins, above the Emperors' home. . . .

We saw the Emperors standing all together, huddled under the Barrier cliff some hundreds of yards away. The little light was going fast : we were much more excited about the approach of complete darkness and the look of wind in the south than we were about our triumph. After indescribable effort and hardship we were witnessing a marvel of the natural world, and we were the first and only men who had ever done so ; we had within our grasp material which might prove of the utmost importance to science ; we were turning theories into facts with every observation we made—and we had but a moment to give.

. . . And so Bill and Birdie rapidly collected five eggs, which we hoped to carry safely in our fur mitts to our igloo on Mount Terror, where we could pickle them in the alcohol we had brought for the purpose. We also wanted oil for our blubber stove, and they killed and skinned three birds—an Emperor weighs up to $6\frac{1}{2}$ stones. . . . We legged it back as hard as we could go : five eggs in our fur mitts, Birdie with two skins tied to him and trailing behind, and myself with one. . . . We found the sledge, and none too soon, and now had three eggs left, more or less whole. Both mine had burst in my mitts . . . on the return journey I had my mitts

far more easily thawed out than Birdie's (Bill had none)
and I believe the grease in the egg did them good. . . .

As we groped our way back that night, sleepless, icy
and dog-tired in the dark and the wind and the drift, a
crevasse seemed almost a friendly gift.

'Things must improve,' said Bill next day, 'I think
we reached bed-rock last night.' We hadn't, by a long
way. . . . With great difficulty we got the blubber stove
to start, and it spouted a blob of boiling oil into Bill's
eye. For the rest of the night he lay, quite unable to
stifle his groans, obviously in very great pain ; he told
us afterwards that he thought his eye was gone.

It is extraordinary how often angels and fools do the
same thing in this life, and I have never been able to
settle which we were on this journey. I never heard
an angry word : once only (when this same day I could
not pull Bill up the cliff out of the penguin rookery) I
heard an impatient one : and these groans were the
nearest approach to complaint. Most men would have
howled. 'I think we reached bed-rock last night,' was
strong language for Bill. 'I was incapacitated for a
short time,' he says in his report to Scott. Endurance
was tested on this journey under unique circumstances,
and always these two men with all the burden of responsibility which did not fall upon myself, displayed that
quality which is perhaps the only one which may be
said with certainty to make for success, self-control.[1]

They had pitched their tent to shelter their gear
outside the igloo. There was an ominous calm in
the night. 'Then there came a sob of wind, and
all was still again. Ten minutes later and it was
blowing as if the world was having a fit of hysterics.'
'Bill, Bill, the tent has gone,'—from Bowers shouting
at the door. The tent, sole refuge of their return,
had been blown to the winds. Then these vikings
of the New Age, in bloodless war with elemental
forces, fought their way time and time again from

[1] *ibid.*, pp. 267–273.

the igloo door to where the tent had been to try and save their gear. They saved it, or all of it that mattered—got inside—' We're all right ! ' yelled Bowers—and for twenty-four hours lay and waited for the roof to go above them, while the drift poured in between the opening crevices of the walls. Above their igloo was a vacuum, and the suction of the wind lifted the canvas by successive jerks with deafening bangs like pistol-shots above the fury of the storm, hour after hour. At last it went, whipped to shreds and strips by the wind as hands rip linen. The rocks that had secured it fell in on them ; they were half-buried now in drift. And for forty-eight more hours they lay in their sleeping-bags, without food, exposed to a blizzard such as only blows in this wild corner of the Antarctic coast. ' It happened,' wrote Wilson afterwards, allowing himself one personal reference, ' to be my birthday.' It was his last ; and he spent it partly wondering whether the blizzard would last as long as eight years previously when he was in this spot with Cross and Whitfield, partly in revolving a plan for getting back with the floor-cloth for tent, and partly (the others said) in singing hymns in which Bowers joined him, and ' I,' says Cherry-Garrard, ' chimed in, somewhat feebly I suspect.' . . . ' I can well believe,' he continues, ' that neither of my companions gave up hope for an instant. They must have been frightened, but they were never disturbed.'

When on the 25th the wind abated, ' bitterly cold and utterly miserable though I don't think we showed it,' they crawled out of their sopping bags into the thick darkness to search for the tent—in

vain. Then they cooked a meal under the floor-
cloth, in their bags. At last the snow in the cooker
melted, and then a hoosh of tea and pemmican
' full of hairs, penguin feathers, dirt and debris,
but delicious,—and that burnt taste will always
bring back the memory.'

Then they fared forth again in a forlorn quest of
the tent.

Birdie went off before Bill and me. I followed Bill
down the slope. We could find nothing. But as we
searched, we heard a shout somewhere below and to the
right. We got on a slope, slipped, and went sliding down,
quite unable to stop ourselves, and came upon Birdie
with the tent, the outer lining still on the bamboos. Our
lives had been taken away and given back to us. We
were so thankful that we said nothing.[1]

They had another meal, and discussed what
they should do next. Bowers the undaunted was
all for ' one other tap at the Rookery.' But
Wilson, weighing up the situation calmly as ever,
considered that ' with one can of oil only, and
sleeping-bags in such a state as might make them
quite unusable should we again meet with really
low temperatures, we ought to return to Cape
Evans.' Cherry-Garrard says simply, 'There
really could be no common-sense doubt.' Even
so Wilson, though every ounce of baggage was a
toll on their strength, was unwilling to leave more
gear than absolutely necessary ; and only what
he felt should be spared he left carefully depoted
in a corner of the stone hut for future use, weighted
with rocks and the second sledge ; and there they
probably remain till this day. Bowers roped the

tent about his body whenever they camped ; ' if it went away he was going with it.'

Then they went back. Add to the conditions which they had experienced on their outward march, these : ice-sheeted garments cracking and no longer wind-proof ; sleeping-bags like coffins for solidity, piled high upon the sledge, the flaps of them stuffed with clothing to ensure an entry at night ; imprisonment in them for six hours' misery, seldom for conscious sleep, until the bags split and they got frost-bitten where they lay ; to rise each morning from an icy, or from a sodden, grave (according to the temperature) ; the flesh of their hands flabby with saturation and all the readier to freeze ; an hour's delay now to cook each meal, handling frozen metal ; Bowers down a crevasse to the length of his harness, saved by his comrades and his own wits ; Wilson leading thereafter, sounding as before, often guessing his direction ; the others sleeping at intervals even as they marched ; the luck changing for the better— longer marches with the lighter load—' How are your feet, Cherry ? ' from Bill. ' Very cold.' ' That's all right ; so are mine ' ; camp only when the feeling goes ; Hut Point at last ; and as they rounded it, walked into what seemed to them a blaze of light : it was the pale foreglow of the Antarctic dawn hitherto hidden from them by the black shadow of Erebus and Terror, just showing now above the northern horizon ; lunch-camp at Glacier Tongue, and then in quiet tones—' I want to thank you two for what you have done. I couldn't have found two better companions—and what is more I never shall.' Home in sight now—

' Spread out well,' said Bill, ' and they will be able to see that there are three men.' Eight days in.

How good [writes Cherry-Garrard] the memories of those days are. With jokes about Birdie's picture hat : with songs we remembered off the gramophone : with ready words of sympathy for frost-bitten feet : with generous smiles for poor jests : with suggestions of happy beds to come. We did not forget the Please and Thank you, which mean much in such circumstances, and all the little links with decent civilization which we could still keep going. I'll swear there was still a grace about us when we staggered in.[1]

The net result of their achievement ?—Three Penguins' eggs. Worth the cost of them ?—A thousand times yes ! How, it may be asked, did they survive ? Physique ?—But only one of them was unusually physically strong. Morale ?—They all had that. But neither physique nor morale combined could have stood that strain without another factor. The secret then, what was it ?— These men loved each other.

---

[1] *ibid.*, p. 296

CHAPTER XVIII

The Last Expedition (continued)

THE POLAR JOURNEY

I. PREPARATIONS

There is nothing in the world, or even out of it, which can be called good without qualification, save only the good will. . . . Even if it should happen that, by some special misfortune or adversity, this will should entirely lack power to accomplish its purpose, even if with the greatest efforts it should yet achieve nothing, and there should remain only the good will, then like a jewel it would still shine by its own light, having its whole value in itself.

KANT.

SCOTT'S relief was considerable. The day after their return he wrote (August 2) :

Wilson is very thin, but this morning very much his keen, wiry self. Bowers quite himself to-day. Cherry-Garrard still looks worn. It is evident that he has suffered most severely, but Wilson tells me that his spirit never wavered for a moment. Bowers has come through best—never was such a sturdy, active, undefeatable little man.

But the reaction lasted for weeks longer, especially in the circulation of the blood to hands and feet ; and although on the 7th Wilson recommended his daily climbs to the Ramp to take observations,[1]

---

[1] Ponting's photograph of him at the Sunshine Recorder on Wind Vane Hill (*Scott's Last Expedition*, I, 393) was taken on August 26.

the writing up of his Report was a difficulty, and
his fingers were still partially numb when on the
10th he took up his paint-brush again. Two days
later he joined Bowers at the snow-tub, as usual.
Of the journey itself he says little in his letters,
though to his wife he confided :

We were close up against trouble that might have
finished the three of us, but we were helped out of it by
the grace of God. On our wedding day we began the
building of Oriana Hut on Oriana Ridge. They want
to cancel the name now because the blizzard blew the
roof off and played such games with us there—but I
won't ever cancel the name, for I learned so much good
there in a very short time, and therefore I love the place
as I love you.

He was now adding picture after picture to his
portfolio, and was planning arrangements for their
exhibition in London the following year ; and
well over a hundred, of which some appear as
illustrations to *Scott's Last Expedition*, were completed before November. A critical description of
them has thus been given by one who is well
qualified to do so.

I have spoken of the drawings which he made when
sledging or when otherwise engaged away from painting
facilities, as at Hut Point. He brought back to Winter
Quarters a notebook filled with such sketches of outlines
and colours : of sunsets behind the Western Mountains :
of lights reflected in the freezing sea or in the glass houses
of the ice-foot : of the steam clouds on Erebus by day
and of the Aurora Australis by night. Next door to
Scott he rigged up for himself a table, consisting of two
venesta cases on end supporting a large drawing-board
some 4 feet square. On this he set to work systematic-
ally to paint the effects which he had seen and noted.
He painted with his paper wet, and necessarily, there-

fore, he worked quickly. An admirer of Ruskin, he wished to paint what he saw as truly as possible. If he failed to catch the effect he wished, he tore up the picture however beautiful the result he had obtained. There is no doubt as to the faithfulness of his colouring : the pictures recalled then and will still recall now in intimate detail the effects which we saw together. . . . In addition to the drawings of land, pack, icebergs and Barrier, the primary object of which was scientific and geographical, Wilson has left a number of paintings of atmospheric phenomena which are not only scientifically accurate but are also exceedingly beautiful. Of such are the records of auroral displays, parhelions, paraselenes, lunar haloes, fog bows, iridescent clouds, refracted images of mountains and mirage generally. If you look at a picture of a parhelion by Wilson not only can you be sure that the mock suns, circles and shafts appeared in the sky as they are shown on paper, but you can also rest assured that the number of degrees between, say, the sun and the outer ring of light were in fact such as he has represented them. You can also be certain in looking at his pictures that if cirrus cloud is shown, then cirrus and not stratus cloud was in the sky : if it is not shown, then the sky was clear. It is accuracy such as this which gives an exceptional value to work viewed from a scientific standpoint. Mention should also be made of the paintings and drawings made constantly by Wilson for the various specialists on the expedition whenever they wished for colour records of their specimens ; in this connection the paintings of fish and various parasites are especially valuable. . . .

Wilson himself set a low value on his artistic capacity. We used to discuss what Turner would have produced in a land which offered colour effects of such beauty. If we urged him to try and paint some peculiar effect and he felt that to do so was beyond his powers, he made no scruple of saying so. His colour is clear, his brushwork clean : and he handled sledging subjects with the vigour of a professional who knew all there was to be known about a sledging life. . . .[1]

---

[1] A. Cherry-Garrard, *The Worst Journey in the World*, I, 204–6.

SUNSET ON MOUNT EREBUS.

Scott's plan of campaign for the Polar Journey was that the motor transport should precede the main party and depot the bulk of the provisions at a point on the Barrier midway between the base and the Beardmore Glacier : that the pony-teams and dog-teams should be taken as far as to the foot of the Glacier, when the dog-teams should return, and the remainder of the ponies which had lasted so far be killed for food for the return. From the foot of the Glacier to the Pole and back (that is, roughly three-quarters of the total distance travelled, or 1,200 geographical miles) all should be done by man-haulage, unless any of the ponies were fit for the ascent. Wilson had always been somewhat sceptical of the value of motor-tractors in the Antarctic, and Scott's early expectations in this respect which had been encouraged by trials of them in Norway were shaken, so that the loss of one of the three tractors immediately on landing was not such a disaster as it then appeared. But since then half his ponies, including his three best, were already lost ; the remainder were far below expectations, and he started on his last journey fully handicapped indeed. It is small wonder that ' the immense fits of depression which attacked him ' sometimes gave way during these final weeks of anxiety to surface irritabilities.

Something has been said of Wilson's dealings with the dogs : he was now practising with the ponies.

I am very anxious about Titus Oates, who has had a great string of rotten unsound ponies thrown on his hands, and who is spoken to rather as though he was to blame whenever anything goes wrong with them, and of course he doesn't like it.

I am glad we have such an excellent man as the Inniskilling Dragoon to manage these beasts. We should be in great trouble without him. Of course they are all more troublesome now than they will be when it comes to heavy and continued work on the Barrier, but there will be some excitement during the first few days before they settle down. . . .

Bowers had hold of the three horses' heads—Victor, Snatcher and Nobby—Petty-officer Evans and I were busy with the sledge-straps, when Victor caught his nostril on the harness of Snatcher's hames and tore a piece of skin off. This frightened him so that he reared and frightened Snatcher, who immediately plunged and broke away with his empty sledge and galloped off towards home. Nobby, seeing Snatcher gallop off and Victor rearing, then jumped over Victor's sledge and galloped off also with his empty sledge swinging behind him. Bowers still held Victor. Evans ran after Snatcher. I ran after Nobby who was running due west out into the middle of the Strait. Every now and then they jumped a ridge of ice and plunged into a drift, and then a cloud of snow would bury them, and then the wind came up and raised so much drift that I lost sight of the other two, and didn't dare stop running for fear of losing sight of mine. I came up with him after running close on 3 miles. Happily I had a biscuit with me, and held it out to him a long way off : and he spotted it and allowed me to come up with it, and so I got hold of his head again, and we then walked home.

Some of the ponies were really dangerous animals, especially ' Christopher,' which Oates managed. It is to be noted that the ' Soldier ' never once hit a pony, however fractious he might be, and his patience and courage were admired as much as his skill in horse management. Here is an experience of Wilson's with another pony.

His favourite game is first to shake his head violently when he thinks you are off your guard ; this hits you indiscriminately in the chest or in the face or in the

stomach ; and then he tries to rear, comes down with
straight fore-legs on your feet which are now in just the
right place for them, and then you see his heels somewhere over your shoulder. The only thing to do is to
hold him tight by the head with a stiff arm, then his
heels can't reach you when he jumps—and knowing this,
he tries to bite you in the leg ! Take him all round on
a breezy day he keeps one busy, and yet he is one of the
quietest animals of the whole lot when on the march.
Some of them are much worse ; they seem to have
learned every trick a horse ever knew : the worst is
striking with the fore-feet, which is difficult (to prevent).
The comfort is that they will all give up these tricks when
they have been in harness on the Barrier for a few days.
Their one idea then is to eat everything—their hobbles,
picketing-lines, puttees, if they have any, or their head-
ropes, and if they get loose they will go for a sack of
oats on the sledge or else for our biscuits, which they
reach by eating through a canvas tank.

By October 17 the personnel for the main
Southern Journey had been selected, and Wilson's
Journal has this entry :

I don't see any other course open to me than to carry
through the job I came here for, which was in the main
this sledge-journey for the Pole. ' *L'homme propose, mais
le bon Dieu dispose* ' is an honest creed, and in this case
l'homme hasn't decided to do anything from first to last
that he wasn't convinced would be approved by his
infinitely better half, and *le bon Dieu* will do the rest.
Whatever happens, even if it's worse than anything one
can bring oneself to imagine, there is no more to be
said or done than this.

Oct. 23. Working at the taking of latitude sights—
mathematics, which I hate. It will be wiser to know a
little navigation on this Southern Sledge Journey.

By October 24 he had completed a summary
of all the reports sent in to him by ' his flock '
the Scientific Staff, with whose work he was immensely pleased. It was told later, as a thing

pleasant to see, how not only they but the other
officers also would ' hover ' about him, anxious to
win his approval to some piece of work they had
done. On the same day the motor-tractors started
from Cape Evans. On the same day also :

I stowed away all my damageable goods for my long
absence. We have very damp places in the Hut and I
had to make certain that all my drawing paper and
drawing material, medical stores and surgical instruments, gun and what-not, wouldn't be mildewed and
rusted by the time we return in March. I'm afraid
there is hardly a chance of my being back here in time
to read my mails and send an answer back by the ship.
She will almost certainly have gone home by the time
we return from our Southern Journey.

His high personal regard for Scott, ' with whom
I have been on the most pleasant and intimate
terms all the time,' had increased with their close
co-operation. ' There is nothing,' he writes, ' that
I would not do for him. He is a really good man,
and a perfect marvel in brain power : the cleverest
man all round I have ever known. His grasp of
things is quite wonderful.'

And now with feelings of deep thankfulness he
could record that the real purpose of his coming
South again was already achieved, whatever the
final issue might prove to be.

Oct. 31. . . . Since I wrote to you on Friday I have
had ample proof that I had a work to do down here,
for I have been having talks with several people, and
hearing grievances and confidences. It is a great thing
to know that one has had a job to do and that one has
been doing it more or less unconsciously and that to
some extent it has come off. . . . It isn't what I should
like to write to you about most of all, but it is what is
much in my mind last thing at night and first thing in
the morning, and it is a huge comfort to me to be able

to voice it to someone : for I only listen to what people
like to tell me here, and like Brer Rabbit lie low and
say nothing all the time, and keep on saying nothing
which seems to encourage confidences. My goodness !
I had hours of it yesterday ; as though I was a bucket
it was poured into me ; I suppose because this is the
last chance for some months, but it's a very great thing
to know what is going on in the minds of everyone here.
. . . Grievances there are bound to be and disagree-
ments, but as long as everyone can keep them from
boiling over I think we can rightly say that we have
been extraordinarily free from any want of unity. . . .
It will comfort you to know that I haven't a single un-
friend here in the whole party, positively not one, and
that puts me in a much better position for being useful.
I think having a wife who is all the world and all the
next world too to me, makes it impossible for me to
want another person to confide in. . . .

. . . Be assured I am content to feel that I was really
wanted here after all, as you assured me I was and
would be when we parted. . . . Whether we reach the
Pole or not I really care very little so long as we feel
we have done all we could. I feel I am here for a
better purpose than to merely get to the Pole. My next
few notes will be in small envelopes from camps on the
Barrier—God comfort you, my own dear wife.

At the same time Scott wrote to his wife the
words with which this book opens, and to Mr.
Reginald Smith as follows :

Wilson has been all that you expected of him. I find
myself wondering at his energy, his tact, or his unselfishness : such qualities have made him beloved by
all, and in return he wields the power of an oracle : he
is consulted in everything, from the larger issues to ridicu-
lously small details of life and work. I hold him mainly
responsible for the extraordinarily amicable relations which
have existed amongst us ; it is really a fact that there
have been no quarrels or other social troubles since the
expedition started. To sum up, he has proved himself
a greater treasure than even I expected to find him.

TABLE OF MILES AND DAYS TAKEN ON POLAR JOURNEY

	Geog. Miles (approx.)	Stat. Miles (approx.)	Outward Journey	General Conditions	Return Journey	General Conditions
Main Hut—One Ton Depot	130	150	Nov. 15	Blizzards and soft snow.		
One Ton Depot—Mid-Barrier	123	142	Nov. 26	The same.	Mar. 21 (less 11 miles)	Same as below. Death of Oates. Fatal blizzard.
Mid-Barrier—Lower Glacier	116	133	Dec. 9	The same. Four days' delay in blizzard.	Mar. 1	Sandy surfaces and low temperatures. Party weak.
Lower Glacier—Upper Glacier	108	125	Dec. 21	Soft snow in lower reaches. Good weather.	Feb. 18	Desperate descent. Death of Evans.
Upper Glacier—Three Degree Depot	131	151	Jan. 3	Good marching surfaces. Good weather.	Feb. 7	Same as below except for rise.
Three Degree Depot—Pole	192	221	Jan. 17	Gradual decline over sandy surfaces and sastrugi. Party feeling wind and cold.	Jan. 31	Gradual rise over same surfaces. Short spells of blizzards.
	800	922				

The Last Expedition (continued)

2. TO THE POLE

Did we think victory great?—So it is, but now it seems
to me that, when it cannot be helped, defeat is great, and
death and dismay are great.   WHITMAN.

WILSON'S Polar Journal now lies where
all may see it, beside Scott's at the
British Museum. It is confined as
usual to matters of fact dispassionately related,
mainly meteorological, and later, on their return
from the Pole, to geological discoveries also of
great importance. The impression gained is that
he is thoroughly enjoying himself. Otherwise it
is an accurate log, corroborative of Scott's more
descriptive record : the passages which are supplementary to Scott's have been fully quoted in
Mr. Cherry-Garrard's comprehensive account of the
journey. For Scott, the writing up of his *Journal*
each day was a serious matter—he felt it to be part
of his obligation to the public. And the discern-
ing reader, with an eye between the lines of his
reflective pages, may detect, not only the reactions
of a great soul at grips with circumstance, but
also, especially in the earlier stages, an unconscious
note of foreboding.

The story has been often told, but never too
often, by others who have drawn inspiration from
its pages, for as long as there exists among English-

men the passion of enthusiasm for noble deeds, so long will it remain as a heart-stirring heritage to the race.

The start was made on November 1, and at Safety Camp ' the flying rearguard ' of the pony-teams—Scott, Cherry-Garrard and Wilson—outward bound across the Great Ice Barrier—were overtaken by Ponting with his cinematograph ; and Wilson can still be seen, the last of this party of three, turning to wave a final farewell.

The first stages of the journey were indeed calculated to take the heart out of man and beast. Even before reaching One Ton Depot they had encountered a thick summer blizzard, and from there to the Mid-Barrier Depot climatic conditions went from bad to worse. Their course, set to follow the 170th parallel of longitude, was sometimes erratic in the teeth of mists and snow-drifts driving from the south, under clouded skies always, often in a whirl of thick soft snow-flakes, over surfaces in which the ponies sank to the fetlocks, sometimes through crusts with deep subsidences even half-way to the hocks. ' Our luck in the weather,' wrote Scott, ' is preposterous ' ; even Bowers' diary occasionally reflects the general depression. And yet strangely, in Wilson's diary, though it records the mere facts, there is no trace whatever of the prevailing gloom. The Motor Party were to have returned from their large Depot half-way between One Ton Depot and the Mid-Barrier on the 20th, but continued man-hauling for four days longer, so that Wilson was able to send back two short letters telling of their fortunes to within two marches from the latter Depot.

[*To his wife.*]

Nov. 20. Lat. 80° 30′. . . . Here is the first chance of sending you a line from a camp on the Barrier now three weeks out . . . with all our ten ponies still alive and every member of the Expedition as fit as can be. Much depends on what the ponies do during the next 14 days, by which time we shall be at the foot of the Beardmore Glacier. My own pony, Nobby, is the fittest of all still. . . .

We shall not take the dogs up the Glacier either. Well . . . I just hope I shall be one of the four to be chosen to go all the way to the Pole—just for your sake. I couldn't be fitter or harder than I am, and I feel equal to anything in the way of exertion. . . .

This life here has given me a new lease of life for years to come. I am so awfully fit—frightfully sunburnt —and very happy. On my return to Hut Point I shall get your letters ! I live now for that ; not for the Pole, I'm afraid, half so much. . . .

Nov. 24. Lat. 81° 15′. We are getting on splendidly —fine weather, and the horses doing steady solid pulling. We shot the first one to-day.

. . . My mind is much occupied with a hope that we shall be able sometime to go to Japan together. I have a longing to sketch there and see the country and the people more than any other place in the world. They are the only really naturally artistic race living, and I am sure one would learn much from them. . . . I have such happy hours—on the march and in my sleeping-bag, when I lie awake at all (not very often)—about our many happy times together. . . . And in years to come I hope we shall always have much hard, solid, useful work, though I intend to keep fitter than I did during the last 10 years. I see now that it was overdoing things badly, and I should have come a cropper but for this Expedition. Now I am entirely on my legs again. . . . God bless you, dearest—and all at home. My heart goes out to you. . . .

From the Mid-Barrier, reached on the 26th, to the foot of the Beardmore Glacier, plugging on blindly through a blank white wall, weather and surfaces became still worse, and the Expedition's prospects more dismal. When on December 5, these unlooked-for conditions culminated in a blizzard ' such as one might expect to be driven at us by all the powers of darkness ' (Bowers), dismay gave place to something akin to despair. This was actually the fifth blizzard they had encountered since the start, and it held them up for four days of misery. It struck them too at the most unfortunate moment, when they needed ' but one short march and the ponies' task was done.' The Camp was called ' The Slough of Despond.'

The position was now really serious : they were already consuming Summit rations. ' I am glad,' wrote Bowers, ' that he (Capt. Scott) has Dr. Bill in his tent ; there is something always so reassuring about Bill—he comes out best in adversity.' The worst feature of the blizzard was that the temperature rose to above freezing-point, so that men lay in their bags in slush and even pools of thawed snow : Wilson reading a copy of ' In Memoriam ' (lent to him by Cherry-Garrard). This, and a pocket Testament and Prayer Book, were the only books that he took on to the Pole.

What a perfect piece of faith and hope ! Makes me feel that if the end comes to me here or hereabouts there will be no great time for O. to sorrow. All will be as it was meant to be, and her faith and hope and trust will be to her what Tennyson's was to him. ' In Memoriam ' is difficult reading and the beauty of it wants pains to find, but it is splendid when found.

Still no trace of depression in Wilson's diary, only distress for the ponies : constantly up with

the others feeding them, digging them out, caring
for them. His own concern found practical expression in that on the last day of the blizzard
he sacrificed his whole biscuit-ration to his pony,
and after a day's march knee-deep in snow reached
'Shambles Camp' 'ravenously hungry,' where
the last ponies were shot. 'Thank God,' he
wrote in his Journal, 'the horses are now all done
with and we begin the heavy work ourselves.'

[*To his wife.*]
Dec. 10, '11.   Lat. 83° 35'.   Just South of Mount Hope
and on the Beardmore Glacier. All is well with us,
and as for me I was never stronger or fitter in all my
life. Meares leaves us to-morrow to return with the two
dog-teams and Dimitri—and I must send you just a word.
We have had very difficult weather lately—really very
difficult—but we have got through so far all right. Our
surfaces are dreadfully heavy with a phenomenal amount
of fresh-fallen snow, but thank God the horses are all
dead now. We shot the last 5 last night as we reached
the entrance to the Beardmore, having no more food
for them, and having been on the march with them
yesterday for eleven hours with no halt and no food
ourselves : and when we camped we had to skin them
all and cut them up and depot the meat before turning
in. But I am as fit as can be and just thrive on it : I
am afraid one or two of the others are not. It is telling
on them a bit : however, such hard work is not the
rule, and we shall have easy days as well. We shall have
another party returning in ten or twelve days' time,
reducing us then to 8. I expect to be one of the 8 at
any rate : but whether I shall have the good fortune to
be considered strong enough to be one of the final 4 or
not—why, I don't know. No one knows yet who they
will be—but I do hope to be one of them for your dear
sake. . . . Then back to Hut Point with light loads
and a fair wind at times and a sail on the sledge, and
then our mails—waiting for us there—and news of my

beloved—and of home—and of the dear Smiths, and of all that you have been doing . . . we shall be back to our mails in another ten or twelve weeks, and the time is simply flying. . . . It is good to have been loved by you, and oh, a privilege indeed to have been allowed to love you. God keep you.

On the last night of the blizzard, with a more hopeful prospect for the morrow, Scott had written —how prophetically !—' nothing can recall four lost days.' Four days in hand would have saved him at the last. This blizzard was, in actual fact, a death-blow.

Up the Beardmore Glacier now—the gateway to the Pole—terribly severe pulling in deep soft snow where Shackleton had been favoured with blue ice. ' Up along the hostile mountains where the hair-poised snow-slide shivers '—10,000 feet to the summit of the Polar Plateau. Wilson's Journal becomes descriptive of the appearance and geological formation of the immense mountain walls above them : his marvellous series of panoramic sketches begin to unfold page after page : in spite of a consequent attack of snow-blindness he is feeling ' as fit as a fiddler, and the surroundings are glorious.' With Mount Kyffin left behind, and the Cloudmaker passed, the Glacier widened out, and the spirits of the party rose with a better pulling surface : and when the Upper Glacier Depot just beyond Buckley Island was reached the heartrending decision must be made—who was to go back with the First Supporting Party.

[*To his wife.*]
Dec. 21, '11. S. lat. 85°. Upper Glacier Depot, by Mt. Darwin. We have now less than 300 miles to go to reach the Pole and we are well in hand for time. . . .

I am as fit and strong as a horse and have great hopes of being one of the final party. The first returning party leaves us to-morrow morning. They are Atkinson, Cherry-Garrard, Wright, and the youngest seaman, Keohane. They will be back in heaps of time to catch the ship, so this letter goes with them. In another fortnight the next four will return. I may be one of them. We shall see.

In another two months we shall be well on the way home towards Hut Point where we shall get our mails ; and news—news of my beloved wife. God knows how I long for it : and then I shall know whether the last six years' work has been satisfactory or not, too ; that is a little nervous outlook—for I hope you will let me know whether my efforts at the Grouse and the British Mammals have been decently reviewed or slated as bad work. I am prepared for either ; I only know they were the best I could do under the circumstances, and as you liked them I can swallow anything that is said besides. Only I *hope*, for Reginald Smith's sake, that the Grouse Disease Report is to be a very great success.

Please write to Mrs. Cherry-Garrard and say how splendidly her son has worked on this sledge journey. He has been a real trump, and has made himself beloved by everyone—a regular brick to work and a splendid tent-mate. I am simply proud of having had something to do with getting him on to this Expedition. Tell the Smiths I am very proud of him.

He is very disappointed at having to go back with the first four ; but it is right, because he is the youngest. He is not worn out in the least, though he has worked his utmost all the way. I am very fond of him. Everyone on this journey is as fit as can be. We have all got thinner in the face, of course, but Scott says I have lost less than anyone else. I believe it is so, though the work up the Glacier has been heavy. We are over the worst of it all now though, and we come home with light loads from depot to depot. All my love is rolled up in this. . . .

Conditions now seem to show a sudden and surprising change. The sympathetic reader of *Scott's*

Journal feels that he can breathe again. No longer those desperately short marches at the cost of excessive physical and mental weariness, but marches on ski over the comparatively level surface of the Plateau averaging 15 miles a day, in improved weather if with a steadily searching south-east wind. A Happy Christmas and a good filling meal. By December 30 Scott's party, which had lost 6½ days altogether in the fatal blizzard and the soft snow of the lower slopes of the Glacier, had actually overhauled Shackleton's dates, but the effort of doing so was a severe tax, greater than they realized at the time. Here, too, Scott showed his qualities as a leader, steering his course to the avoidance of crevasses and disturbances with unerring judgment. The extraordinary sight of a Skua gull on the wing the day before reaching ' Three Degree Depot ' evidently raised conjecture in his mind and Wilson's. Midway between the Upper Glacier Depot and the Pole the Last Supporting Party—Lieutenant Evans, with Petty-Officers Lashly and Crean—was sent back.[1] At the last moment Scott decided on a five-man party for the Pole, and Bowers was added to his tent, with Wilson, Oates, and Petty-Officer Evans.

[*To his wife.*]
Jan. 3, '12. S. lat. 87° 32'. To-morrow . . . the last supporting party returns to the winter quarters—and they will take this note home, arriving probably in time to catch the ship. I am one of the five to go on to the Pole. So this may be the last you hear of me for an-

---

[1] The tale of their perilous return has been finely told by Evans in *South with Scott*, chap. xv, and by Lashly in his diary, quoted in *The Worst Journey in the World*, pp. 384–406.

other whole year . . . only I am glad for your sake
that I am one of the five . . . all fit and strong and
well, and only 148 more miles to go. . . . It seems too
good to be true that this long journey to the Pole should
be realizing itself—we ought to be there in less than a
fortnight now. . . . Our five are all very nice together
and we shall be a very happy party. . . . You know
my love for you—it's just myself, and all I do and all I
pray for is your good. Be strong in hope and in faith
if you hear no more of me after this till next year. . . .
I believe firmly that we have a lot to do together when
we meet again. I am full of plans and possibilities as
we stolidly plod along with our sledges—but oh, how I
long to be with you again ! Give my dearest love to
dear old Dad and Mother and all the family, and to your
dear folk and the Aunts and the Smiths and all. God
bless them and you.

Those fine fast marches over the Plateau must
have been very heartening. Hopes were high as
they set forth to cover the last lap, daily diminish-
ing the miles between them and their goal : Scott
and Wilson pulling on ski in front, Oates and
Petty Officer Evans also on ski behind them : while
Bowers pluckily made his own pace on foot between
the four. Scott seems, for the first time on the
whole journey, to have been happy.

It is quite impossible to speak too highly of my companions. Each fulfils his office to the party—Wilson,
first as doctor, ever on the look-out to alleviate the small
pains and troubles incidental to the work ; now as cook,
quick, careful and dexterous, ever thinking of some fresh
expedient to help the camp life ; tough as steel on the
traces, never wavering from start to finish. . . .

And yet, from now onward, a little doubt begins
to creep into the mind of the reader. Seaman
Evans had cut his hand and Wilson was daily
dressing it—a trifle perhaps in the ordinary way :

but when 100 miles from their goal and with 800 more to go, a slight mishap may have far-reaching consequences. The party as a whole, though fit and sound, were for some unexplainable reason beginning to feel the cold, though the temperatures were not yet really low, and Oates more than the rest of them. There were probably climatic reasons for this—'some damp quality' in the air perhaps; but further, those cruelly severe marches up the lower reaches of the Beardmore had tried them more than they knew. And the surfaces were getting worse—loose 'sandy' snow, and 'bearded' sastrugi. 'It's going to be a stiff pull *both ways* apparently,' Scott wrote; and again, 'It takes it out of us like anything. None of us ever had such hard work before.'

Wilson's Journal maintains the same equable level—neither minimizing nor magnifying the difficulties: his eyes are on the sky, noting the shape and colours of the clouds, or on the surface of the wind-swept snow, crested with ice-crystals, which he sketches: the sastrugi and sandy drifts make the going difficult sometimes.

On the 16th, Bowers' 'sharp eyes' detected a black speck ahead. Wilson's account is as follows :—

Jan. 16. We got away at 8 a.m. and made 7·5 miles by 1.15, lunched, and then in 5·3 miles came on a black flag and the Norwegian's sledge, ski and dog-tracks running about N.E. and S.W. both ways. The flag was of black bunting tied with string to a fore and after which had evidently been taken off a finished-up sledge. The age of the tracks was hard to guess—but probably a couple of weeks—or three or more—the flag was fairly well frayed at the edges. We camped here and examined the tracks and discussed things. The surface was fairly

good in the forenoon—23°, and all the afternoon we were
coming down hill with again a rise to the W., and a
fall and a scoop to the East where the Norwegians came
up evidently by another glacier.

Jan. 17. We camped on the Pole itself at 6.30 p.m.
this evening. In the morning we were up at 5 a.m. and got
away on Amundsen's tracks, going S.S.W. for 3 hours, passing two small snow cairns, and then, finding his tracks too
much snowed up to follow, we made our own bee-line for
the Pole. Camped for lunch at 12.30 and off again from
3 to 6.30 p.m. It blew from force 4 to 6 all day in our
teeth with temp. –22°, the coldest march I ever remember. It was difficult to keep one's hands from freezing in
double woollen and fur mitts. Oates, Evans and Bowers
all have pretty severe frost-bitten noses and cheeks and we
had to camp early for lunch on account of Evans's hands.

It was a very bitter day. Sun was out now and again,
and observations taken at lunch, and before and after
supper, and at night, at 7 p.m. and at 2 a.m. by our
time. The weather was not clear—the air was full of
crystals driving towards us as we came South, and making
the horizon grey and thick and hazy. We could see no
sign of cairn or flag, and from Amundsen's direction
of tracks this morning he has probably hit a point about
3 miles off. We hope for clear weather to-morrow, but
in any case are all agreed that he can claim prior right
to the Pole itself. He has beaten us in so far as he
made a race of it. We have done what we came for
all the same and as our programme was made out.
From his tracks we think there were only 2 men—on
ski, with plenty of dogs on rather low diet. They seem
to have had an oval tent. We sleep one night at the
Pole and have had a double hoosh with some last bits
of chocolate, and Ber's [Bernard Rendall's] cigarettes
have been much appreciated by Scott and Oates and
Evans. A tiring day : now turning into a somewhat
starchy frozen bag. To-morrow we start for home and
shall do our utmost to get back in time to send the
news to the ship.

Jan. 18. Sights were taken in the night, and at about
5 a.m. we turned out and marched from this night-camp
about 3¾ miles back in a S.E.¹ʸ direction to a spot which

we judged from our last night's sights to be the Pole. Here we lunched—camp—built a cairn—took photos— flew the Queen-Mother's Union Jack and all our own flags. We call this the Pole—though as a matter of fact we went ½ a mile further on in a S.E.^{ly} direction, after taking further sights, to the actual final spot, and here we left the Union Jack flying. During the forenoon we passed the Norwegian's last S.^{ly} camp. They called it Polheim, and left here a small tent, with Norwegian and Fram flags flying, and a considerable amount of gear in the tent—half reindeer sleeping-bags, sleeping-socks— reinskin trousers, 2 pair—a sextant and artif. horizon—a hypsometer with all the thermoms broken. I took away the spirit lamp of it which I have wanted for sterilizing and making disinfectant lotions of snow. There were also letters there—one from Amundsen to King Haakon with a request that Scott should send it to him. There was also a list of the 5 men who made up their party, but no news as to what they had done. I made some sketches here, but it was blowing very cold, − 22°. Birdie took some photos. We found no sledge there, though they said there was one—it may have been buried in drift. The tent was a funny little thing for 2 men, pegged out with white line and tent-pegs of yellow wood. I took some strips of blue-grey silk off the tent seams—it was perished. The Norskies had got to the Pole on Dec. 16th and were here from 15th to 17th. At our lunch South Pole Camp we saw a sledge-runner with a black flag about ½ a mile away blowing from it. Scott sent me on ski to fetch it and I found a note tied to it showing that this was the Norskies' actual final Pole position. I was given the flag and the note with Amundsen's signature,[1] and I got a piece of the sledge-runner as well. The small chart of our wanderings shows best how all these things lie. After lunch we made 6·2 miles from the Pole Camp to the North again—and here we are camped for the night.

The pencil sketches which he made at the Pole are in the possession of the King. ' It was blowing

---

[1] Now in the Scott Polar Research Institute, Cambridge, with the Wilson relics.

very cold, −22°,' and it had been ' the coldest march I ever remember.' [1]

A comparison of the photographs taken at the Pole shows Wilson the fittest of the party : his face is full, and appears free from frost-bite. In one of these groups taken by Bowers, Scott and Wilson are seen with heads thrown back, roaring with laughter, evidently at some remark of the photographer. That men could laugh at all under such conditions is something that calls for more than a passing comment.

There is no hint of any ' collapse of morale ' here—' We have done what we came for.' That was enough for Wilson. Effort with him was always worth more than achievement : sincerity of purpose and purity of motive worth much more than success. And if comparisons, always invidious, are needed, why then—

The South Pole was actually attained by Amundsen, but to all time it will be inseparably associated with the name of Scott. . . . It was the early pioneer work of Scott—*not flamboyant nor sensational, but superbly thorough and honest*—which rendered possible the later successes of Shackleton and Amundsen. And henceforth, whenever men speak of the South Pole or of the Antarctic Continent, it is the thought of Scott . . . and of his noble comrades which will be present. Scott and the South Pole are synonymous for all ages. [2]

---

[1] It is not the actual temperature in the Polar Regions, but the presence of wind, that most affects the explorer. On January 31 in the same temperature with no wind Wilson notes ' delightfully warm.' The altitude also makes a difference, perhaps a great difference. Cp. *The Polar Regions*, p. 21 *et seq.* (F. Debenham) and *The Worst Journey*, II, 502–8.

[2] Extract from a balanced survey of Antarctic exploration in *Geographical Discovery*, by Joseph Jacobs. The italics are ours.

The Last Expedition (continued)

3. THE LAST JOURNEY

*This is the most fascinating ideal I think I ever imagined,
to become entirely careless of your own soul or body in
looking after the welfare of others.*

E. A. W. (from an early letter).

THE orb of a world swung below them :
800 miles to go ! No wonder that Scott,
looking back across the immense wastes
of the frozen fields they had striven through,
wrote : 'Now for the run home and a desperate
struggle. I wonder if we can do it.'

His fears about stiff pulling both ways from the
88th parallel to the Pole and back were well
founded. The Pole lies 1,000 feet below the
summit of the Plateau. They were pulling up a
steady rise across the undulating surface of which
minute particles of snow, frozen too hard to melt
with the friction of the sledge-runners, blew hither
and thither like sand-drifts in a desert ; where
also, even when sledging under sail (the tent's
bamboo support for mast, a Norwegian ski-runner
for yard, and the floor-cloth for sail), occasional
blizzards made the picking up of cairns and depots
difficult, and threatened a break-up of the weather.
'Wilson and Bowers are my stand-by : I don't
like the easy way Oates and Evans get frost-
bitten.'

Half-way from the Pole to the Glacier, surface
conditions improved and the miles came faster.
On February 7, relief was great at being off the
Summit, after 20 days from the Pole : but now
they were in the crevassed region of the Upper
Glacier again. Wilson was snow-blind and had
severely strained a tendon of his leg, Scott had
bruised his shoulder, Evans's frost-bitten fingers
were suppurating ; all were cold and very
tired, especially Oates : Bowers, if anything, was
fittest.

Wilson's Journal is still filled with observations
of meteorology and glaciation, sketches of parhelia
and ice-crystals ; some of the latter resemble the
structure of ' gorse,' others are ' minute agglo-
merate spicules like tiny sea-urchins,' the ripples
in the snow remind him of the scales on the wings
of butterflies, or sometimes of shell-porcelain : and
when he notes that Titus picked up his lost pipe
he must have been reminded of old days when he
flung his own away in Crippetts woods and found
it again. He does not extenuate the awful nature
of the surfaces and the weather, but always there is
the ring of hope, despite the fact that for five days
he pulled blindfold in agony with snow-blindness
without complaint : for five more similarly with a
badly swollen leg.

On February 8, at Buckley Island by Mount
Darwin in the upper reaches of the Glacier, he
had ' a regular field-day geologizing,' and (though
every minute stolen from sleep was precious now)
' was very late turning in.' Next day the same—
' and got some good things written up in Sketch
Book.' These notes are of the utmost value to

science ; and from five of the neatly written pages
two are here reproduced, to show the care and
precision of the writer under conditions which can
only be imagined.[1] His deductions from these
finds are as valuable as his observations both here
and on the ' Cloudmaker ' half-way down the
glacier ; and at his special request 35 lbs. weight
of specimens was added to the sledge, and carried
to the end.

The descent of the Beardmore Glacier was undoubtedly the most difficult and dangerous feat
on the whole of the Polar Journey. It took only
a day less to accomplish than the ascent had done.
Every mountaineer knows how much easier it is
to climb up than down ; but here were not only
a chaos of deceptively lidded crevasses and steeply
terraced ice-slopes down which the sledge was
always on the point of over-running, but also

---

[1] Below the snow-tops of Mount Buckley dolerite crags fall
in red-brown perpendicular columns to vertical cliffs of light
yellow sandstone weathering to red terra-cotta with bands
of coal and shale.　Huge blocks of limestone, sandstone and
dolerite moraine are strewn about its base, and with them
are large quartzite pebbles mixed—true water-worn—in
which were also to be seen long stalks of vegetable origin
with cellular markings in cast, and black crystalline coal fragments in the pits.　Most of the bigger leaves are distinctly
beech-like in shape and variation, like British beech but
smaller, and the venation much more abundant and finer in
character.

One fragment of coal yielded a lump of solid iron pyrites
breaking down into a yellow efflorescence of sulphur on the
outside, but shiny and metallic within.　Iron-stone there is,
hard and heavy in squarish blocks, but nothing like hæmatite
proper.　The bluish limestone blocks disclosed one minute
fragment of *possible* archeo-cyathus with a doubtful ring.

Buckley Id. (1.)

The Limestone in situ above the top of Sandstone?
Water pools & runnels in moraine – no water
Coarse grained sandstone – with pebble size of hazel
nuts. not common. Easily broken up & generally breaking
White masses of Quartzite – dead white – like chalk. but
not much grit and much worn on outside
Limestone in large boulders & multitude of small bol. in
the moraine of Mt Buckley – all lying below & out
side the debris from the Sandstone cliffs. none
up the slope. Must have come from higher
up somewhere. possibly from between Mt Darwin
& Mt Buckley – where a very heavy glacier comes
down from mountains at the back & from the
summit. Don't think it can be the stratum
of paler grey rock above the sandstone as
there were no blocks of it on the sandstone
debris slopes.

Snow top

Dolerite crags – & columns – dark chocolate
or red brown –

Sandstone, vertical cliffs. light yellow.
weathering to red terra cotta.
Bands of no great breadth of coal
& shale & slaty coal.

angle up to glacier slope
10° to 15°

Section of Upper part
of moraine:

Sandstone blocks only
and dolerite

Debris slope

grey part
of moraine

Limestone. Sandstone
+ dolerite
moraine

Tent

PAGE FROM POLAR SKETCH BOOK

Buckley I? (5).

The large limestone blocks which characterized the moraine all along its upper & middle length were of pale bluish French chalk grey. Sometimes a little greenish in tint — Sometimes streaked with a rich green matter in irregular veins. breaking often with a clean surface. The large blocks are heavily & richly veined often with white calcite. & the amount of this limestone. gave a quite distinct colour to the moraine from the sandstone debris bank above which was all yellow & terracotta red with dark red brown blocks of weathered dolerite. We found no limestone that could be called pink or dark. it was all pale grey. I hunted these blocks over & over for Archaeocyathus. & found only nothing. except one minute fragment chipped out with a doubtful ring. Amongst the gravel fragments of the moraine however were a number of small pieces of grey limestone almost like oolite. full of small round spheres the size of hard fish roe. which were to be seen on many faces in cross section as small double rings. These I at first took for Archaeocyathus but soon saw there was no linear arrangement on any face. They may be connected with the foraminif. ruminants found by Shackleton. or radiolarians. don't know. but brought a number of bits for section. The one fragment which may be an archaeocyatn is this size

Nat. size

PAGE FROM POLAR SKETCH BOOK

[284]

sheer landfalls and icefalls whose whereabouts could only be guessed at from above. Again and again they tried to cut corners, winding in and out amongst the pressure, 'crossing multitudes of bridges,' or 'plunging into an icefall in which we wandered for hours and hours.' Added to the physical dangers of the descent was the mental anxiety of keeping the track and, worst of all, the uncertainty of finding the mid-Glacier Depot. On February 13, when nearing the region of the 'Cloudmaker' in a turmoil of broken ice and through a baffling fog, with food enough for barely one meal, their hopes of finding the Depot had nearly ebbed when, after a false alarm, 'Wilson saw the actual Depot flag, and the relief to all was inexpressible.' Safety was thus achieved, but again at the price of severe snow-blindness.

On February 17, at the foot of the Glacier, occurred the death of the strongest man of the party—Seaman Evans. Though for a month (that is, even before reaching the Pole) his condition had been such as to cause increasing anxiety, and though his collapse was hastened by heavy falls in the Glacier, this gallant petty-officer was actually pulling in harness the day he died. His death it was that affected the spirits of the party ; not the disappointment in priority at the Pole. 'It is a very terrible thing to lose a companion in this way'; but they stood by him and tended him to the last, even 'when the safety of the remainder seemed to demand his abandonment.'

And so they went out on to the Barrier, and at once 'the surfaces were terrible, like pulling over desert sand.'

In estimating the preliminary causes that led to the disaster, Scott in his Last Message says, 'We fought these untoward events with a will and conquered . . . but all the facts above enumerated were as nothing to the surprise that awaited us on the Barrier.' Instead of the southerly wind which they had anticipated, and which would have enabled them to sledge under sail as on the Plateau, they encountered either no wind at all or light northerly airs. These northerly airs, though warmer in their upper currents, are cold on the Barrier level, where they cause, and lack the force to scatter, a deposit of ice-crystals on the snow. Moreover, though the sun shone brightly it had no warmth, and by excessive radiation hardened the ice-crystals to an extent which made any glide for the sledge-runners impossible. Further, it is precisely at the end of February that the dip of the sun below the Southern horizon occurs. Thus, temperatures were in the minus thirties by day and in the minus forties by night : an average of ten degrees lower than on the Plateau 10,000 feet above. And further, the season was rapidly closing in ; the travellers' vitality was depleted ; it was now more than ever a race against time.

On February 24 Wilson was stricken with another bout of snow-blindness ; he was ever too ready not only to sketch but also, we are told, to sacrifice his eyes to track-finding without goggles, but he still wrote up his diary despite it as before, until February 27—when his diary ceases. The last entry is :

Overcast all forenoon and cleared to splendid weather afternoon. Good march on ski—some fair breeze. 12·2 miles. Turned in at -37°.

All his life Wilson had kept a diary, recording the events and work done for each day as an act of thanksgiving. Time and the spending of time were so precious in his eyes that he regarded the record of the hours as a sacred duty. Here for the first time it ceases : and this has significance. For it is certain that he would never have abandoned it now unless circumstances had dictated a more urgent duty. On the same day Scott's diary, which for some days had lapsed to hurried short sentences, has the entry : ' It is a critical position.' The inference is clear—each minute in camp was now required for attention to his companions : ' Wilson, the best fellow that ever stepped, has sacrificed himself again and again to the sick men of the party.' This was his Odyssey : for weeks he had been ' striving to win his own soul and his comrades' homeward way ' : now, in the supreme hour of his life he could realize an ideal higher still—the highest that his young imagination had conceived. ' This is the most fascinating ideal I think I ever imagined, to become entirely careless of your own soul or body in looking after the welfare of others.'

From February 21 to March 2 the mileages covered show a desperate struggle, and on that day they reached the mid-Barrier Depot. Here three distinct blows awaited them. First, a shortage of fuel, insufficient to last till the next Depot (One Ton), due to the perishing of the leather washers ; second, Oates disclosed his badly frost-bitten feet which he had till then concealed ; third, a south wind in the night which brought bad weather.

[From *Scott's Journal*.]

2nd. We are in a *very* queer street since there is no doubt we cannot do the extra marches and feel the cold horribly.

3rd. God help us, we can't keep up this pulling, that is certain. Amongst ourselves we are unendingly cheerful, but what each man feels in his heart I can only guess.

4th. We are in a very tight place indeed, but none of us are despondent yet, or at least we preserve every semblance of good cheer, but one's heart sinks as the sledge stops dead at some sastrugi behind which the surface sand lies thickly heaped. . . . Providence to our aid ! We can expect little from man now. . . . I don't know what I should do if Wilson and Bowers weren't so determinedly cheerful over things.

5th. Our fuel dreadfully low and the poor Soldier nearly done. . . . We none of us expected these terribly low temperatures, and of the rest of us Wilson is feeling them most ; mainly, I fear, from his self-sacrificing devotion in doctoring Oates' feet.

6th. Poor Oates is unable to pull, sits on the sledge when we are search-tracking—he is wonderfully plucky, as his feet must be giving him great pain. He makes no complaint, but his spirits only come up in spurts now, and he grows more silent in the tent.

7th. One feels that for poor Oates the crisis is near, but none of us are improving, though we are wonderfully fit considering the really excessive work we are doing. . . . I should like to keep the track to the end.

8th. Worse and worse this morning; poor Oates' left foot can never last out, and time over foot gear something awful. . . . Wilson's feet giving trouble now, but this mainly because he gives so much help to others.

9th. (No entry.)

10th. Things steadily downhill. Oates' foot worse. He has rare pluck and must know that he can never get through. He asked Wilson if he had a chance this morning, and of course Bill had to say he didn't know. In point of fact he has none. . . .

11*th.* Titus Oates is very near the end, one feels. What we or he will do, God only knows. We discussed the matter after breakfast : he is a brave fine fellow and understands the situation, but he practically asked for advice. Nothing could be said but to urge him to march as long as he could. One satisfactory result of the discussion : I practically ordered Wilson to hand over the means of ending our troubles to us, so that any of us may know how to do so. Wilson had no choice between doing so and our ransacking the medicine case.

' Slog on, just slog on,' was all that Wilson could now reply to Oates, and for four more days the gallant Soldier struggled on, until on March 16, the eve of his birthday, he took the course that has passed into history.

We knew that poor Oates was walking to his death, but though we tried to dissuade him we knew it was the act of a brave man and an English gentleman. We all hope to meet the end with a similar spirit, and assuredly the end is not far. I can only write at lunch and then only occasionally. The cold is intense, −40 at midday. My companions are unendingly cheerful . . . still confident of getting through—or pretend to be—I don't know !

Another march they made, carrying their lost comrade's sleeping-bag and finnesko upon the sledge, when they abandoned them and their theodolite, and covering 17 miles in four marches pitched their last camp as truly as ever on March 21 at a point 11 miles distant from One Ton Depot when the nine days' blizzard fell on them. Their fuel was finished, their food nearly : at One Ton Depot lay provisions sufficient to keep them alive for weeks. At One Ton Depot also on March 4, with food for that journey but no more, Cherry-

Garrard had arrived with the dog-teams to meet them, to be held up by a four-days' blizzard there. But diminish the 11 miles by half, and halve that again, and suppose each to have been cognizant of the other's whereabouts, and suppose further the dates to have coincided ; in that ' scene of whirling drift ' they could never have come together.

Warming his numbed fingers at the flame of a lamp improvised by a tin and wick from a finnesko, Scott wrote his Message to the Public and his last letters. And if ever the depth of this man's nature was apparent it was so in the high tide of soul which inspired these unforgettable sentences. A characteristic of the faultlessness of great literature is the ease with which it lives in the memory, and these sentences once read can never be forgotten.

The causes of the disaster are not due to faulty organization, but to misfortune in all risks which had to be undertaken. . . . But it would do your heart good to be in our tent, and to hear our songs and the cheery conversation. . . . We have decided to die naturally in the track. . . . We could have got through if we had neglected our sick. . . .

We are weak, writing is difficult, but for my own sake I do not regret this journey, which has shown that Englishmen can endure hardships, help one another, and meet death with as great a fortitude as ever in the past. We took risks, we knew we took them ; things have come out against us, and therefore we have no cause for complaint, but bow to the will of Providence, determined still to do our best to the last. . . . Had we lived, I should have had a tale to tell of the hardihood, endurance and courage of my companions which would have stirred the heart of every Englishman. These rough notes and our dead bodies must tell the tale. . . .

To Mrs. E. A. Wilson.

MY DEAR MRS. WILSON,—

If this letter reaches you Bill and I will have gone out together. We are very near it now and I should like you to know how splendid he was at the end—everlastingly cheerful and ready to sacrifice himself for others, never a word of blame to me for leading him into this mess. He is not suffering, luckily, at least only minor discomforts.

His eyes have a comfortable blue look of hope and his mind is peaceful with the satisfaction of his faith in regarding himself as part of the great scheme of the Almighty. I can do no more to comfort you than to tell you that he died as he lived, a brave, true man— the best of comrades and staunchest of friends.

My whole heart goes out to you in pity,

Yours,

R. SCOTT.

Over the lonely tent on the Great Ice Barrier the darkness of the long winter night fell and deepened, and over the bereaved party in the Hut 150 miles away. The *Terra Nova*, bringing the long-hoped-for mails, had come and gone.

Eight months later the Search Party took the trail again for the last time south across the Great Ice Barrier. On November 11, 1912, they reached One Ton Depot on a day of bright sunshine radiant with iridescent alto-stratus clouds. In the afternoon they continued south when the scarce-seen hint of a hummock in the snow, a thought to westward of the line of cairns, called a halt.

Wright came across to us. ' It is the tent.' I do not know how he knew. Just a waste of snow : to our right the remains of one of last year's cairns, a mere mound : and then three feet of bamboo sticking quite alone out of the snow : and then another mound of snow, perhaps a trifle more pointed. We walked up to it. I do not think we quite realized—not for very long —but someone reached up to a projection of snow, and brushed it away. The green flap of the ventilator of the tent appeared, and we knew that the door was below.[1]

They found the tent pitched as truly as ever. Atkinson and Cherry-Garrard first entered it :

Bill especially had died very quietly with his hands folded over his chest, Birdie also quietly.[2]
Wilson and Bowers were found in the attitude of sleep, their sleeping-bags closed over their heads as they would naturally close them. Scott died later. He had thrown back the flaps of his sleeping-bag and opened his coat. The little wallet containing the three notebooks was under his shoulders and his arm flung across Wilson.[3]

They left them where they lay, the world their couch, the snow their coverlet, the sky their canopy. They removed the bamboo supports of the tent and let it cover them, and raised a mighty cairn of snow above them surmounted with the symbol of self-sacrifice, far-seen, and ' it is a grave that kings must envy.'

There alone in their greatness they will lie without change or bodily decay with the most fitting tomb in the world above them. [While for Oates]—the kindly snow had covered his body, giving him a fitting burial.[4]
And on that gaunt white cross on Observation Hill— mute memorial in a land where there are none to read— are carved the words that have raised a glow extending far beyond these college walls, words which may be applied to the life of Edward Adrian Wilson without prejudice to those of his brave companions :

TO STRIVE, TO SEEK, TO FIND AND NOT TO YIELD.[5]

---

[1] Cherry-Garrard.   [2] *ibid*.   [3] Atkinson.   [4] *ibid*.
[5] Debenham, *The ' Caian.'*

EDWARD WILSON

Last Letters of Dr. Wilson

March 21 or 22, '12.

To Reginald Smith, Esq., K.C.

MY DEAR GOOD FRIEND, AND MY DEAR MRS. SMITH,—
This looks like a finish to our undertaking for we are out of food and oil, and not able to move now for 3 days on account of the blizzard.

We have had a long struggle against intense cold on very short fuel, and it has done us up. We shall make a forlorn-hope effort to reach the next depot to-morrow, but it means 22 miles, and we are none of us fit to face it.

I want to say how I have valued your friendship and your example, and how I and my beloved wife have loved you both from first to last. God be thanked for such as you. We shall meet in the hereafter.

I have no fear of death—only sorrow for my wife and for my dear people—otherwise all is well. I should like to have seen the Grouse Book, but it is not allowed me. God's will be done. I am only hopeful that this note may reach you some day to tell you how your goodness has helped me and my beloved Ory. I know she will come to you in her trouble and find consolation, thank God. Your loving TED WILSON.

To my Beloved Wife.

Life has been a struggle for some weeks now on this return journey from the Pole—so much so that I have not been able to keep my diary going. To-day may be the last effort. Birdie and I are going to try and reach the Depot 11 miles north of us and return to this tent where Captain Scott is lying with a frozen foot. . . . I shall simply fall and go to sleep in the snow, and I have your little books with me in my breast-pocket. . . .

Don't be unhappy—all is for the best. We are playing a good part in a great scheme arranged by God himself, and all is well. . . . I am only sorry I couldn't have seen your loving letters, and Mother's and Dad's and the Smiths', and all the happy news I had hoped to see— but all these things are easily seen later, I expect. . . . God be with you—my love is as living for you as ever.

I would like to have written to Mother and Dad and all at home, but it has been impossible. We will all meet after death, and death has no terrors. . . . We have done what we thought was best. . . . My own dear wife, good-bye for the present. . . . I do not cease to pray for you,—to the very last. . . .

To my Most Beloved Wife.

God be with you in your trouble, dear, when I have gone. I have written another short letter to you. . . . I leave this life in absolute faith and happy belief that if God wishes you to wait long without me it will be to some good purpose. All is for the best to those that love God, and oh, my Ory, we have both loved Him with all our lives. All is well. . . .

We have struggled to the end and we have nothing to regret. Our whole journey record is clean, and Scott's diary gives the account. . . . The Barrier has beaten us—though we got to the Pole.

My beloved wife, these are small things, life itself is a small thing to me now, but my love for you is for ever and a part of our love for God. . . . I do not cease to pray for you and to desire that you may be filled with the knowledge of His will. (*Later.*) God knows I am sorry to be the cause of sorrow to anyone in the world, but everyone must die—and at every death there must be some sorrow. . . . All the things I had hoped to do with you after this Expedition are as nothing now, but there are greater things for us to do in the world to come. . . . My only regret is leaving you to struggle through your life alone, but I may be coming to you by a quicker way. I feel so happy now in having got time to write to you. One of my notes will surely reach you. . . . Dad's little compass and Mother's little comb and looking-glass are in my pocket. Your little testament and prayer book will be in my hand or in my breast pocket when the end comes. All is well. . . .

THE END

INDEX

Index

Made and Printed in Great Britain by Butler & Tanner Ltd., Frome and London